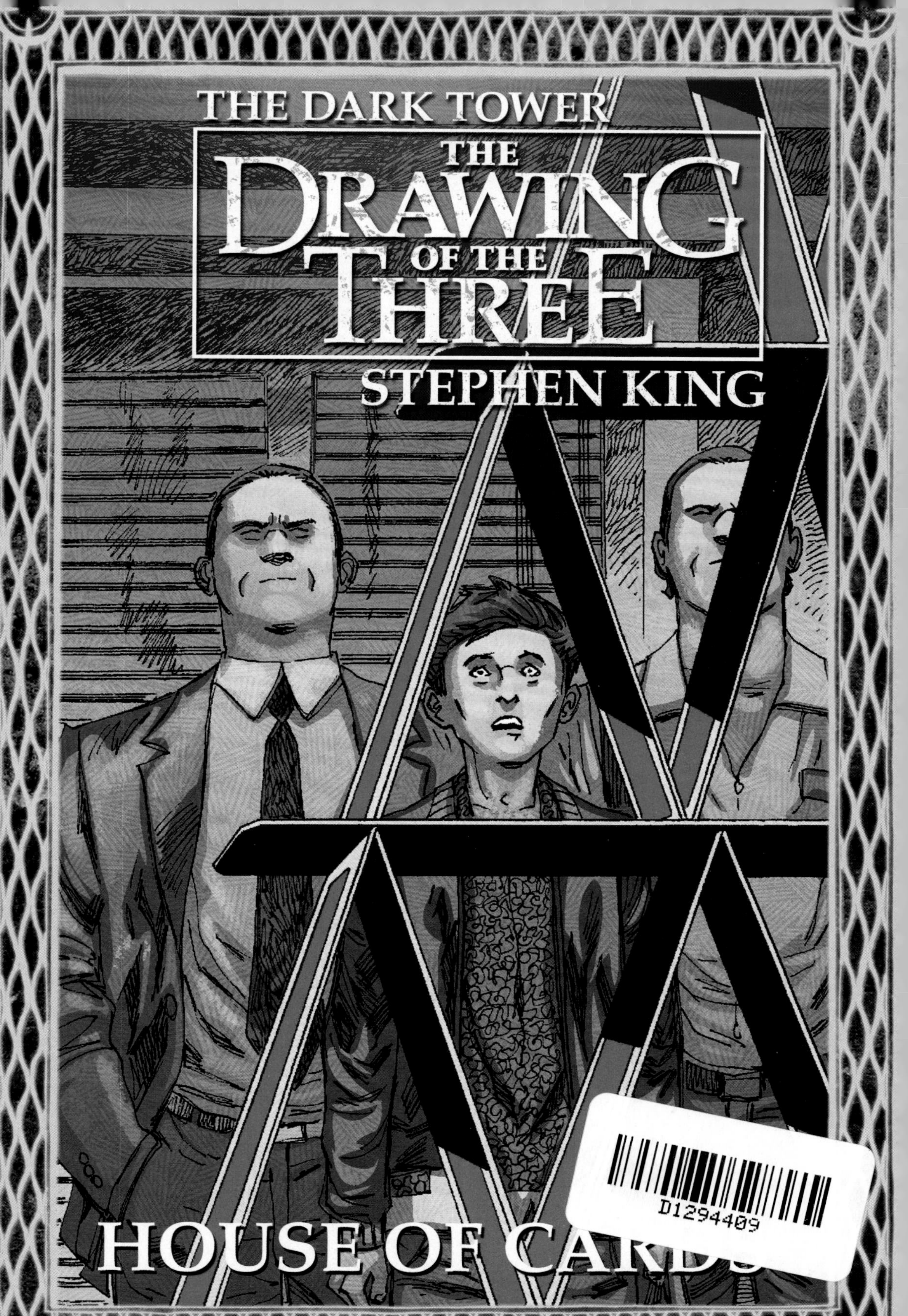
THE DARK TOWER
THE DRAWING OF THE THREE
STEPHEN KING
HOUSE OF CARDS

# THE DARK TOWER

# THE DRAWING OF THE THREE

## STEPHEN KING

CREATIVE DIRECTOR AND EXECUTIVE DIRECTOR
**STEPHEN KING**

PLOT AND CONSULTATION
**ROBIN FURTH**

SCRIPT
**PETER DAVID**

ARTIST
**PIOTR KOWALSKI**

COLORIST
**NICK FILARDI**

LETTERING
**VC'S JOE SABINO**

COVER ARTIST
**JULIAN TOTINO TEDESCO**

EDITORS
**EMILY SHAW** WITH
**MARK BASSO**

CONSULTING EDITORS
**RALPH MACCHIO** WITH
**BILL ROSEMANN**

# HOUSE OF CARDS

COLLECTION EDITOR
**MARK D. BEAZLEY**

ASSISTANT EDITOR
**SARAH BRUNSTAD**

ASSOCIATE MANAGING EDITOR
**ALEX STARBUCK**

EDITOR, SPECIAL PROJECTS
**JENNIFER GRÜNWALD**

SENIOR EDITOR, SPECIAL PROJECTS
**JEFF YOUNGQUIST**

SVP PRINT, SALES & MARKETING
**DAVID GABRIEL**

EDITOR IN CHIEF
**AXEL ALONSO**

CHIEF CREATIVE OFFICER
**JOE QUESADA**

PUBLISHER
**DAN BUCKLEY**

SPECIAL THANKS TO CHUCK VERRILL, MARSHA DEFILIPPO & BRIAN STARK

**DARK TOWER: THE DRAWING OF THE THREE — HOUSE OF CARDS.** Contains material originally published in magazine form as DARK TOWER: THE DRAWING OF THE THREE — HOUSE OF CARDS #1-5. First printing 2015. ISBN# 978-0-7851-9281-7. Published by MARVEL WORLDWIDE, INC., a subsidiary of MARVEL ENTERTAINMENT, LLC. OFFICE OF PUBLICATION: 135 West 50th Street, New York, NY 10020. Copyright © 2015 Stephen King. All rights reserved. All characters featured in this issue and the distinctive names and likenesses thereof, and all related indicia are trademarks of Stephen King. No similarity between any of the names, characters, persons, and/or institutions in this magazine with those of any living or dead person or institution is intended, and any such similarity which may exist is purely coincidental. Marvel and its logos are TM & © Marvel Characters, Inc. **Printed in Canada.** ALAN FINE, President, Marvel Entertainment; DAN BUCKLEY, President, TV, Publishing and Brand Management; JOE QUESADA, Chief Creative Officer; TOM BREVOORT, SVP of Publishing; DAVID BOGART, SVP of Operations & Procurement, Publishing; C.B. CEBULSKI, VP of International Development & Brand Management; DAVID GABRIEL, SVP Print, Sales & Marketing; JIM O'KEEFE, VP of Operations & Logistics; DAN CARR, Executive Director of Publishing Technology; SUSAN CRESPI, Editorial Operations Manager; ALEX MORALES, Publishing Operations Manager; STAN LEE, Chairman Emeritus. For information regarding advertising in Marvel Comics or on Marvel.com, please contact Jonathan Rheingold, VP of Custom Solutions & Ad Sales, at jrheingold@marvel.com. For Marvel subscription inquiries, please call 800-217-9158. **Manufactured between 7/17/2015 and 8/24/2015 by SOLISCO PRINTERS, SCOTT, QC, CANADA.**

10 9 8 7 6 5 4 3 2 1

Greetings, fellow Constant Readers, and welcome to *House of Cards*, a story that grew out of Stephen King's second Dark Tower novel, *The Drawing of the Three*. *House of Cards* is the continuation of Marvel's five-issue story arc entitled *The Prisoner*, which told of the childhood misadventures of Eddie Dean and his no-good big brother, Henry Dean. Like *The Prisoner* before it, Marvel's *House of Cards* is not a strict retelling of Stephen King's tale. Unlike King's books, which focus on the quest of a gunslinger named Roland Deschain (Marvel readers will remember Roland from *The Gunslinger Born*), these two arcs focus upon the life of Eddie Dean, who is one of Roland Deschain's *ka*-mates, or traveling companions.

Like most of Roland's later *ka*-mates, Eddie is not a native of Mid-World but is from our world. When we meet Eddie in King's novel, he is already a grown man seated on a plane flying from Nassau to New York, a large stash of cocaine strapped to his chest.

Since Stephen King has already told the tale of Eddie's adventures with Roland (and who could tell it better?), we decided to tell Eddie's tale from Eddie's perspective. To do this, we gathered all of the flashbacks King shares about Eddie's early life and wove them together to make a coherent whole. Throughout this process, we were careful to remain true to Stephen King's Mid-World, so that Roland's longtime fans will feel at home in the universe they find. A large part of this tale is also unabashed but true-to-source conspiracy theory. In the Dark Tower Universe, a powerful supernatural agency is trying to prevent Roland from fulfilling his quest. It makes sense then that this same force should try to destroy Eddie before he can join Roland. In fact, in Book Six of the Dark Tower series, we learn that Eddie's nemesis, Balazar, is actually in the pay of Roland's enemies.

In *The Prisoner*, we learned that when Eddie was two years old and Henry was ten, their sister Gloria was hit by a car while playing hopscotch. After that, Henry was given the job of watching out for Eddie, but all that Henry really seemed able to do was to get them both into trouble. From a young age, Henry had a taste for drugs, but a knee injury he suffered in Vietnam made his taste for narcotics blossom into a full-blown heroin addiction.

And as always seemed to happen, whatever bad habits Henry developed, Eddie copied, even though he knew better.

By the end of *The Prisoner*, drug-fried Henry owed a significant amount of money to the mobster and drug kingpin Enrico Balazar, and the only way that Eddie could clear the debt was to become Balazar's drug mule, hauling cocaine from the Bahamas to New York City. Eddie hoped that his payment for the run would not only clear Henry's debt but pay for a final blowout before the two brothers checked themselves into rehab. But unluckily for Eddie, the Feds (and *ka*) had other plans for him.

In Mid-World, which is the barren land to which Eddie is transported during this tale, *ka* is a word that has many meanings. It signifies life force, consciousness, duty, and destiny. In the vulgate, or low speech, it means a place to which an individual must go. The closest terms in our language are probably fate and destiny, although *ka* also implies karma, or the accumulated destiny (and accumulated debt) of many existences. We are the servants of *ka*, but we are also its prisoners. *Ka* is the root of many Mid-World terms, such as *ka-tet* (a group of companions bound by fate), *ka-mai* (destiny's fool), and *ka-dinh* (leader).

Although he doesn't know it, Eddie's *ka* is very powerful. In fact, Eddie's future actions will have such far-reaching effects that there are forces in the universe that are trying to stop him from fulfilling his destiny. As we learned in issue #1 of *The Prisoner*, the death of Eddie's sister was no accident. The intended victim was Eddie Dean himself, and it was only chance (or perhaps the tidal force of *ka*) that sacrificed Gloria in Eddie's stead.

The driver that murdered Gloria worked for Enrico Balazar, the very man who helped to get both Eddie and Henry hooked on drugs. And as you have probably guessed, Eddie and Henry's addiction is not an accident either, but something carefully planned by those who would like to obliterate Eddie's future.

So, you might ask yourself, why would a junkie kid from 1987 Brooklyn, New York be so important? The answer lies not in our world, but with Roland and his world, a parallel Earth (or perhaps even a possible future of Earth), but one with a slightly different history.

Born in a walled city called Gilead, Roland was the only son of Steven Deschain, the last *dinh* (or leader) of the city's aristocratic gunslingers. He was also the direct descendant of Arthur Eld, the ancient king of All-World. During Roland's youth, Mid-World was divided into multiple baronies, each ruled by elected officials. But though barony officials and gunslingers worked together in a loose alliance (called the Affiliation), ultimate authority rested with the gunslingers, the aristocratic rulers of the In-World barony of New Canaan.

For centuries, the gunslingers of Gilead (part Arthurian knights, part Western gunmen) were the politicians, lawmen, and diplomats of Mid-World, and their right to rule was unquestioned. However, when Roland was a boy, a powerful challenge arose to the gunslingers' authority. This challenge came from a former outlaw called John Farson, who began to agitate for the downfall of Mid-World's hereditary elite. But despite his talk of democracy and equality, Farson was a madman whose true goals were personal power and cultural anarchy. After a protracted war in which Farson made use of the technologically advanced weapons left by Mid-World's ancient inhabitants (a people known as the Great Old Ones), Farson and his men sacked Gilead. Years later, the few remaining gunslingers made a final stand against Farson's men at the Battle of Jericho Hill. All but Roland were slaughtered.

During the years that followed, Roland wandered across Mid-World's growing deserts, a landscape where reality itself was fraying, and where neither time nor directions held true anymore. Thanks to the anarchy unleashed by Farson, human society had collapsed, as had all distinction between law and lawlessness. More and more mutants were being born, and a terrible desiccation was drying out the land, leaving it lifeless and sterile.

Haunted by the voices of his dead friends as well as that of his combat teacher, Cort, Roland now believes that if he can find the Dark Tower and question whatever god or demon resides at its top, he will be able to heal the ills of his world. According to legend, the Dark Tower is the linchpin of the time-space continuum and exists in a land known as End-World.

But unfortunately for Roland, and for all the worlds connected by it, the Dark Tower itself is no longer stable. Two of the magnetic Beams that hold it in place have snapped, and the others are weakening. To make matters more urgent, it is not only Mid-World that will blink out of existence if the Dark Tower falls; our world will also be lost. In order to reach the Dark Tower and to save the multiverse from annihilation, Roland must draw another *ka-tet* to him, one that will replace his *ka-tet* that died at the Battle of Jericho Hill.

Since Mid-World is dying, Roland must draw his new companions from another world. So, on a beach located on the bleak shoreline of the Western Sea, Roland finds the first of three magical doorways. This doorway is labeled The Prisoner, and leads to the mind of Eddie Dean, a young man who has dreamt of Roland all of his life. (Those who read *The Prisoner* will remember Eddie's gunslinger doll Johnny Bronco, and the doll's enemy, Sam Sidewinder.)

In many ways, Eddie resembles Roland's childhood friend Cuthbert Allgood, whom we came to know so well in *The Gunslinger Born*, *The Long Road Home*, *Treachery*, *The Fall of Gilead*, and *The Battle of Jericho Hill*.

Like Bert, Eddie is a constant joker. In fact, Roland labels them both as *ka-mais*, or *ka*'s fools, and swears that Eddie will die laughing, just as Cuthbert did. When Roland first meets the drug-addled Eddie, he senses the steel in him and knows that he has the makings of a gunslinger, despite his habit. In fact, he compares Eddie to a good gun sinking in quicksand. We have yet to see whether Eddie will be able to quit the drugs (and in fact, whether he will live long enough to do so!).

Another reason Roland needs Eddie is that Eddie is a key maker. In *The Prisoner*, issue #3, we saw Eddie's whittling talent, though as always happened when Eddie outshone his brother, Henry tried to squash Eddie's enthusiasm. Luckily for Roland, Henry wasn't successful. In a multiverse full of parallel worlds, connected by magical doorways, an accomplished key maker is a very valuable companion.

On that note I will leave you, since I don't want to let slip any spoilers! As we say in Mid-World, "Long days and pleasant nights!"

Robin Furth

EDDIE DEAN IS SPECIAL. SO SPECIAL THAT AN UNDERWORLD CRIME BOSS CALLED BALAZAR TRIED TO HAVE HIM KILLED WHEN HE WAS ONLY TWO YEARS OLD. WHY? BECAUSE BALAZAR BELIEVES EDDIE IS ONE OF A SELECT FEW THAT EXIST ON MANY PLANES OF REALITY.

EDDIE HAD A TROUBLED BUT NORMAL CHILDHOOD. GROWING UP IN BROOKLYN IN THE '60S AND '70S, HE IDOLIZED HIS OLDER BROTHER HENRY, EVEN AS HENRY GOT HOOKED ON DRUGS AND RAN JOBS FOR BALAZAR. EDDIE FOLLOWED IN HIS FOOTSTEPS.

WHEN HENRY GOT INTO DEBT WITH BALAZAR, EDDIE DECIDED TO TAKE ON ONE LAST BIG JOB - A JOB THAT WOULD WIPE THE SLATE CLEAN FOR HIM AND HIS BROTHER AND EARN THEM PAID SPOTS IN REHAB.

BUT ON THE FLIGHT BACK, EDDIE HAD THE STRANGEST DREAM. IN HIS DREAM, EDDIE ENCOUNTERED A SINISTER MAN IN BLACK, A MYSTERIOUS COWBOY, AND A GREY BEACH CRAWLING WITH GIANT LOBSTER BEASTS. WHEN HE AWOKE, HE SAW A GLOWING DOORWAY THAT LED TO THE WORLD FROM HIS DREAM.

PANICKED, EDDIE RAN TO THE PLANE BATHROOM AND HIS SUSPICIOUS BEHAVIOR ALARMED THE FLIGHT ATTENDANTS. THERE IN THE LAVATORY, HE SAW THE DOOR AGAIN. TRAPPED BETWEEN ARREST AND THE UNKNOWN, EDDIE STEPPED THROUGH THE DOORWAY AND INTO ANOTHER WORLD, WHERE THE COWBOY WAS WAITING...

WER

THE
WING
THE
REE

HEN KING

F CARDS
R ONE

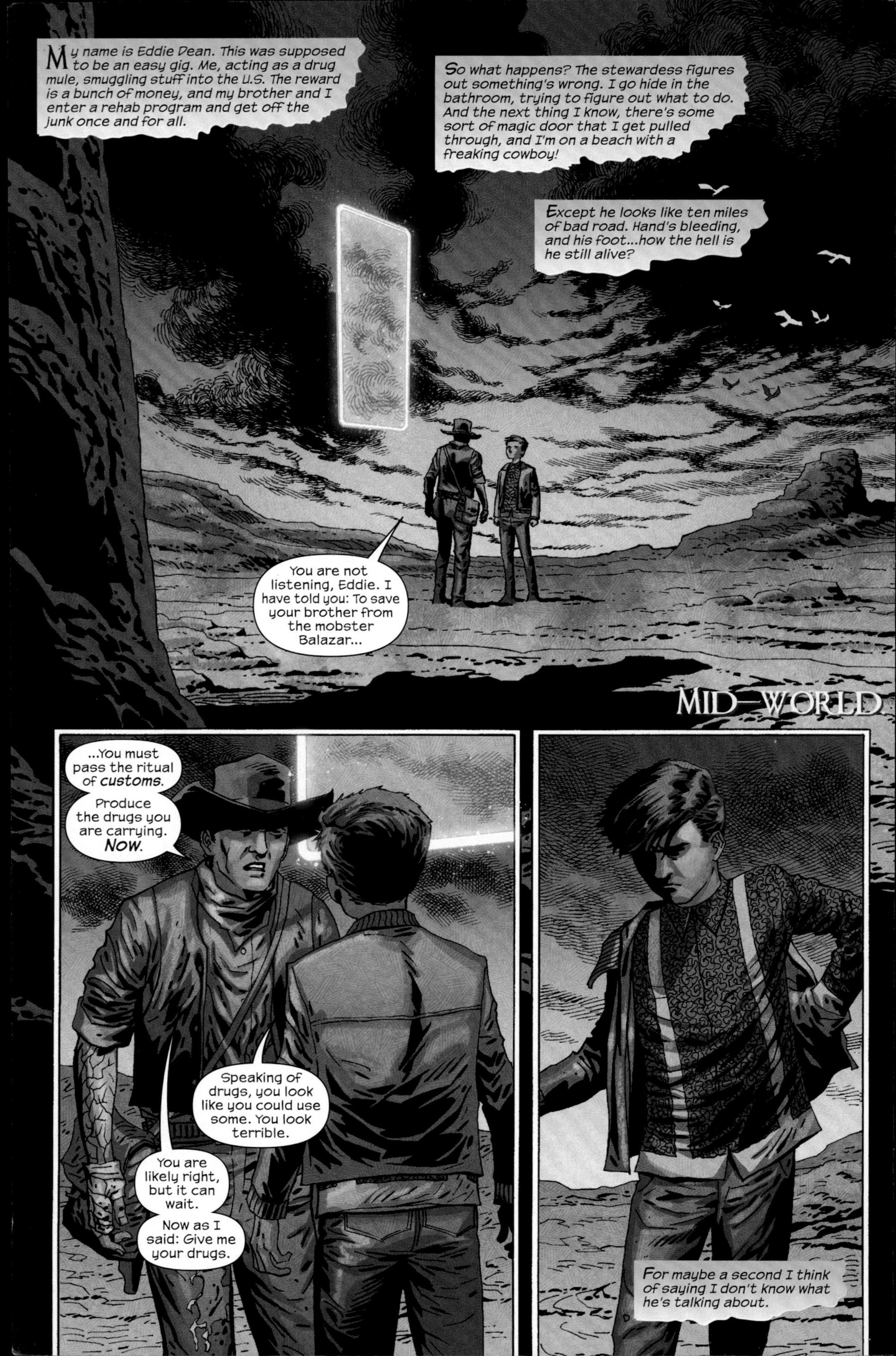
My name is Eddie Dean. This was supposed to be an easy gig. Me, acting as a drug mule, smuggling stuff into the U.S. The reward is a bunch of money, and my brother and I enter a rehab program and get off the junk once and for all.
So what happens? The stewardess figures out something's wrong. I go hide in the bathroom, trying to figure out what to do. And the next thing I know, there's some sort of magic door that I get pulled through, and I'm on a beach with a freaking cowboy!
Except he looks like ten miles of bad road. Hand's bleeding, and his foot...how the hell is he still alive?
You are not listening, Eddie. I have told you: To save your brother from the mobster Balazar...
MID-WORLD.
...You must pass the ritual of *customs*.
Produce the drugs you are carrying. *NOW*.
Speaking of drugs, you look like you could use some. You look terrible.
You are likely right, but it can wait.
Now as I said: Give me your drugs.
For maybe a second I think of saying I don't know what he's talking about.

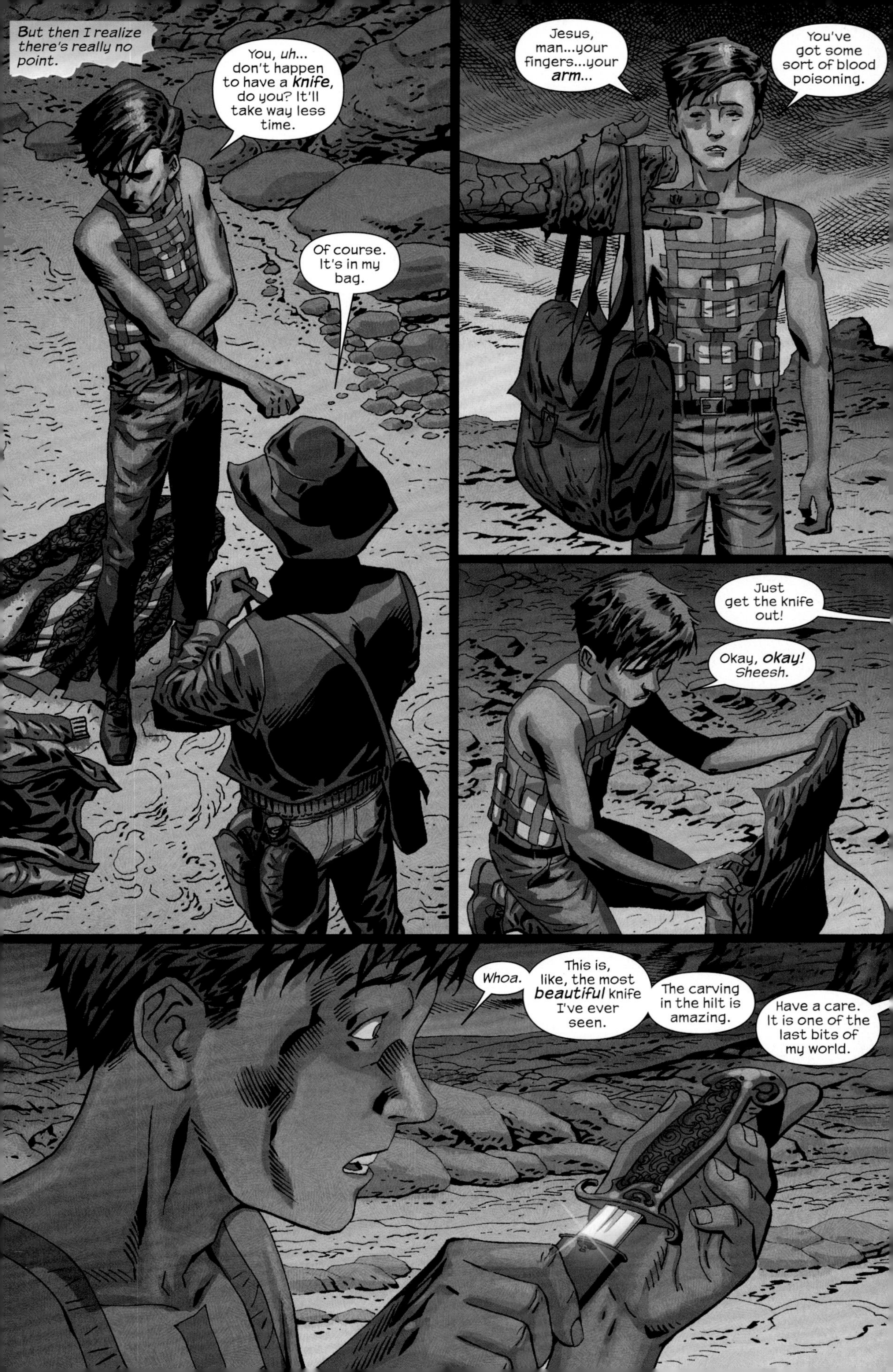
But then I realize there's really no point.
You, *uh*... don't happen to have a ***knife***, do you? It'll take way less time.
Of course. It's in my bag.
Jesus, man...your fingers...your ***arm***...
You've got some sort of blood poisoning.
Just get the knife out!
Okay, ***okay!*** *Sheesh.*
*Whoa.*
This is, like, the most ***beautiful*** knife I've ever seen.
The carving in the hilt is amazing.
Have a care. It is one of the last bits of my world.

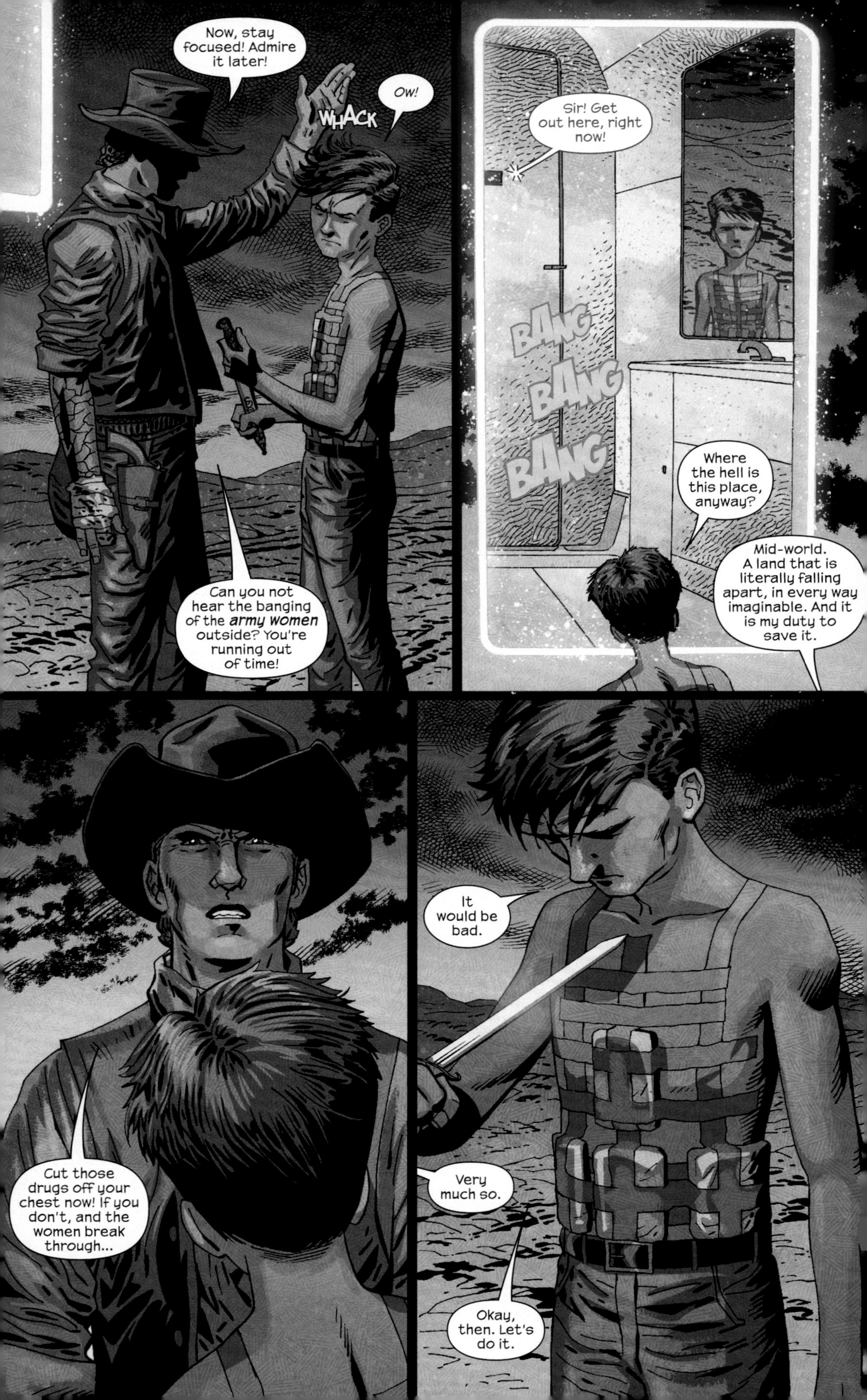
Now, stay focused! Admire it later!
WHACK
Ow!
Can you not hear the banging of the *army women* outside? You're running out of time!
Sir! Get out here, right now!
BANG
BANG
BANG
Where the hell is this place, anyway?
Mid-world. A land that is literally falling apart, in every way imaginable. And it is my duty to save it.
Cut those drugs off your chest now! If you don't, and the women break through...
It would be bad.
Very much so.
Okay, then. Let's do it.

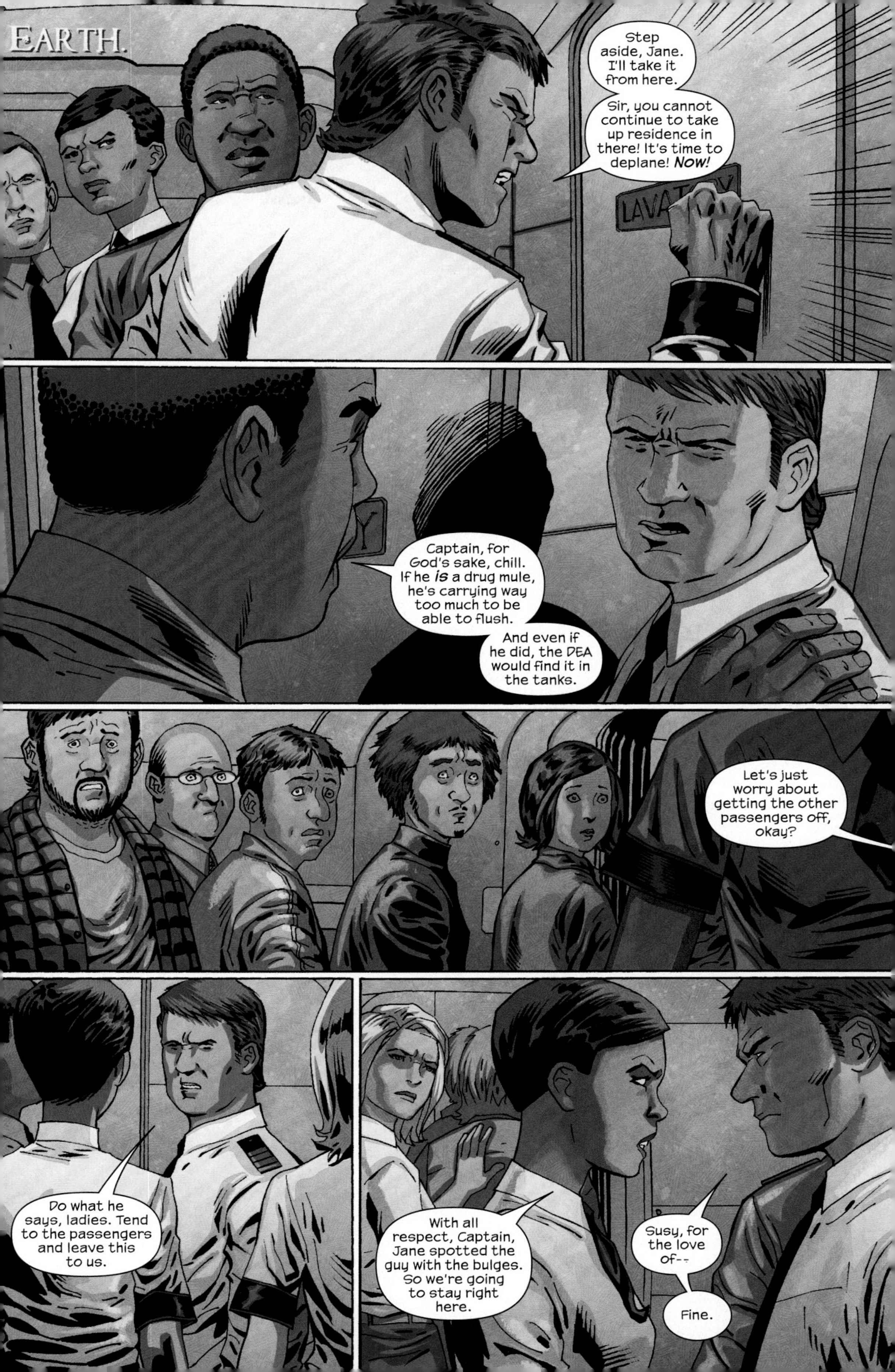
EARTH.
Step aside, Jane. I'll take it from here.
Sir, you cannot continue to take up residence in there! It's time to deplane! NOW!
Captain, for God's sake, chill. If he is a drug mule, he's carrying way too much to be able to flush.
And even if he did, the DEA would find it in the tanks.
Let's just worry about getting the other passengers off, okay?
Do what he says, ladies. Tend to the passengers and leave this to us.
With all respect, Captain, Jane spotted the guy with the bulges. So we're going to stay right here.
Susy, for the love of--
Fine.

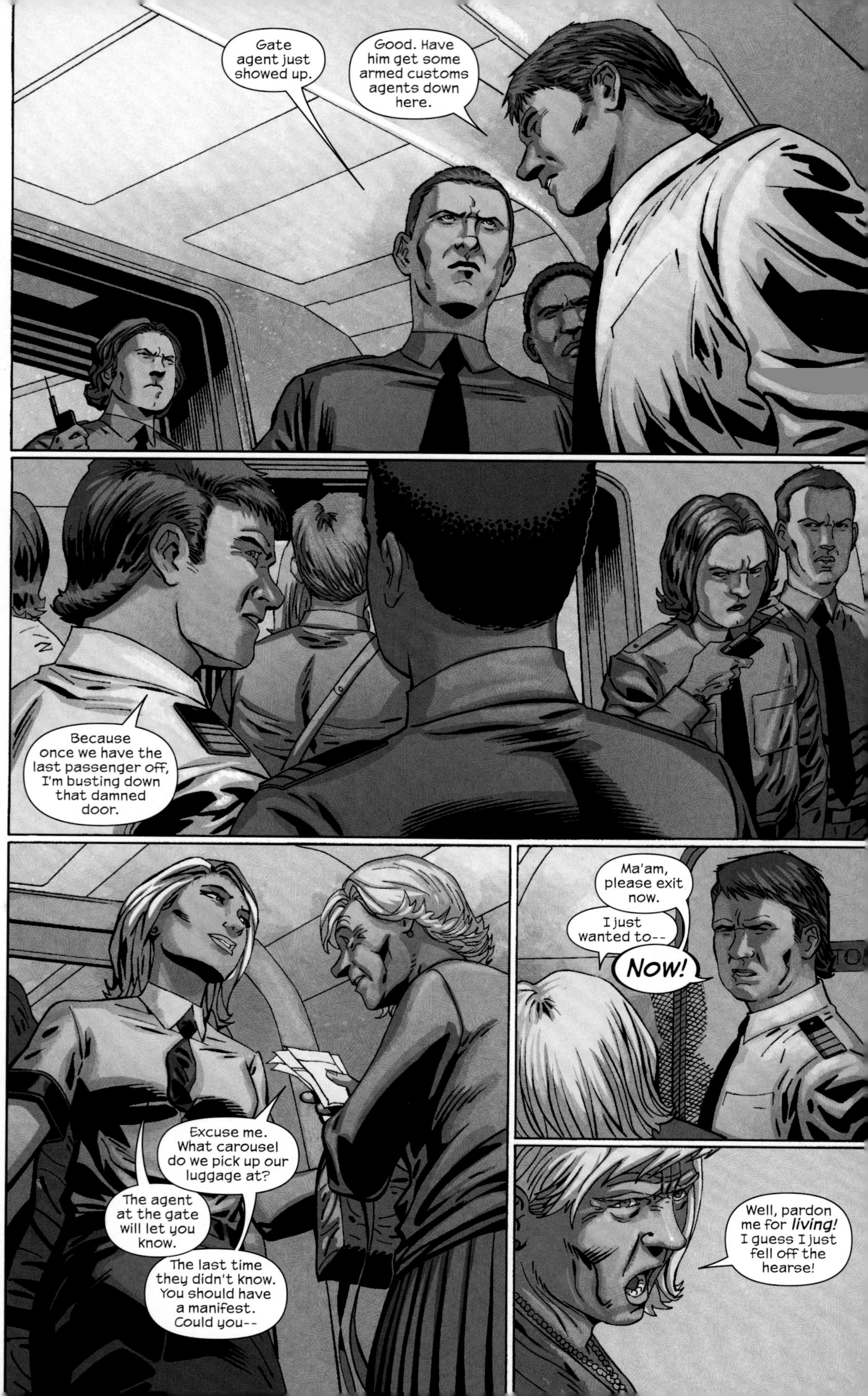

Gate agent just showed up.
Good. Have him get some armed customs agents down here.
Because once we have the last passenger off, I'm busting down that damned door.
Excuse me. What carousel do we pick up our luggage at?
The agent at the gate will let you know.
The last time they didn't know. You should have a manifest. Could you--
Ma'am, please exit now.
I just wanted to--
NOW!
Well, pardon me for *living!* I guess I just fell off the hearse!

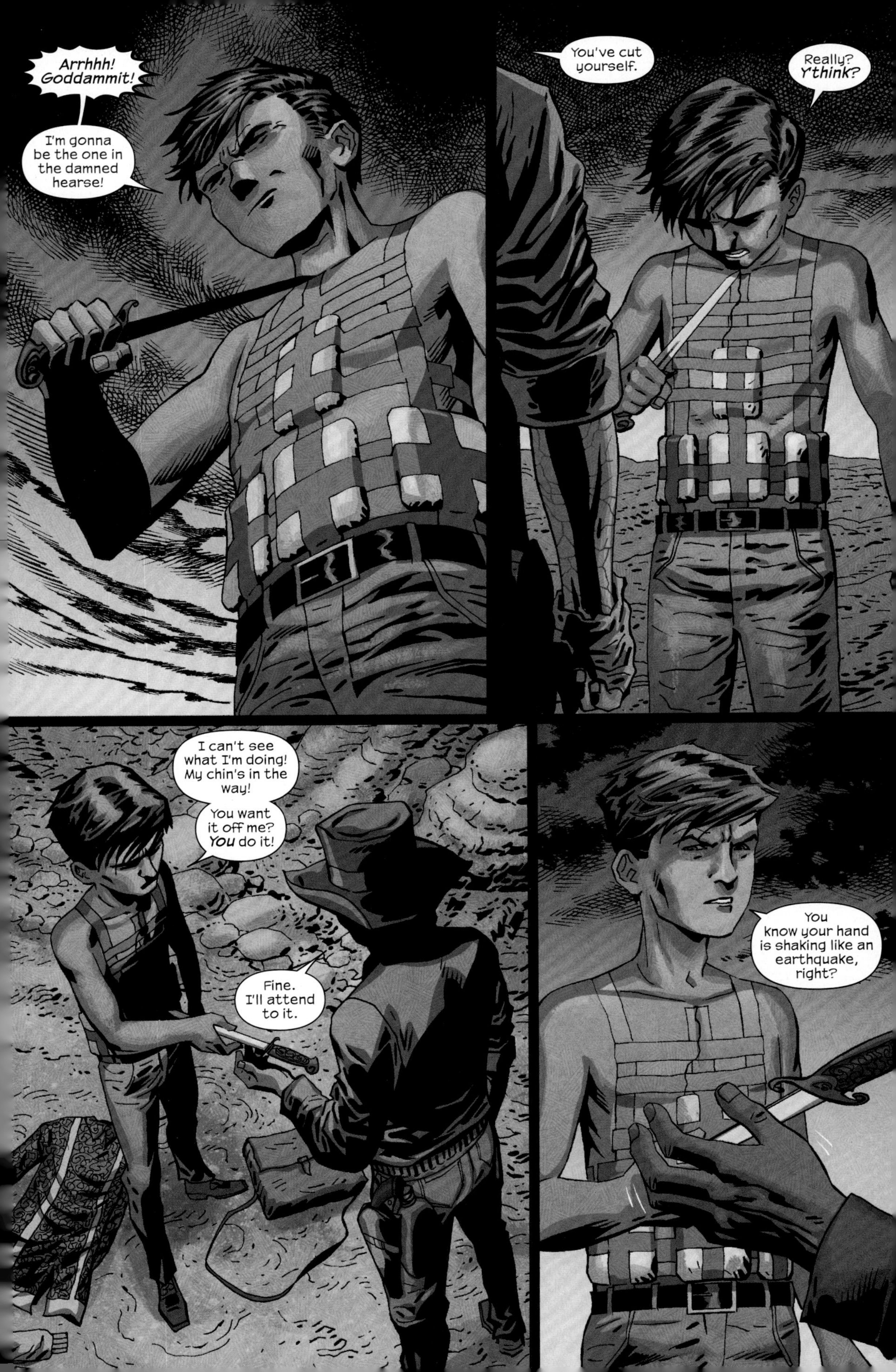
Arrhhh! Goddammit!
I'm gonna be the one in the damned hearse!
You've cut yourself.
Really? Y'think?
I can't see what I'm doing! My chin's in the way!
You want it off me? YOU do it!
Fine. I'll attend to it.
You know your hand is shaking like an earthquake, right?

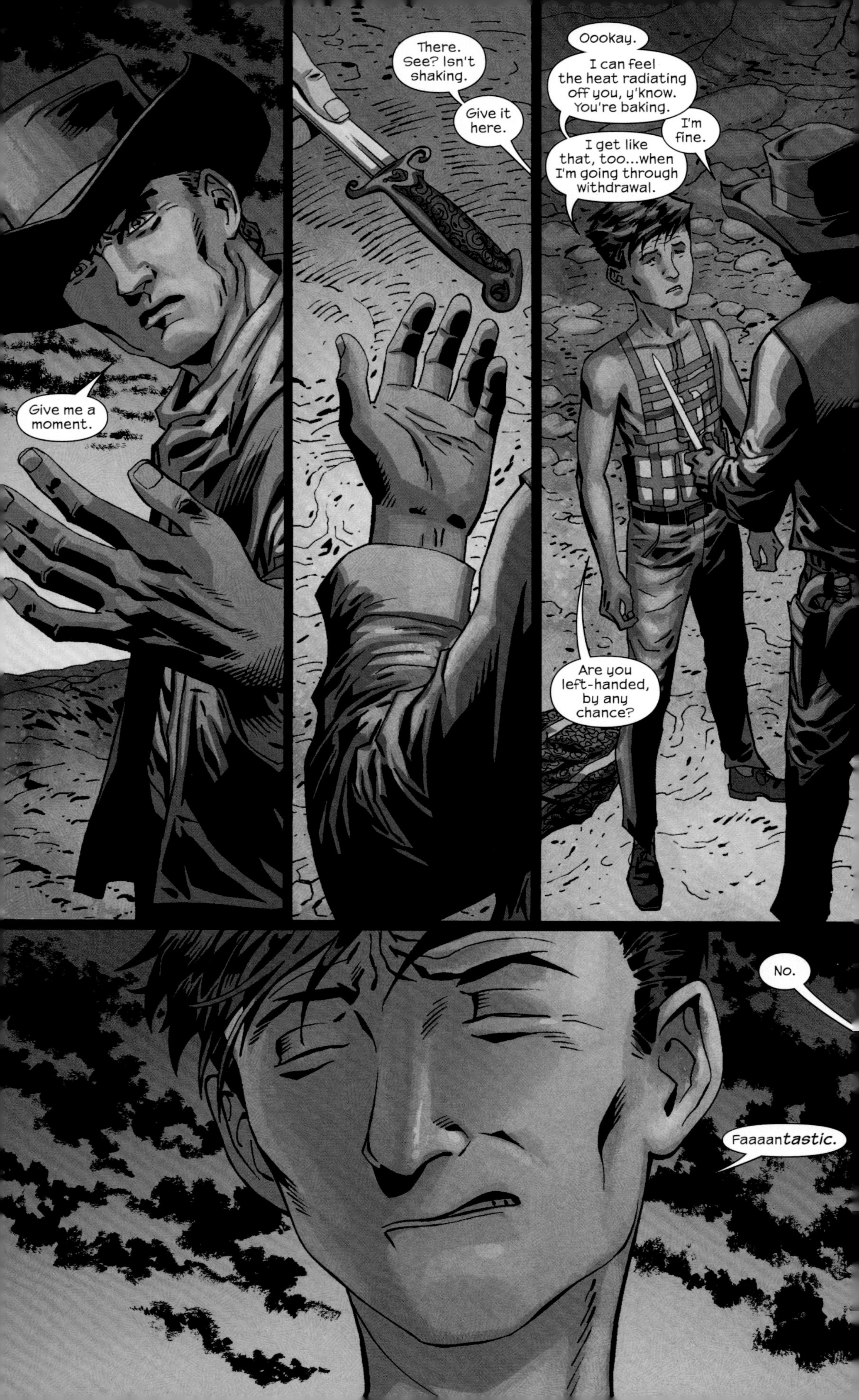
Give me a moment.
There. See? Isn't shaking.
Give it here.
Oookay.
I can feel the heat radiating off you, y'know. You're baking.
I'm fine.
I get like that, too...when I'm going through withdrawal.
Are you left-handed, by any chance?
No.
Faaaantastic.

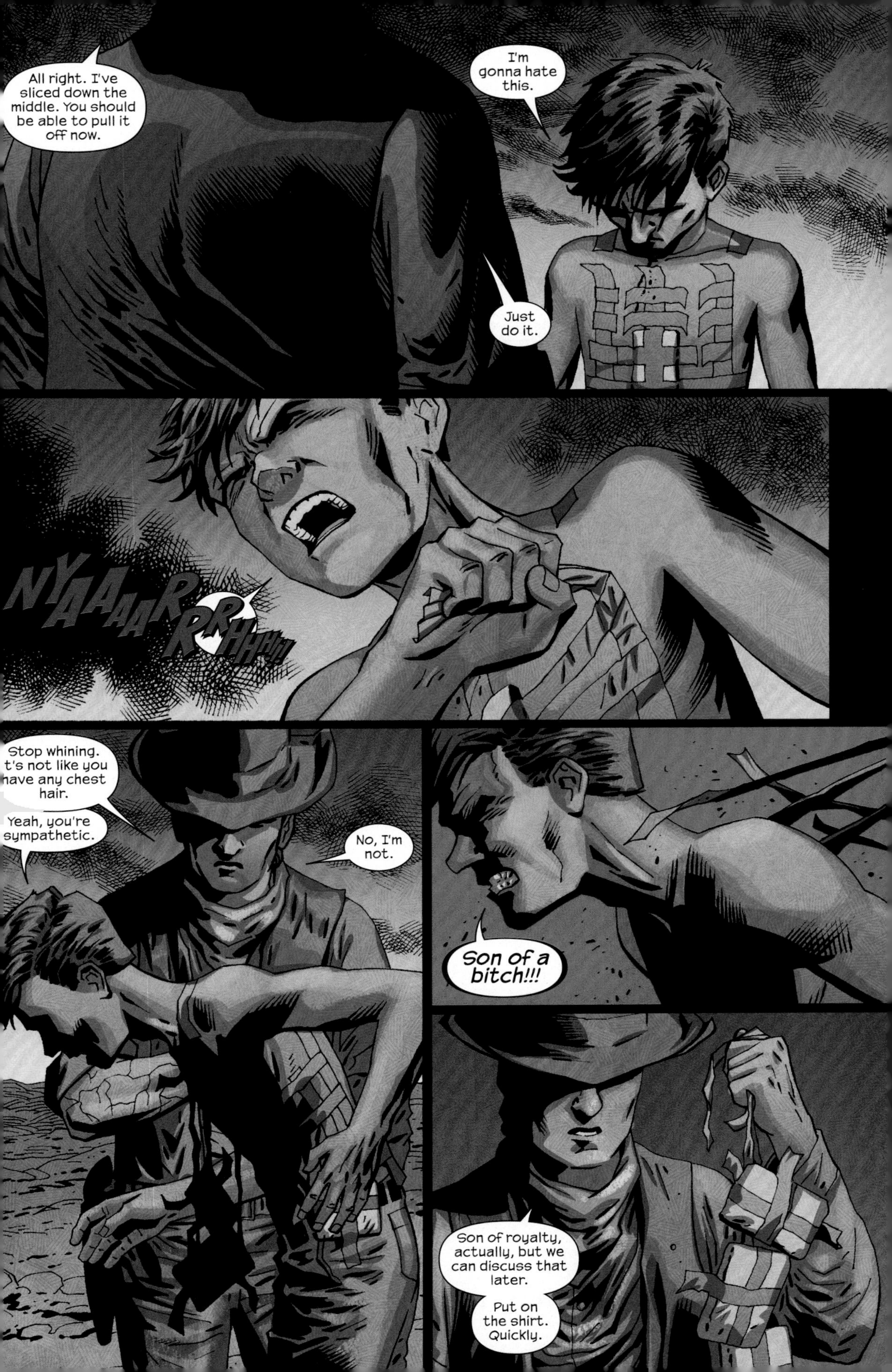
All right. I've sliced down the middle. You should be able to pull it off now.
I'm gonna hate this.
Just do it.
NYAAAARRRHHH!
Stop whining. t's not like you have any chest hair.
Yeah, you're sympathetic.
No, I'm not.
Son of a bitch!!!
Son of royalty, actually, but we can discuss that later.
Put on the shirt. Quickly.

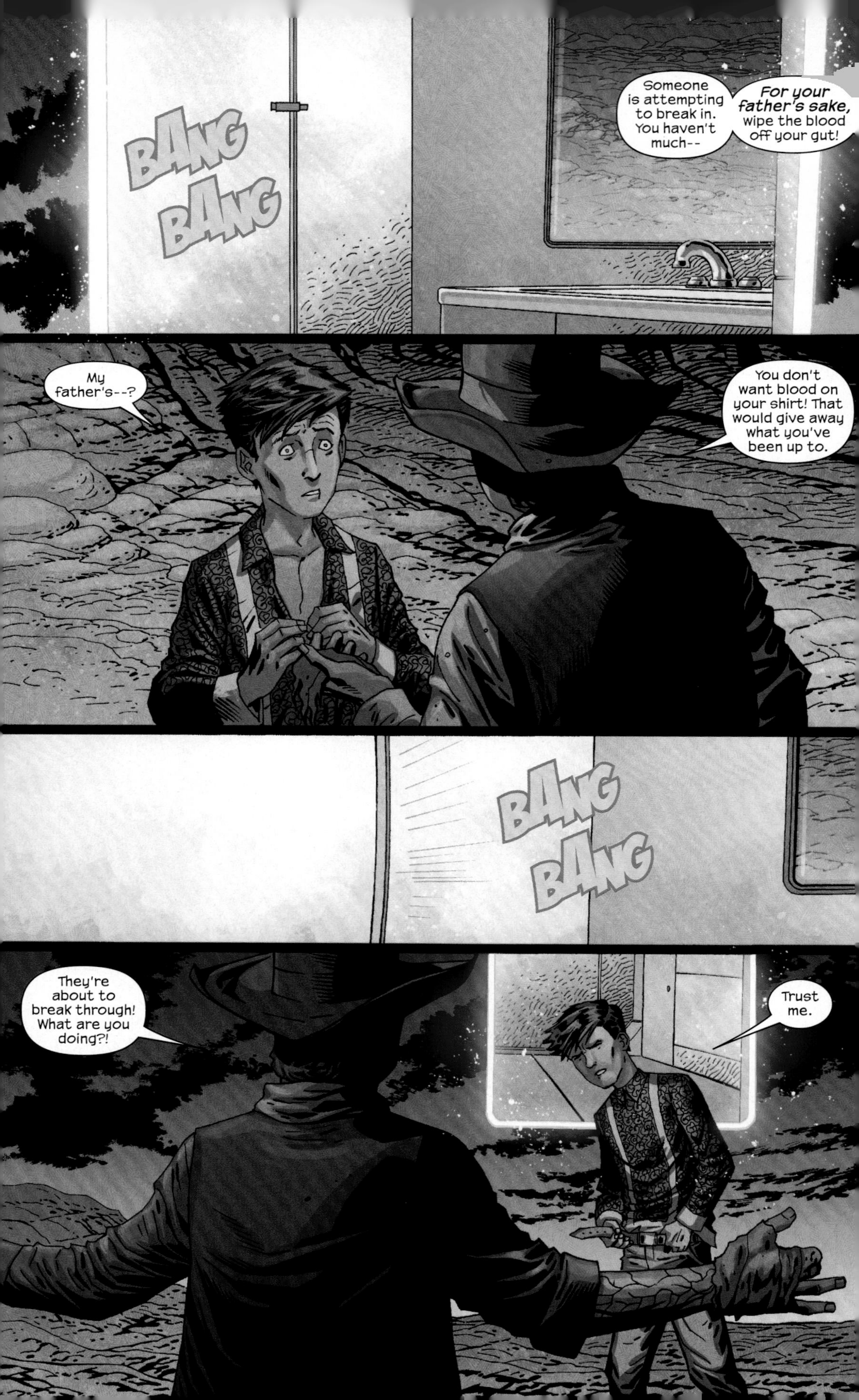
BANG
BANG
Someone is attempting to break in. You haven't much--
For your father's sake, wipe the blood off your gut!
My father's--?
You don't want blood on your shirt! That would give away what you've been up to.
BANG
BANG
They're about to break through! What are you doing?!
Trust me.

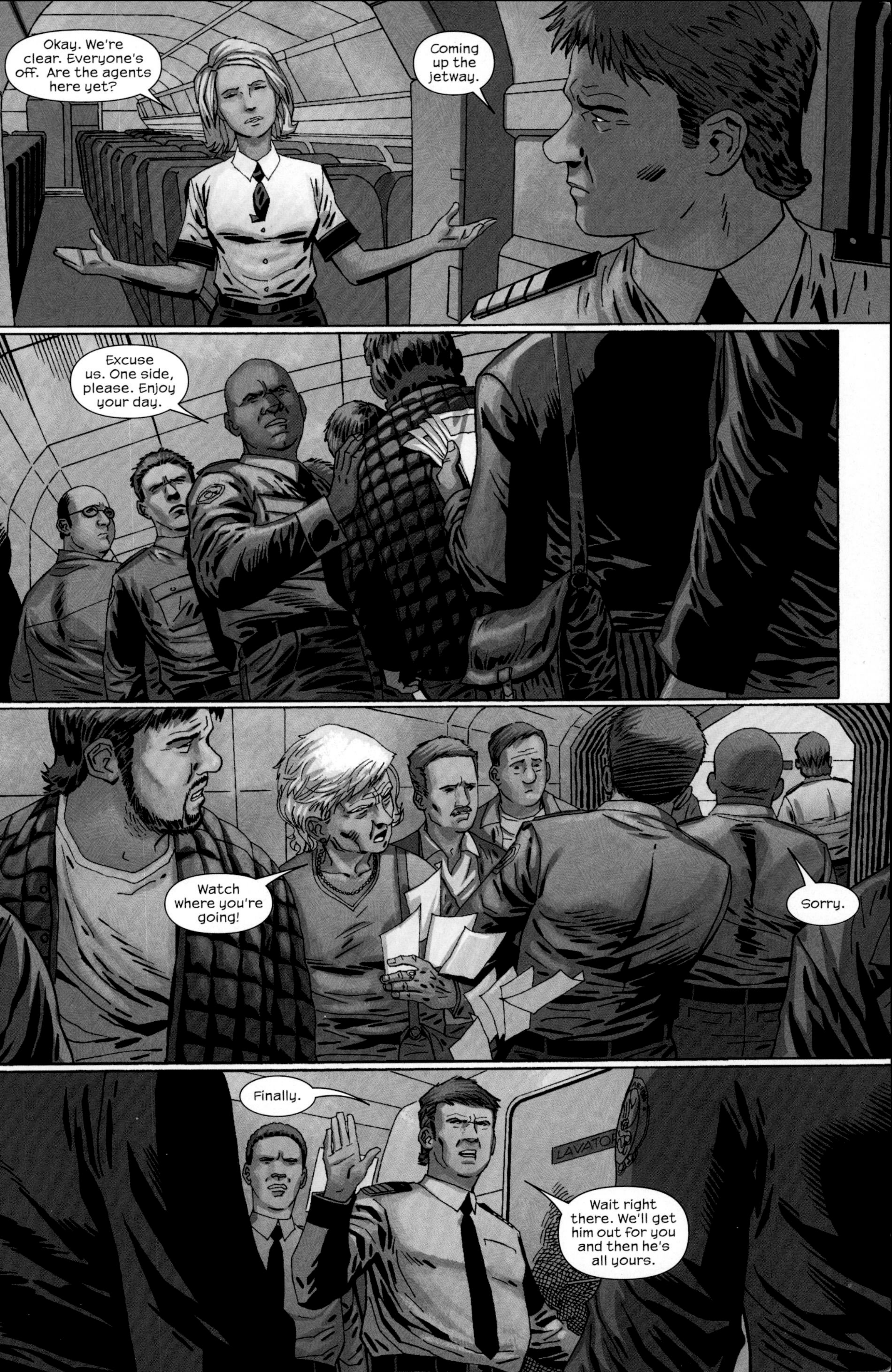
Okay. We're clear. Everyone's off. Are the agents here yet?
Coming up the jetway.
Excuse us. One side, please. Enjoy your day.
Watch where you're going!
Sorry.
Finally.
Wait right there. We'll get him out for you and then he's all yours.

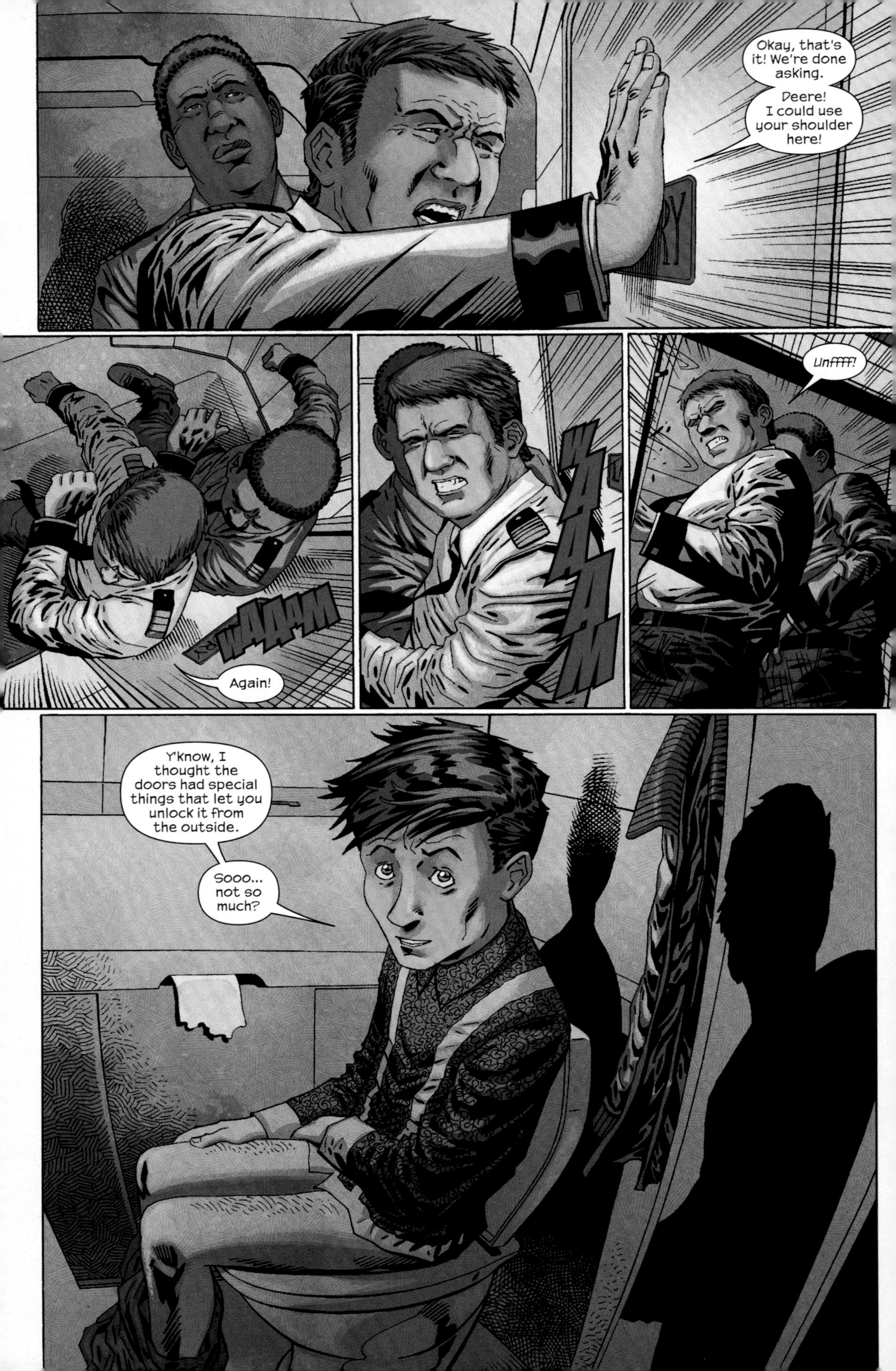
Okay, that's it! We're done asking.
Deere! I could use your shoulder here!
WAAAM
Again!
WAAAM
Unffff!
Y'know, I thought the doors had special things that let you unlock it from the outside.
Sooo... not so much?

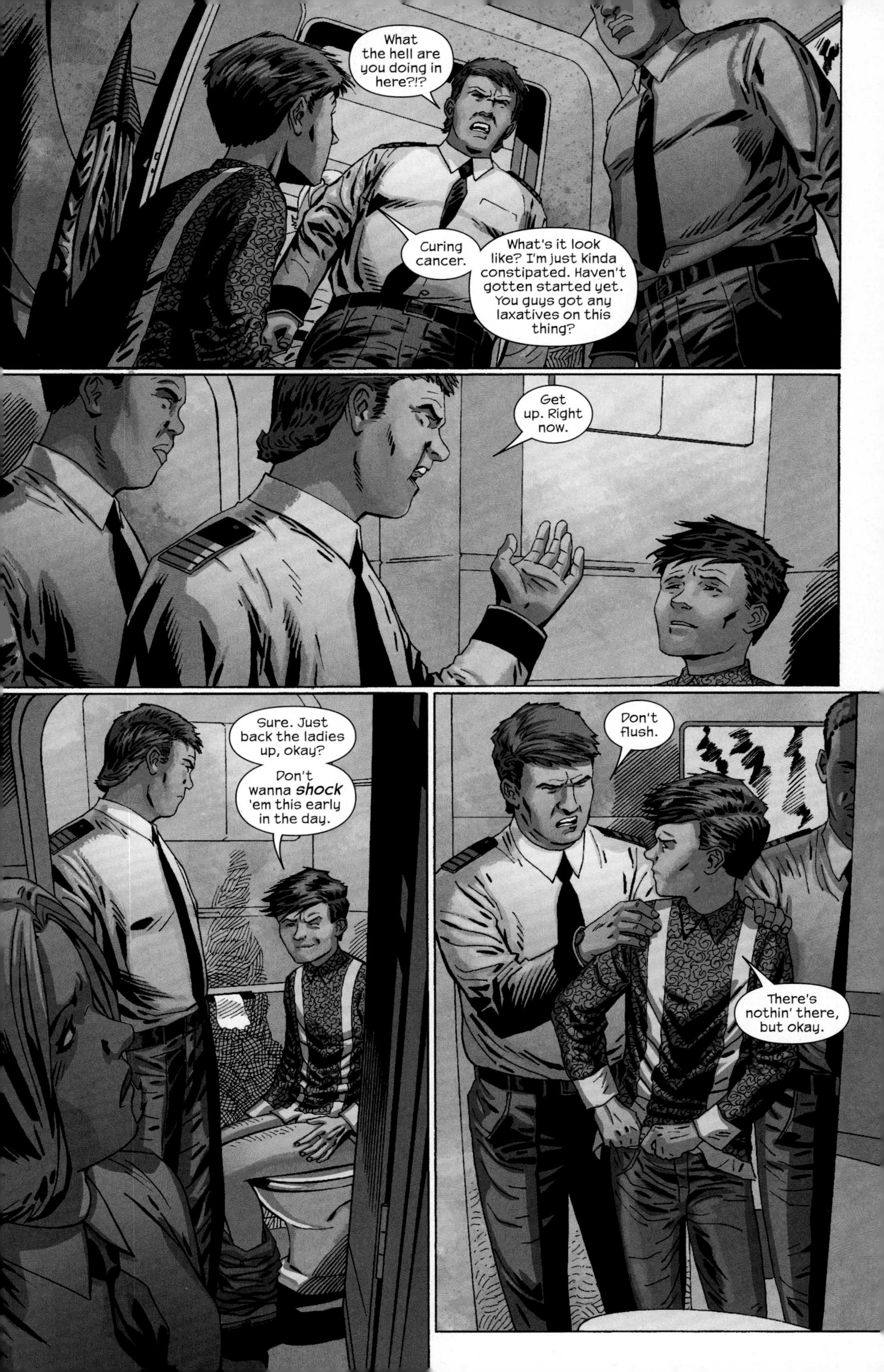
What the hell are you doing in here?!?
Curing cancer.
What's it look like? I'm just kinda constipated. Haven't gotten started yet. You guys got any laxatives on this thing?
Get up. Right now.
Sure. Just back the ladies up, okay?
Don't wanna shock 'em this early in the day.
Don't flush.
There's nothin' there, but okay.

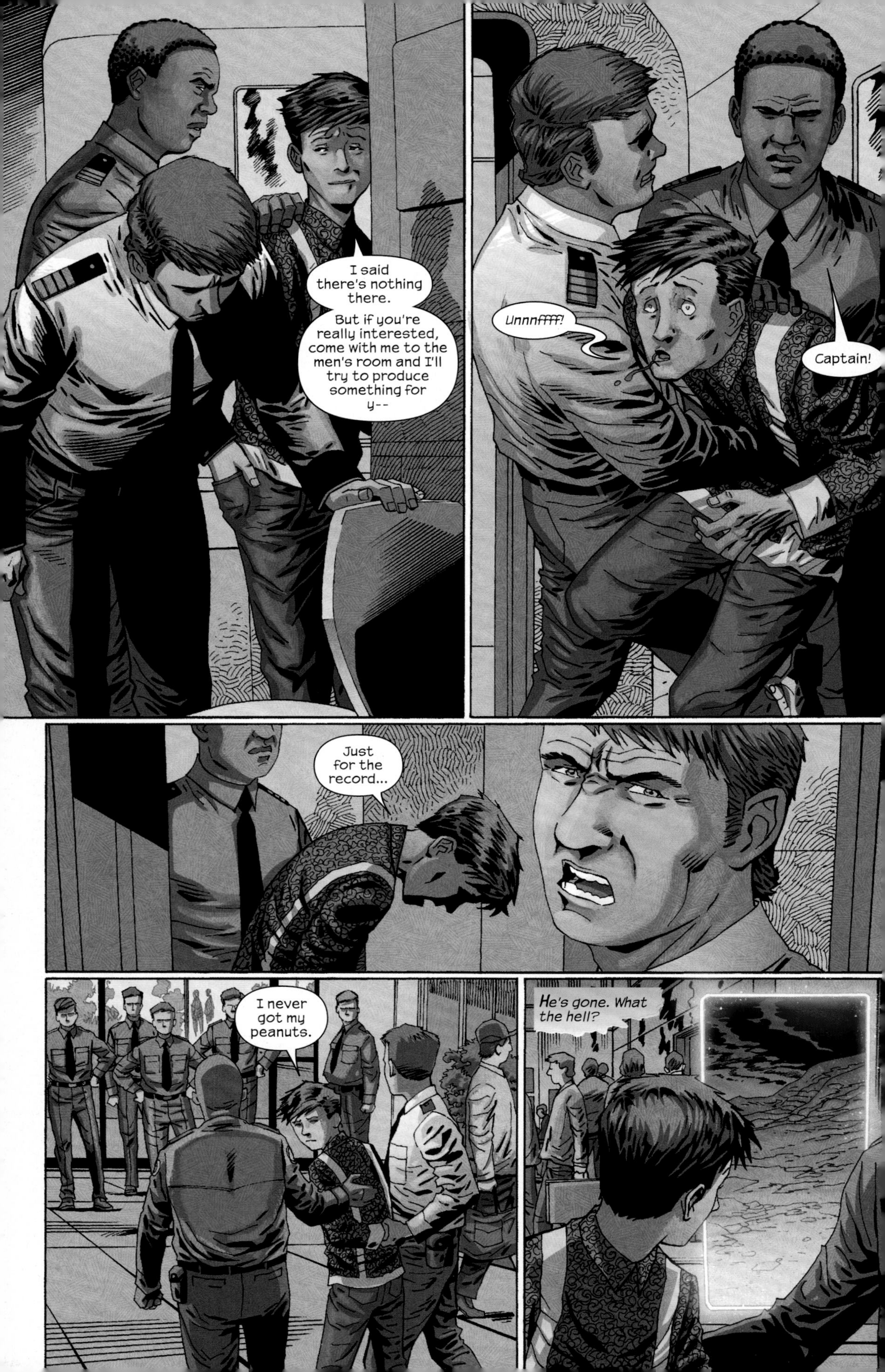
I said there's nothing there.
But if you're really interested, come with me to the men's room and I'll try to produce something for y--
Unnnffff!
Captain!
Just for the record...
I never got my peanuts.
He's gone. What the hell?

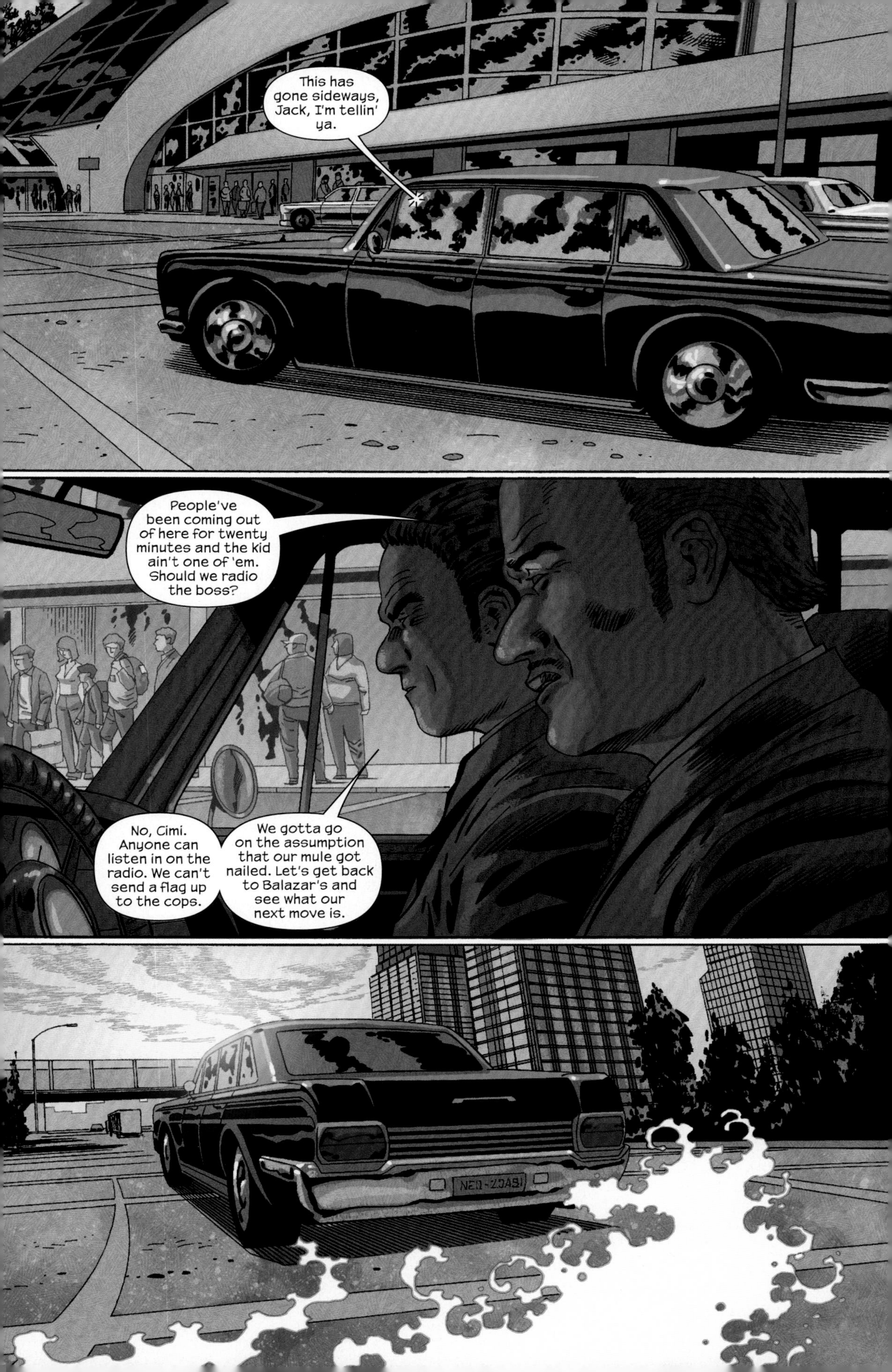

This has gone sideways, Jack, I'm tellin' ya.
People've been coming out of here for twenty minutes and the kid ain't one of 'em. Should we radio the boss?
No, Cimi. Anyone can listen in on the radio. We can't send a flag up to the cops.
We gotta go on the assumption that our mule got nailed. Let's get back to Balazar's and see what our next move is.

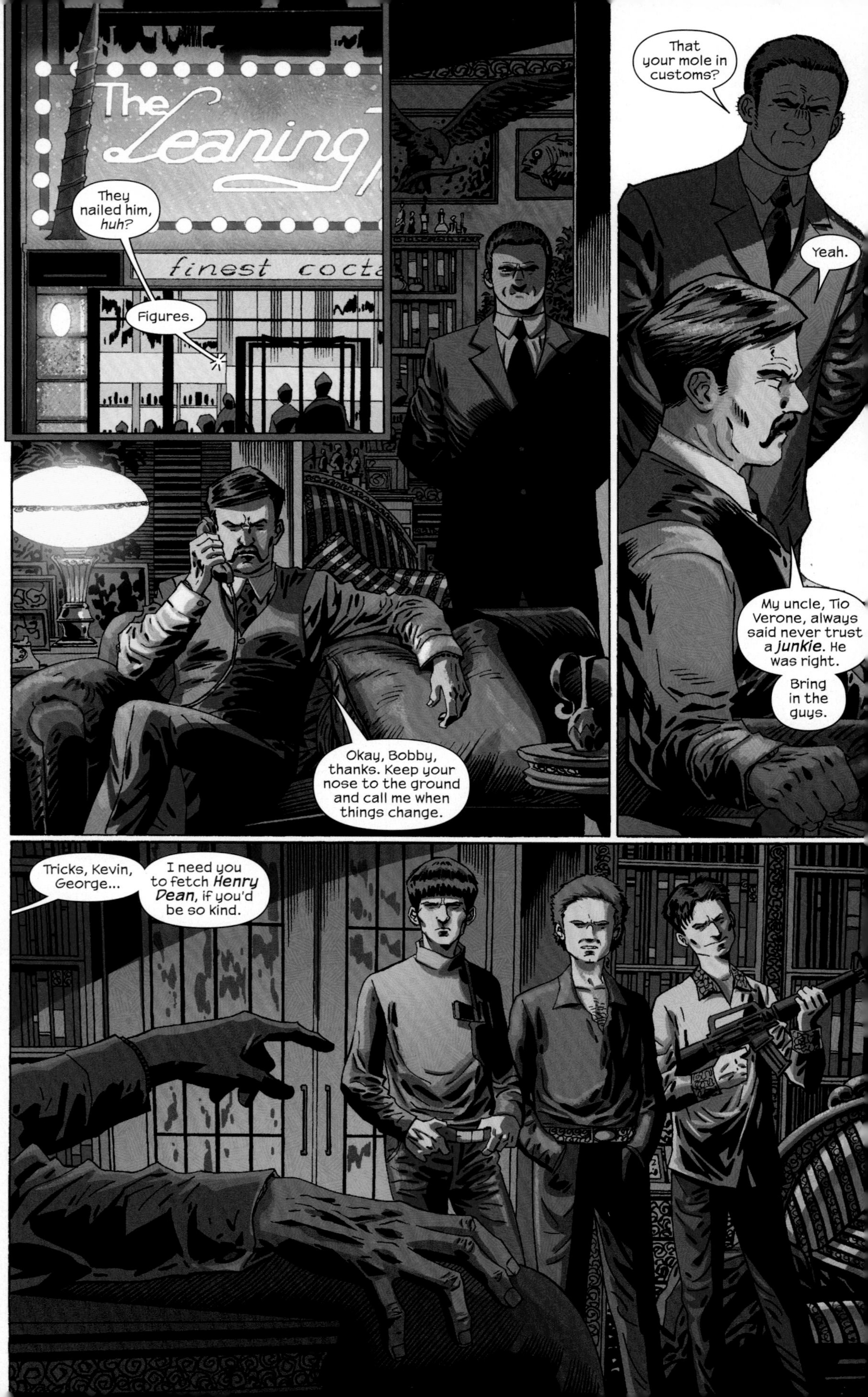
The Leaning T
finest cocta
They nailed him, huh?
Figures.
Okay, Bobby, thanks. Keep your nose to the ground and call me when things change.
That your mole in customs?
Yeah.
My uncle, Tio Verone, always said never trust a junkie. He was right.
Bring in the guys.
Tricks, Kevin, George...
I need you to fetch Henry Dean, if you'd be so kind.

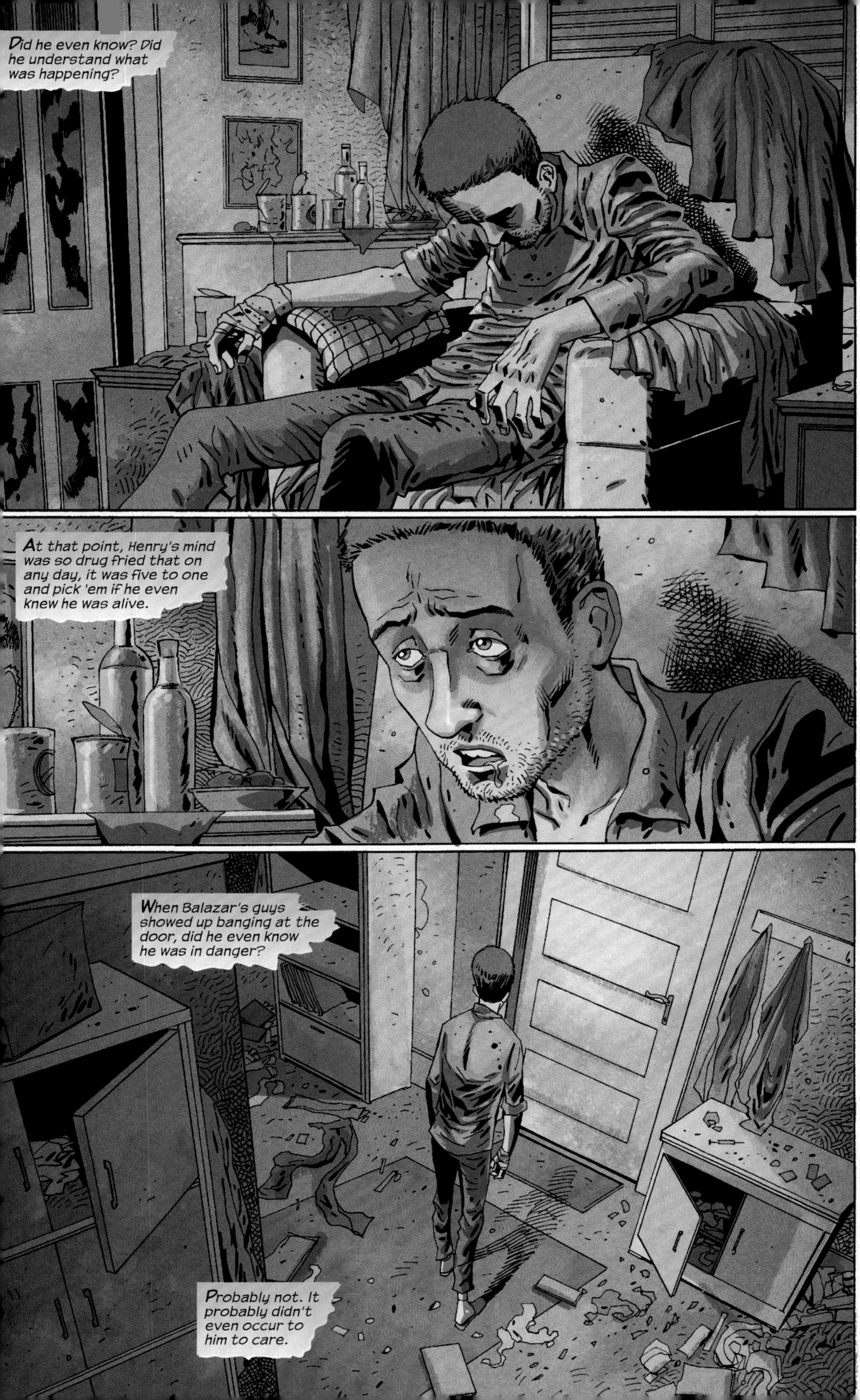
Did he even know? Did he understand what was happening?
At that point, Henry's mind was so drug fried that on any day, it was five to one and pick 'em if he even knew he was alive.
When Balazar's guys showed up banging at the door, did he even know he was in danger?
Probably not. It probably didn't even occur to him to care.

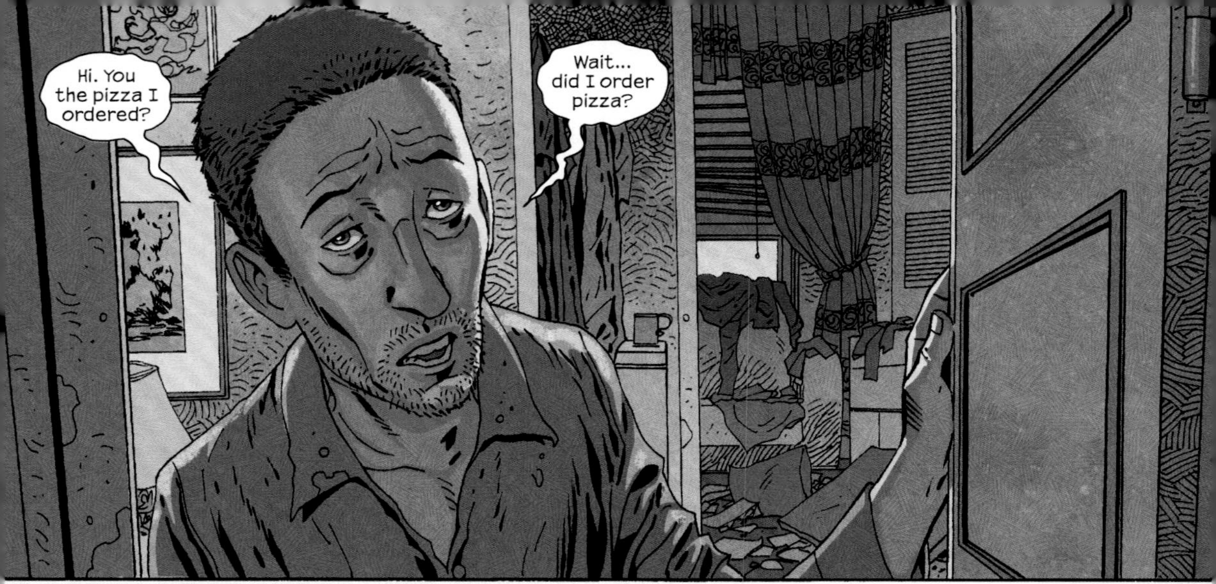
Hi. You the pizza I ordered?
Wait... did I order pizza?

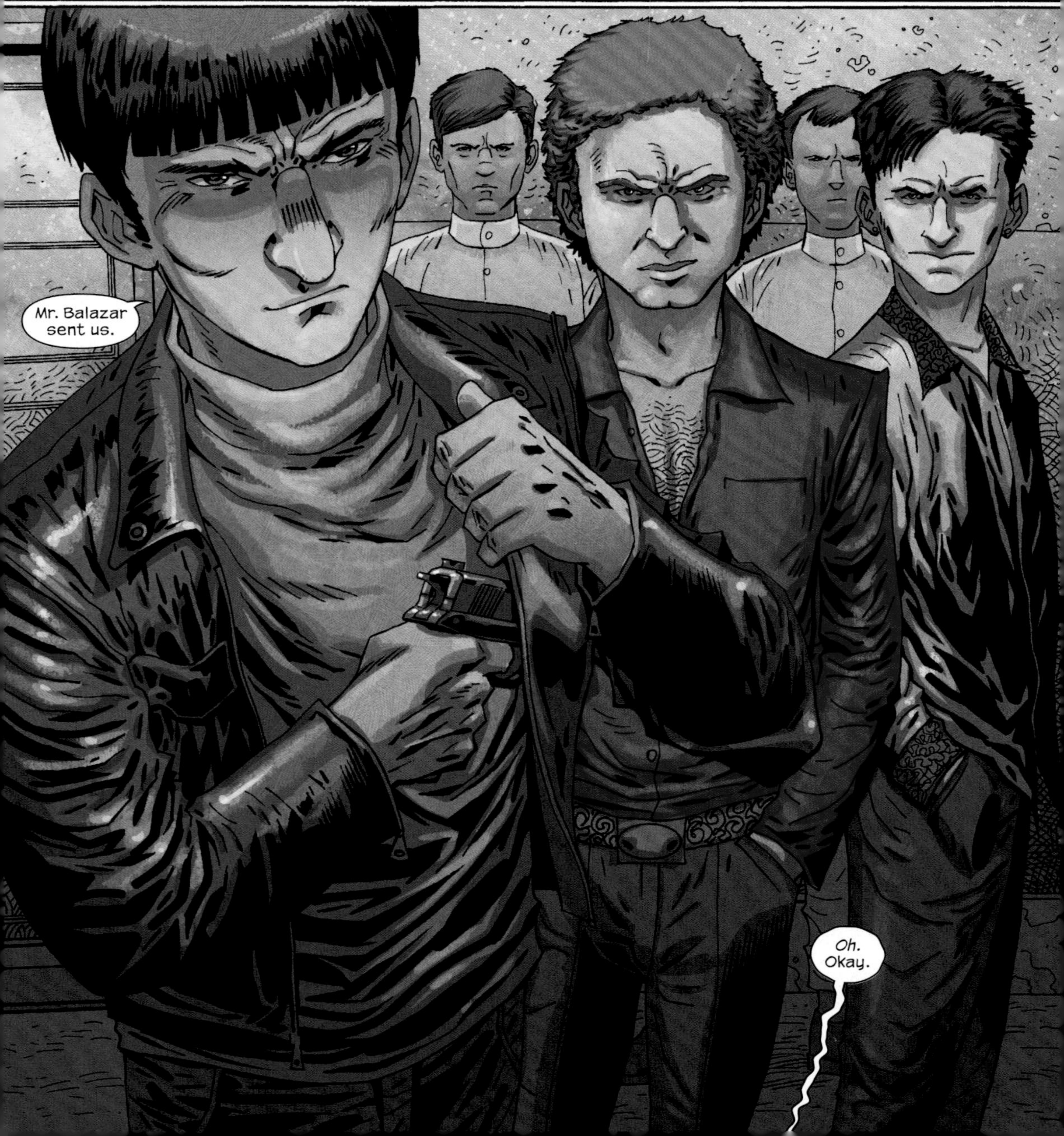
Mr. Balazar sent us.
Oh. Okay.

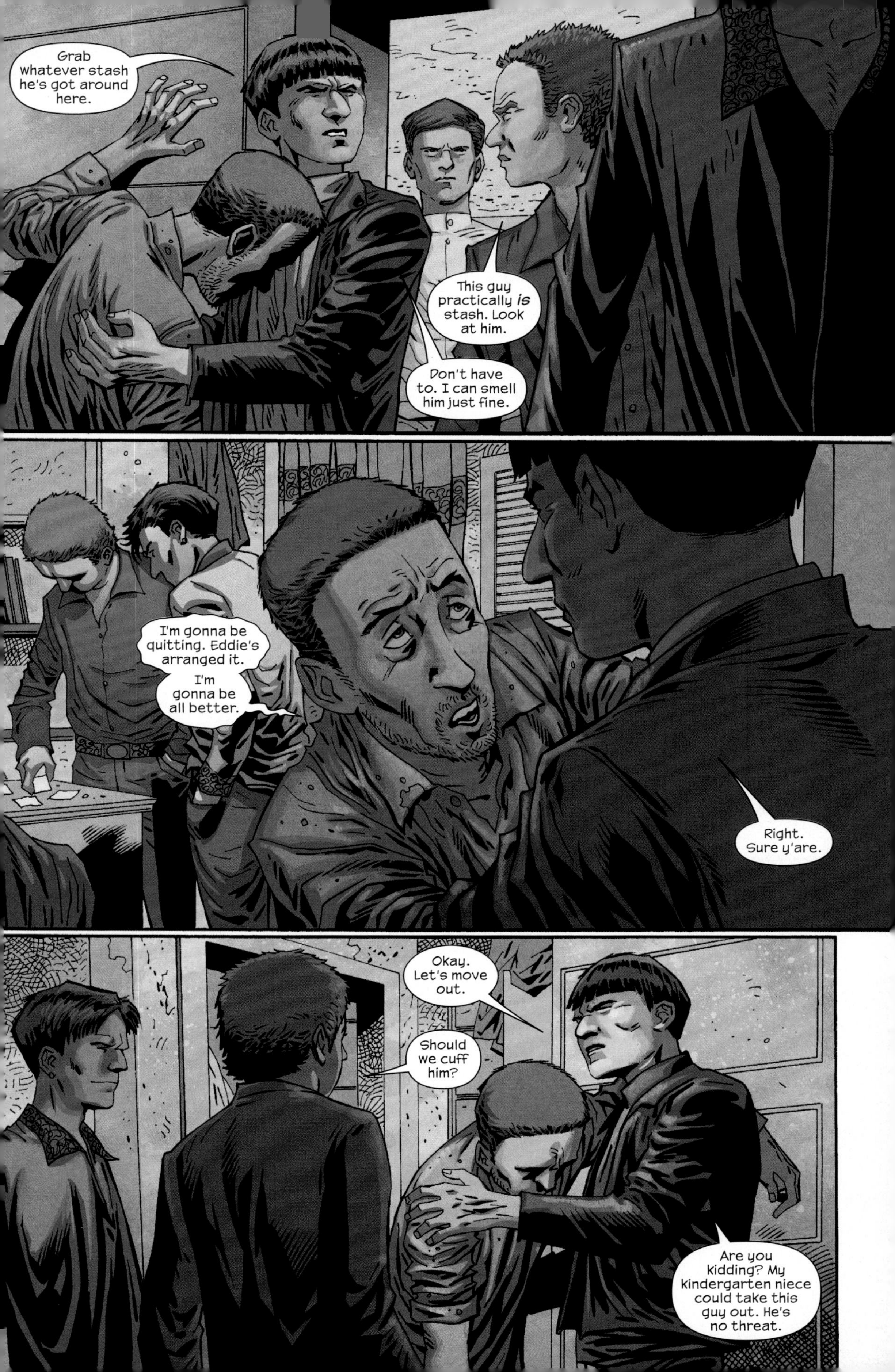
Grab whatever stash he's got around here.
This guy practically *is* stash. Look at him.
Don't have to. I can smell him just fine.
I'm gonna be quitting. Eddie's arranged it.
I'm gonna be all better.
Right. Sure y'are.
Okay. Let's move out.
Should we cuff him?
Are you kidding? My kindergarten niece could take this guy out. He's no threat.

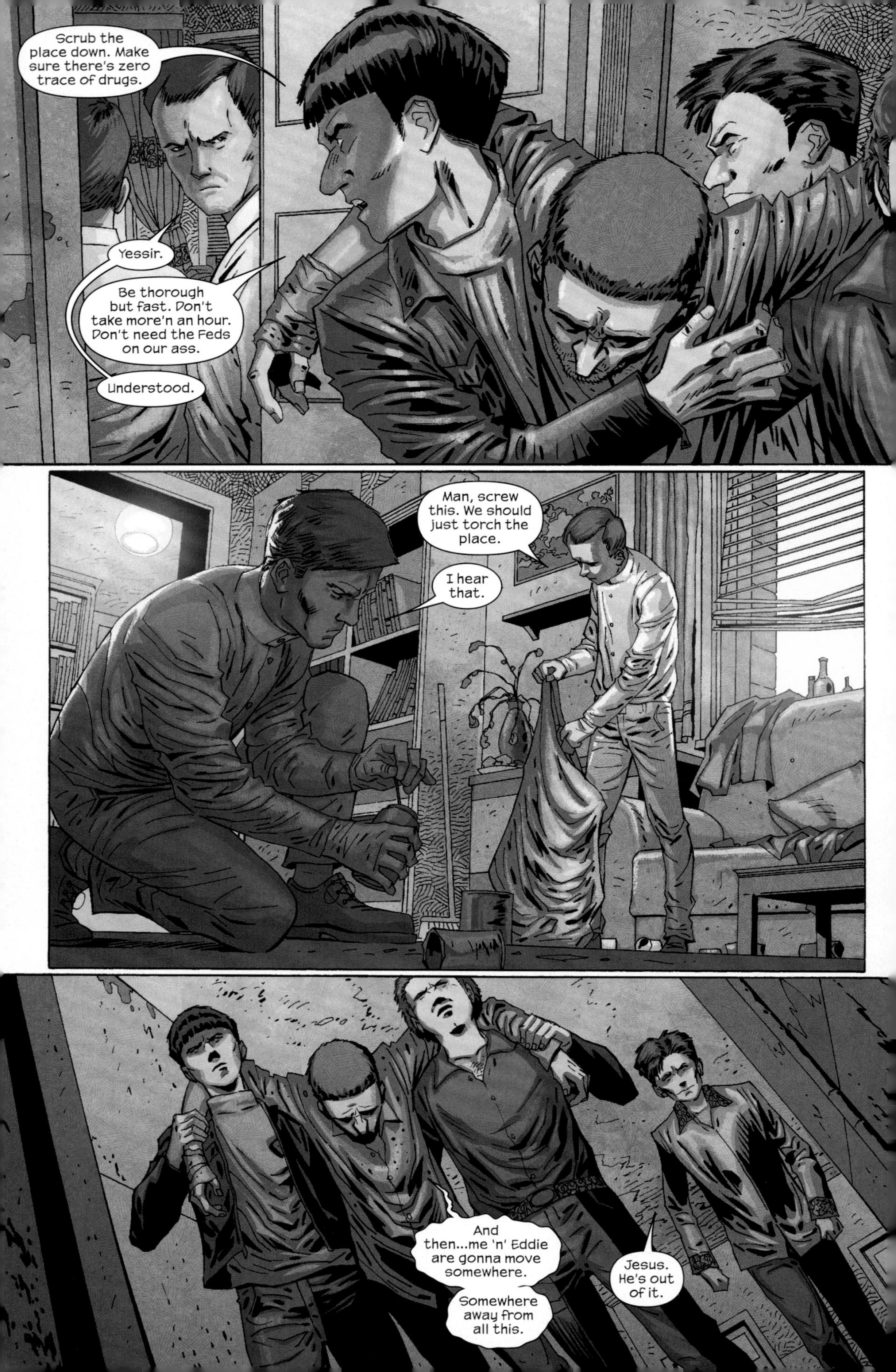
Scrub the place down. Make sure there's zero trace of drugs.
Yessir.
Be thorough but fast. Don't take more'n an hour. Don't need the Feds on our ass.
Understood.
Man, screw this. We should just torch the place.
I hear that.
And then...me 'n' Eddie are gonna move somewhere.
Somewhere away from all this.
Jesus. He's out of it.

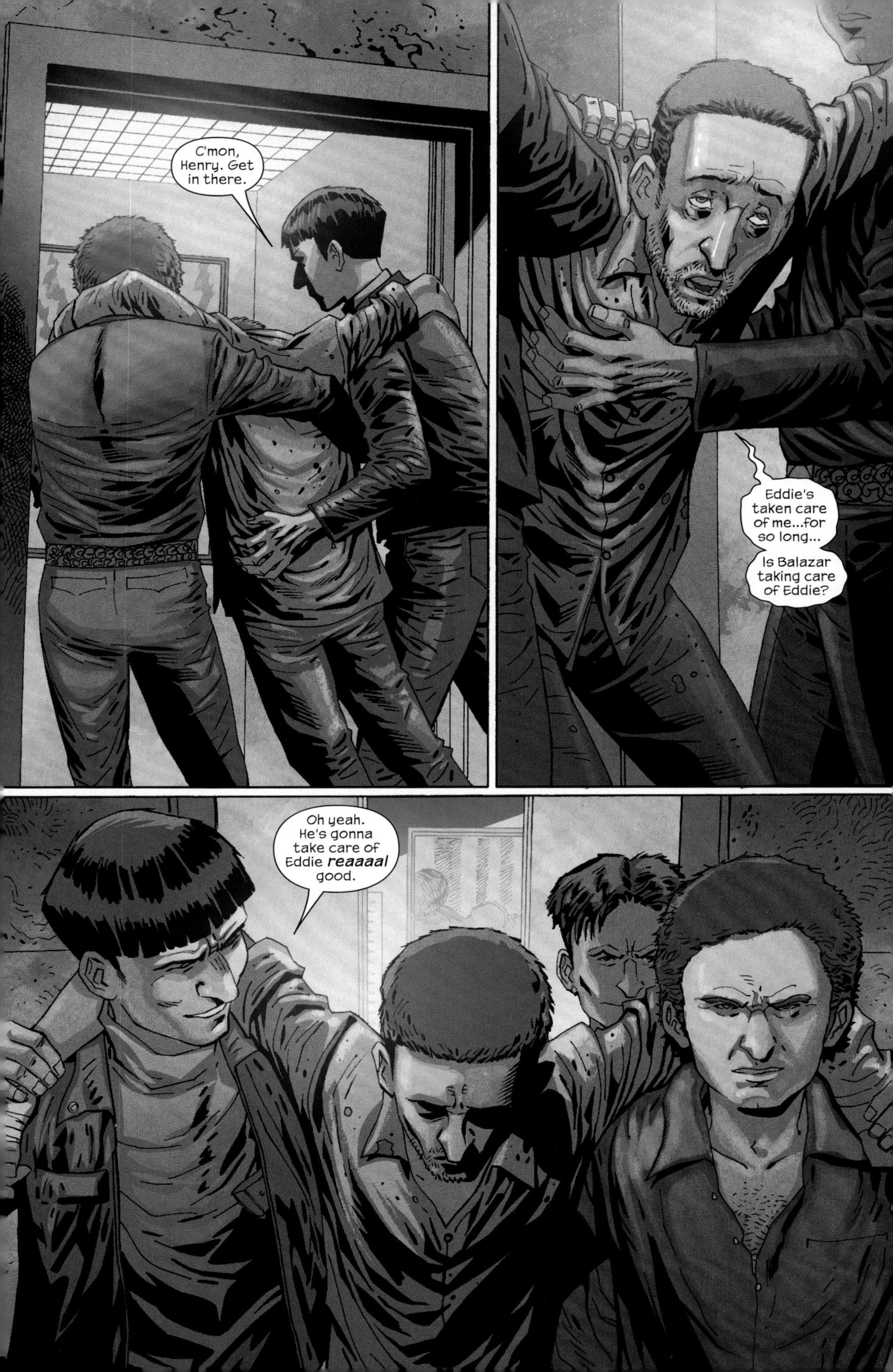
C'mon, Henry. Get in there.
Eddie's taken care of me...for so long...
Is Balazar taking care of Eddie?
Oh yeah. He's gonna take care of Eddie *reaaaal* good.

# THE DARK TOWER
# THE DRAWING OF THE THREE
## STEPHEN KING

# HOUSE OF CARDS
## CHAPTER TWO

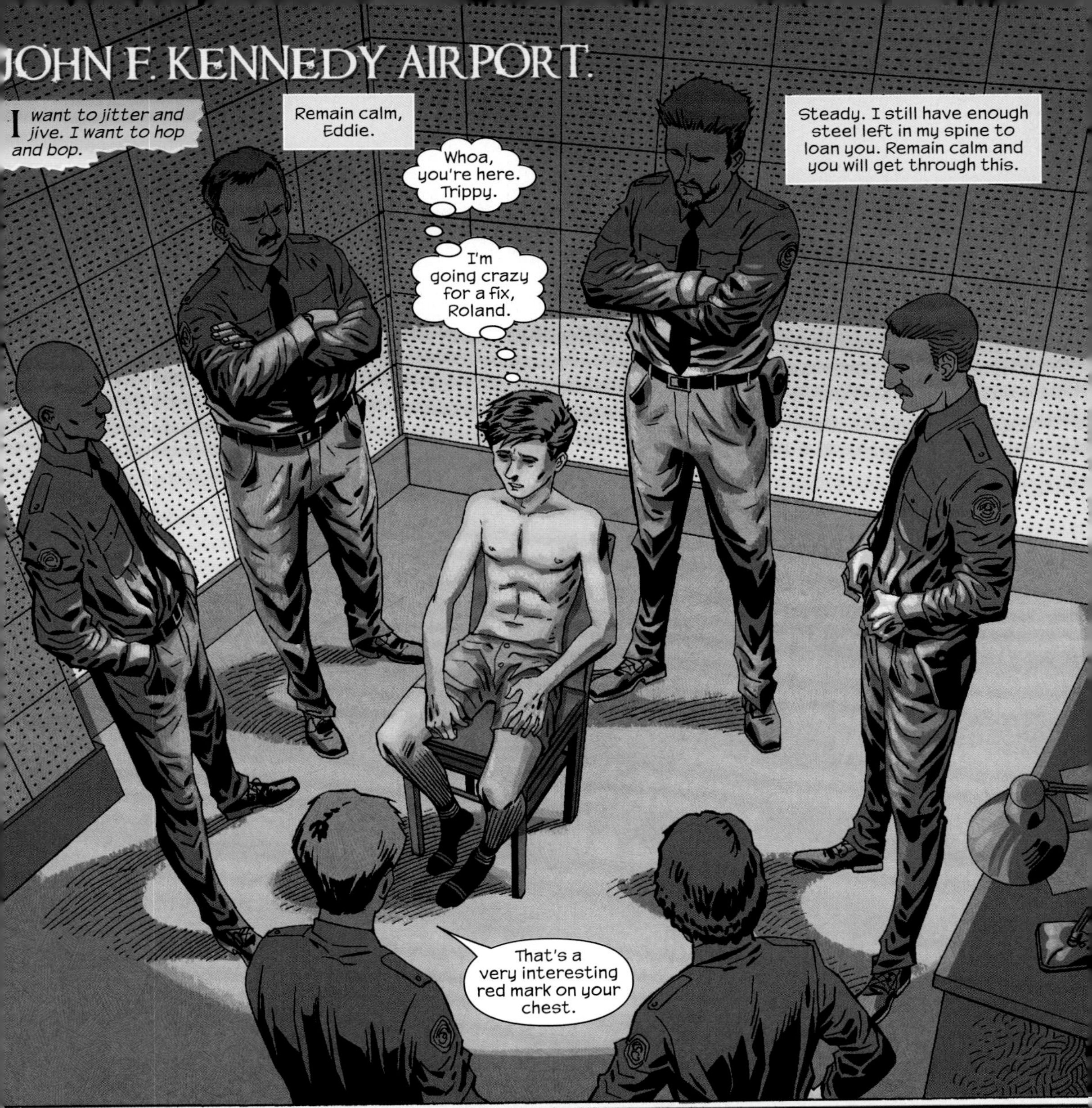
JOHN F. KENNEDY AIRPORT.
I want to jitter and jive. I want to hop and bop.
Remain calm, Eddie.
Whoa, you're here. Trippy.
I'm going crazy for a fix, Roland.
Steady. I still have enough steel left in my spine to loan you. Remain calm and you will get through this.
That's a very interesting red mark on your chest.


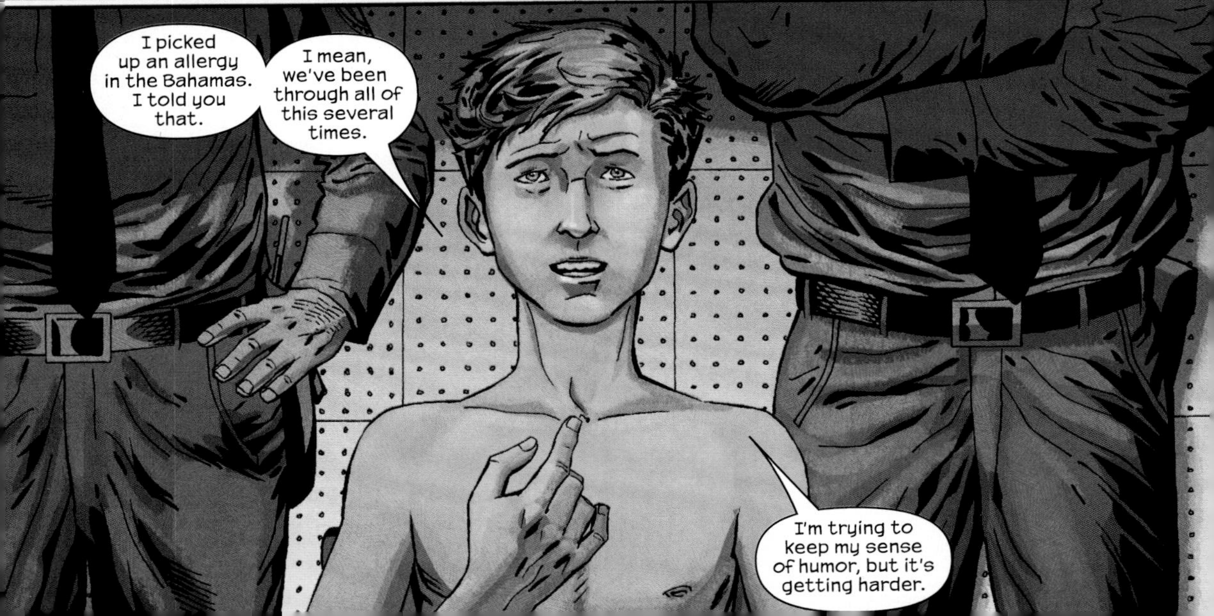
I picked up an allergy in the Bahamas. I told you that.
I mean, we've been through all of this several times.
I'm trying to keep my sense of humor, but it's getting harder.

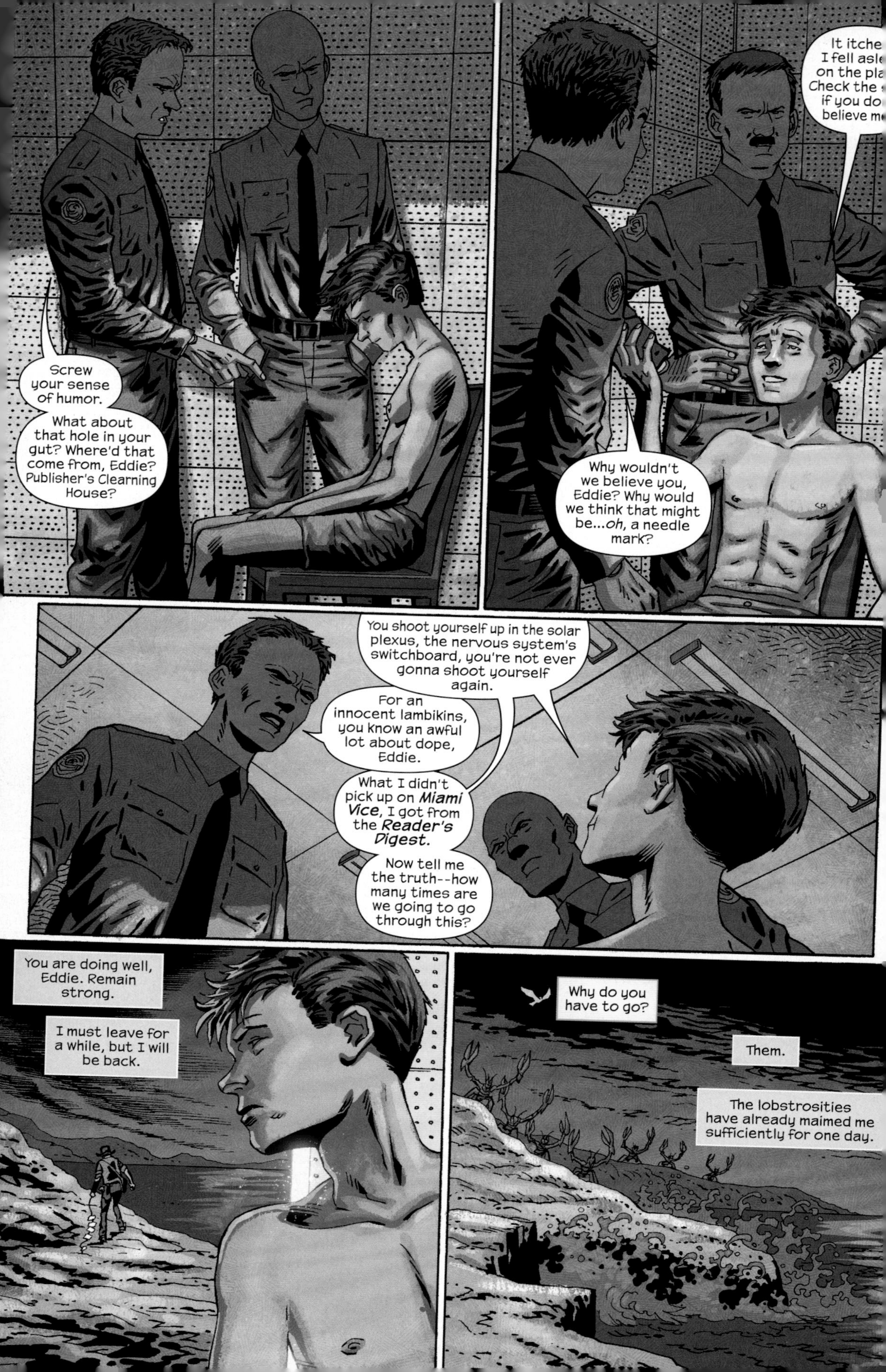
Screw your sense of humor.
What about that hole in your gut? Where'd that come from, Eddie? Publisher's Clearning House?
It itche I fell asle on the pla Check the if you do believe m
Why wouldn't we believe you, Eddie? Why would we think that might be...*oh*, a needle mark?
You shoot yourself up in the solar plexus, the nervous system's switchboard, you're not ever gonna shoot yourself again.
For an innocent lambikins, you know an awful lot about dope, Eddie.
What I didn't pick up on *Miami Vice*, I got from the ***Reader's Digest***.
Now tell me the truth--how many times are we going to go through this?
You are doing well, Eddie. Remain strong.
I must leave for a while, but I will be back.
Why do you have to go?
Them.
The lobstrosities have already maimed me sufficiently for one day.

Jesus.

Yes.

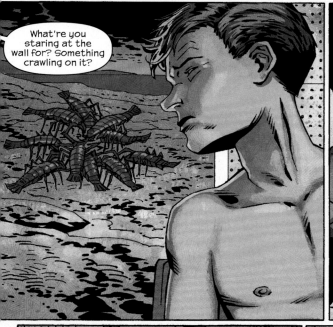

What're you staring at the wall for? Something crawling on it?

Crawling the walls. *Heh. Hehhh heh...*

What's so damned funny?

You are. This is.

These are filaments. We'll get the lab confirmation, but we know what sort they are.

They're filaments of strapping tape. Took these off his chest.

Mosquito bites. I told you. Almost healed. Jesus Christ, you can see that for yourself.

And those marks on your arm? They're not needle tracks?

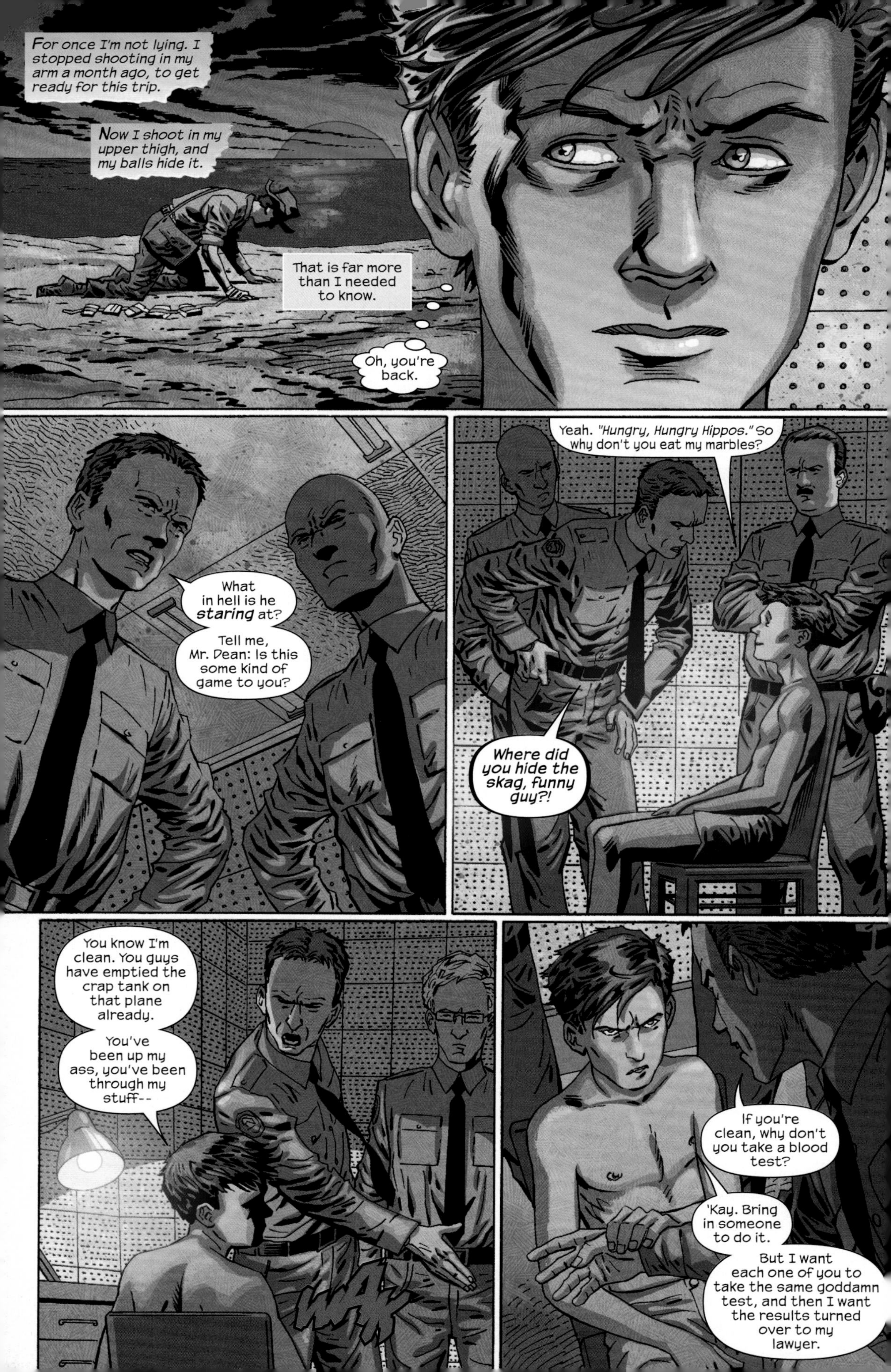

For once I'm not lying. I stopped shooting in my arm a month ago, to get ready for this trip.
Now I shoot in my upper thigh, and my balls hide it.
That is far more than I needed to know.
Oh, you're back.
What in hell is he *staring* at?
Tell me, Mr. Dean: Is this some kind of game to you?
Yeah. *"Hungry, Hungry Hippos."* So why don't you eat my marbles?
*Where did you hide the skag, funny guy?!*
You know I'm clean. You guys have emptied the crap tank on that plane already.
You've been up my ass, you've been through my stuff--
If you're clean, why don't you take a blood test?
'Kay. Bring in someone to do it.
But I want each one of you to take the same goddamn test, and then I want the results turned over to my lawyer.

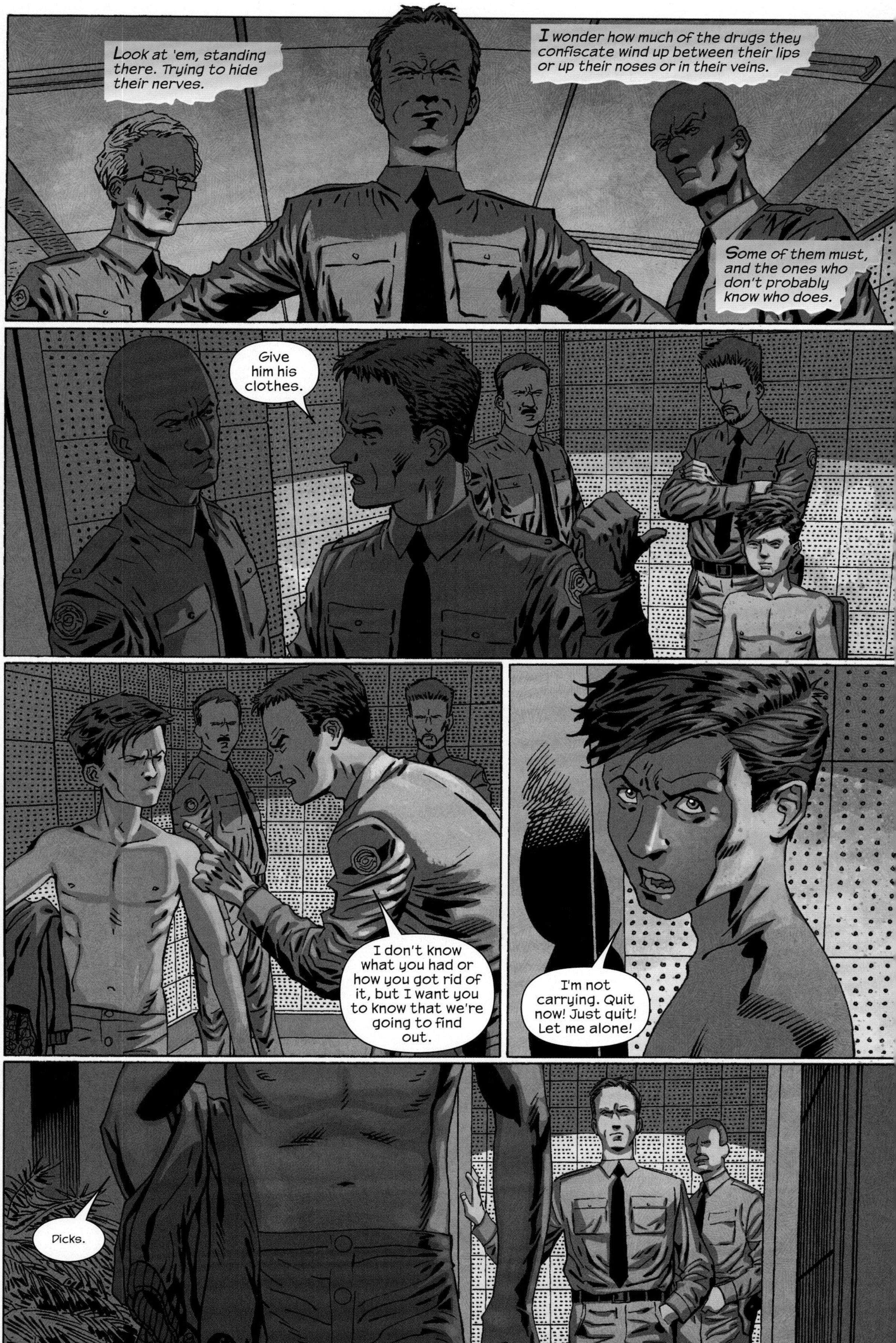
Look at 'em, standing there. Trying to hide their nerves.
I wonder how much of the drugs they confiscate wind up between their lips or up their noses or in their veins.
Some of them must, and the ones who don't probably know who does.
Give him his clothes.
I don't know what you had or how you got rid of it, but I want you to know that we're going to find out.
I'm not carrying. Quit now! Just quit! Let me alone!
Dicks.

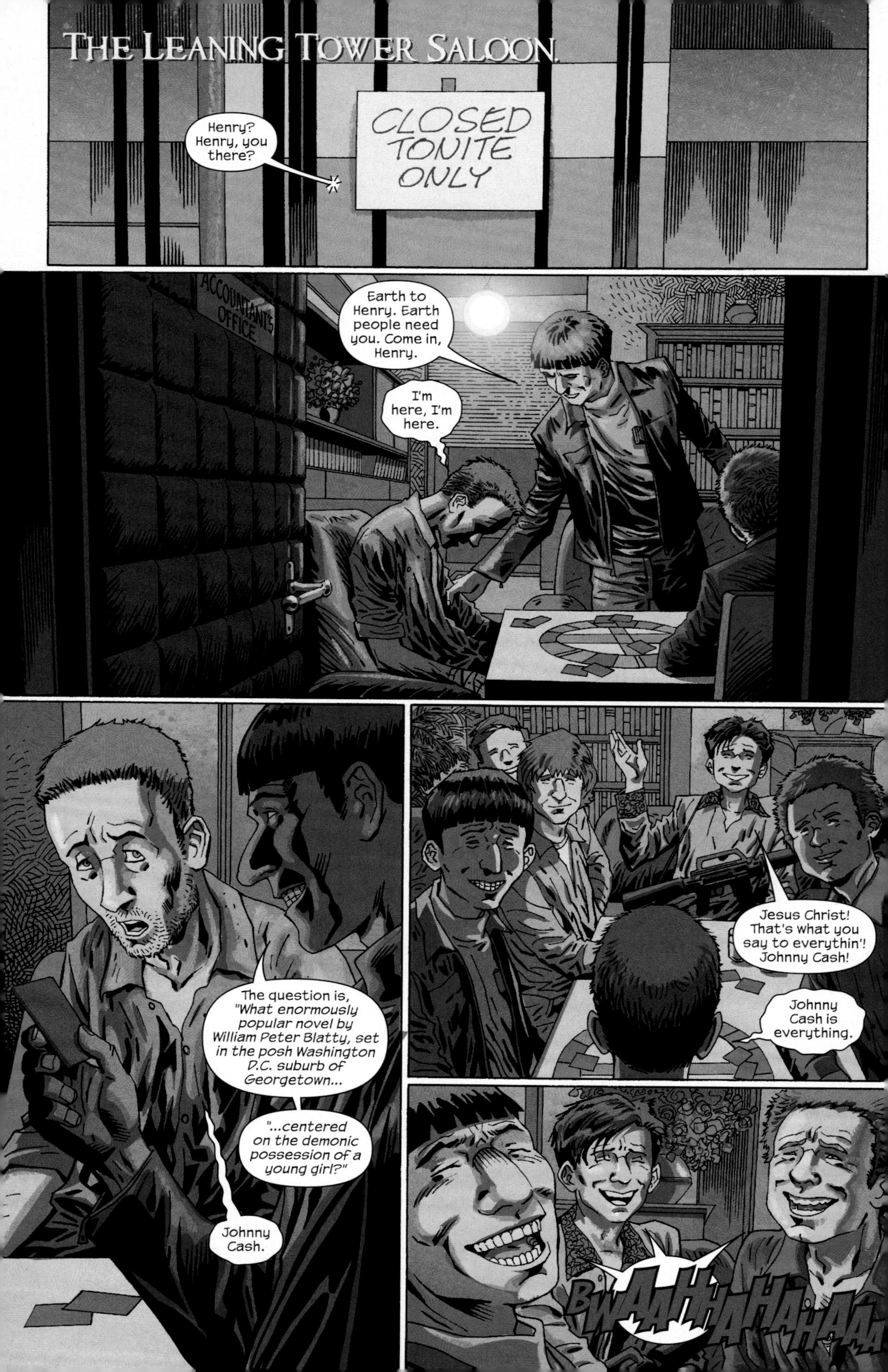
THE LEANING TOWER SALOON.
CLOSED TONITE ONLY
Henry? Henry, you there?
Earth to Henry. Earth people need you. Come in, Henry.
I'm here, I'm here.
ACCOUNTANT'S OFFICE
The question is, "What enormously popular novel by William Peter Blatty, set in the posh Washington D.C. suburb of Georgetown...
"...centered on the demonic possession of a young girl?"
Johnny Cash.
Jesus Christ! That's what you say to everythin'! Johnny Cash!
Johnny Cash is everything.
BWAHHAHAHAA

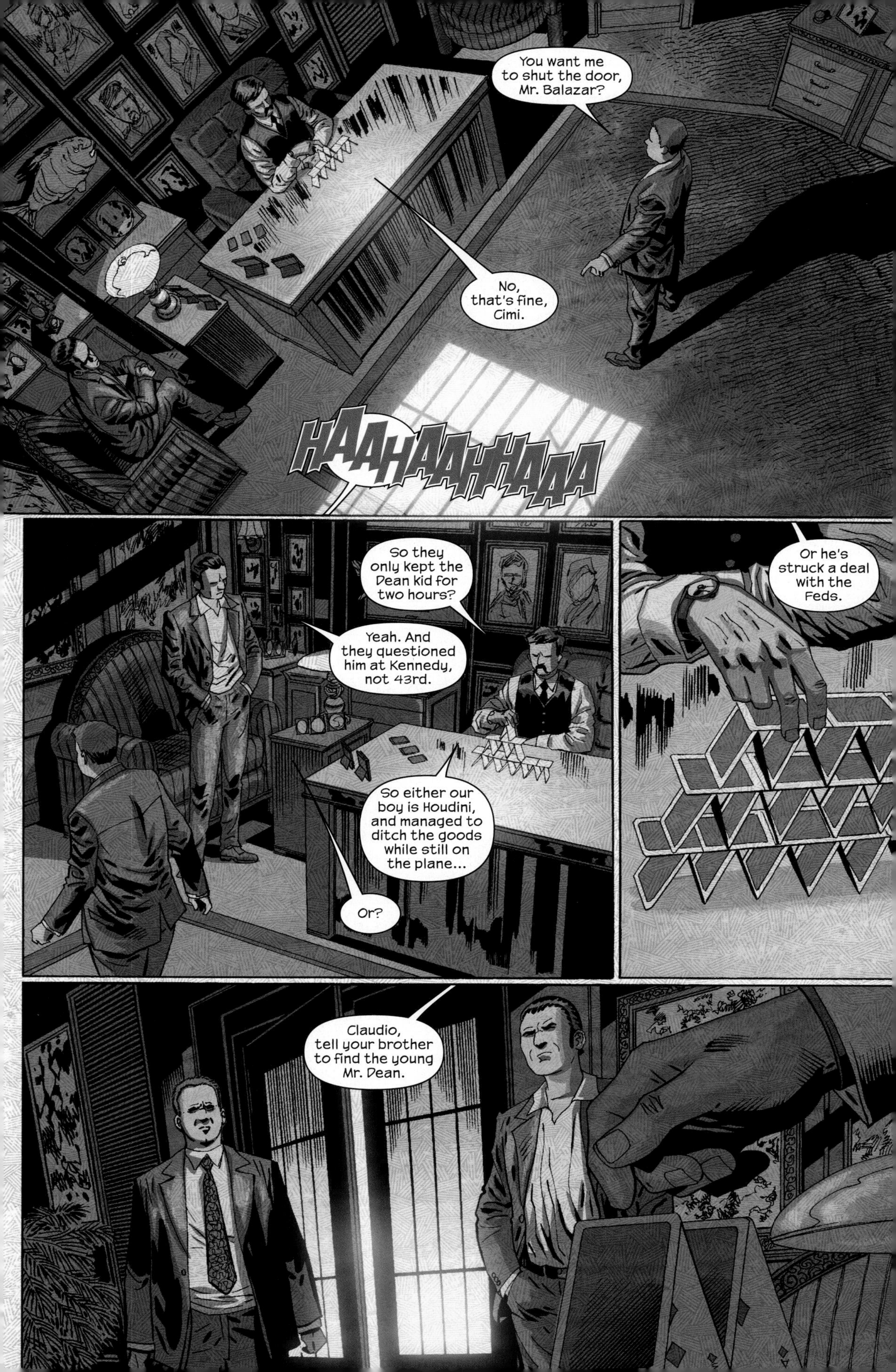

You want me to shut the door, Mr. Balazar?
No, that's fine, Cimi.
HAAHAAHHAAA
So they only kept the Dean kid for two hours?
Yeah. And they questioned him at Kennedy, not 43rd.
So either our boy is Houdini, and managed to ditch the goods while still on the plane...
Or?
Or he's struck a deal with the Feds.
Claudio, tell your brother to find the young Mr. Dean.

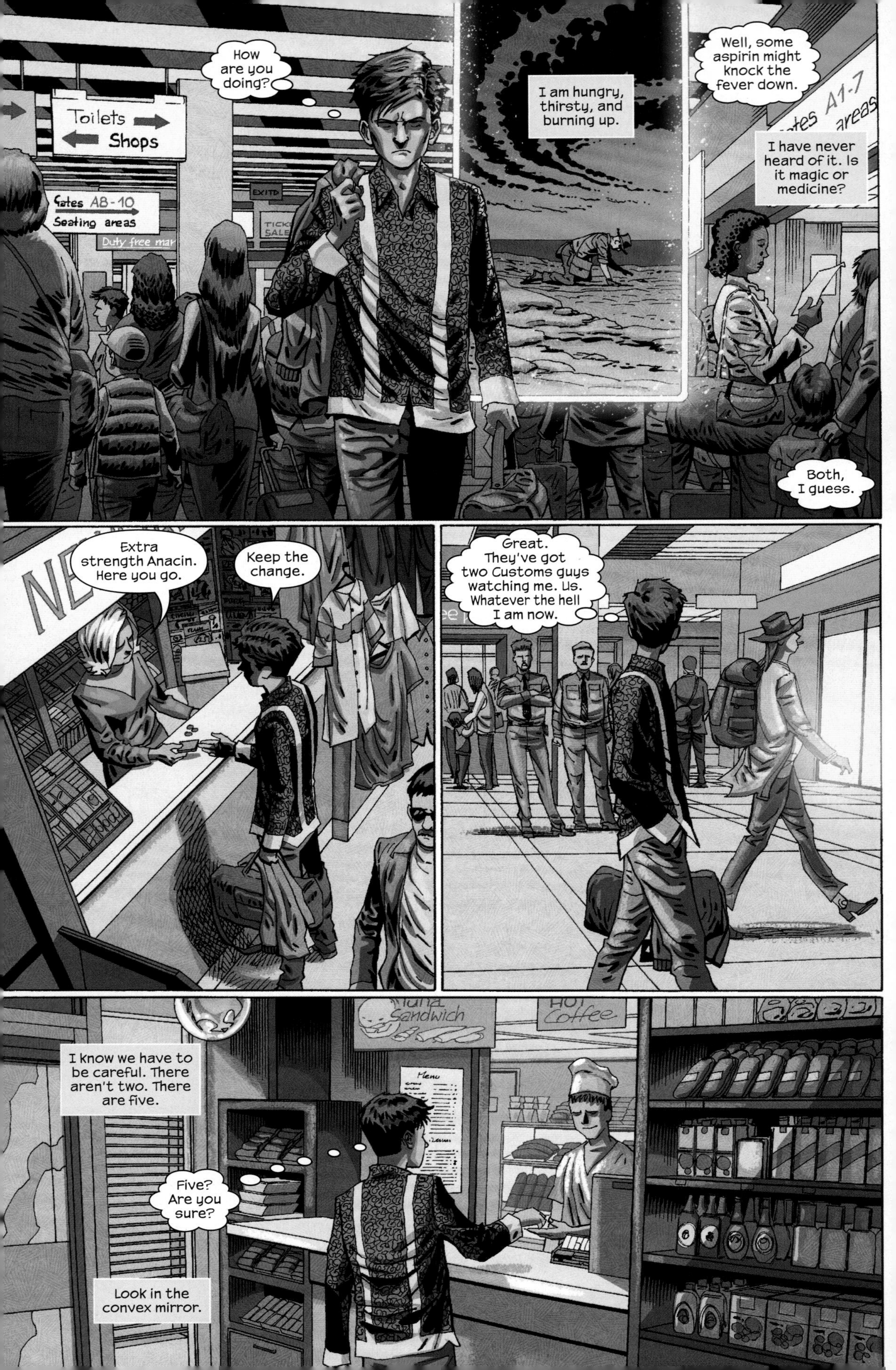
How are you doing?
Toilets
Shops
Gates A8-10
Seating areas
I am hungry, thirsty, and burning up.
Well, some aspirin might knock the fever down.
Gates A1-7
areas
I have never heard of it. Is it magic or medicine?
Both, I guess.
Extra strength Anacin. Here you go.
Keep the change.
Great. They've got two Customs guys watching me. Us. Whatever the hell I am now.
Tuna Sandwich
Hot Coffee
Menu
I know we have to be careful. There aren't two. There are five.
Five? Are you sure?
Look in the convex mirror.

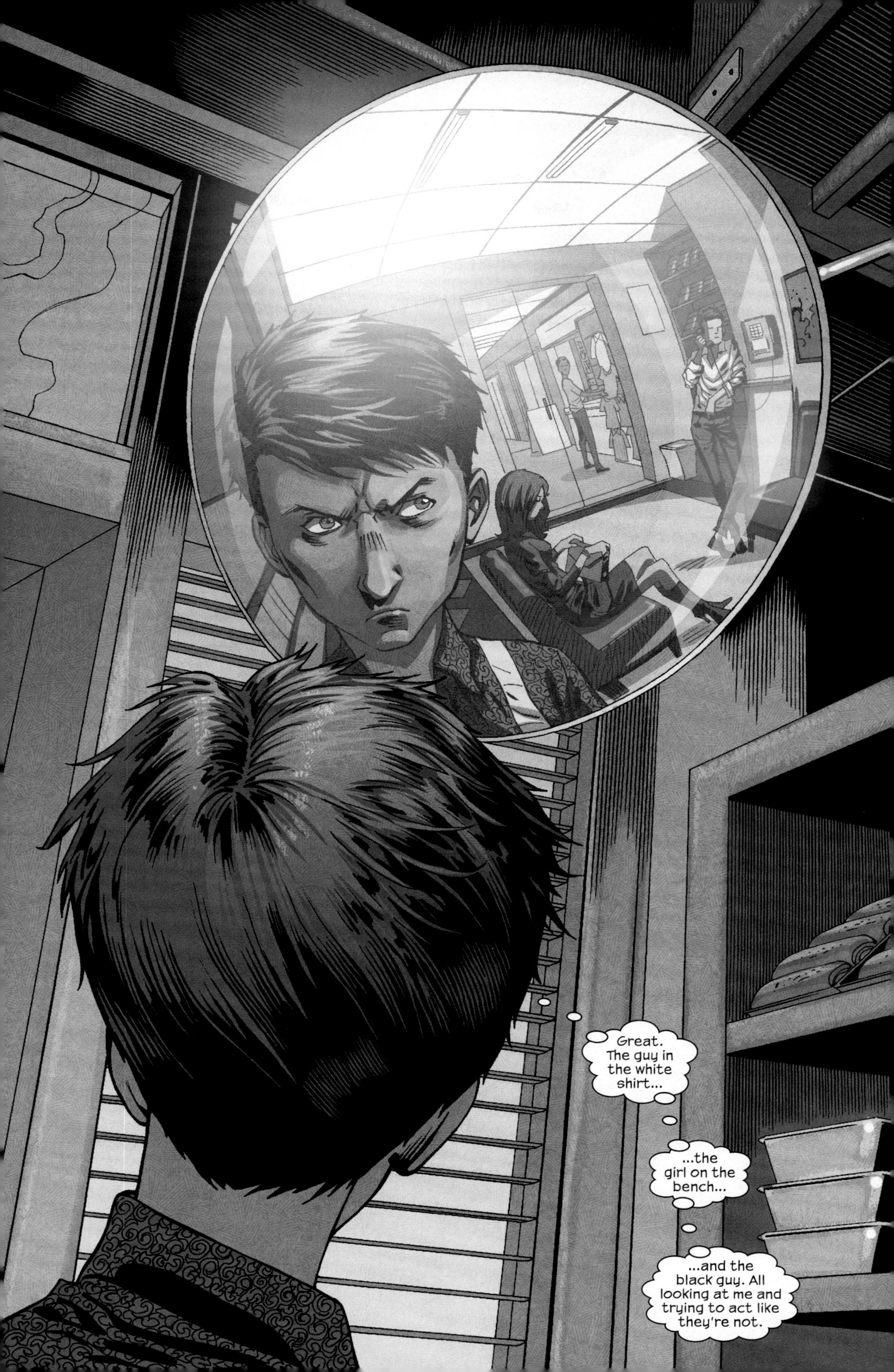
Great. The guy in the white shirt...
...the girl on the bench...
...and the black guy. All looking at me and trying to act like they're not.

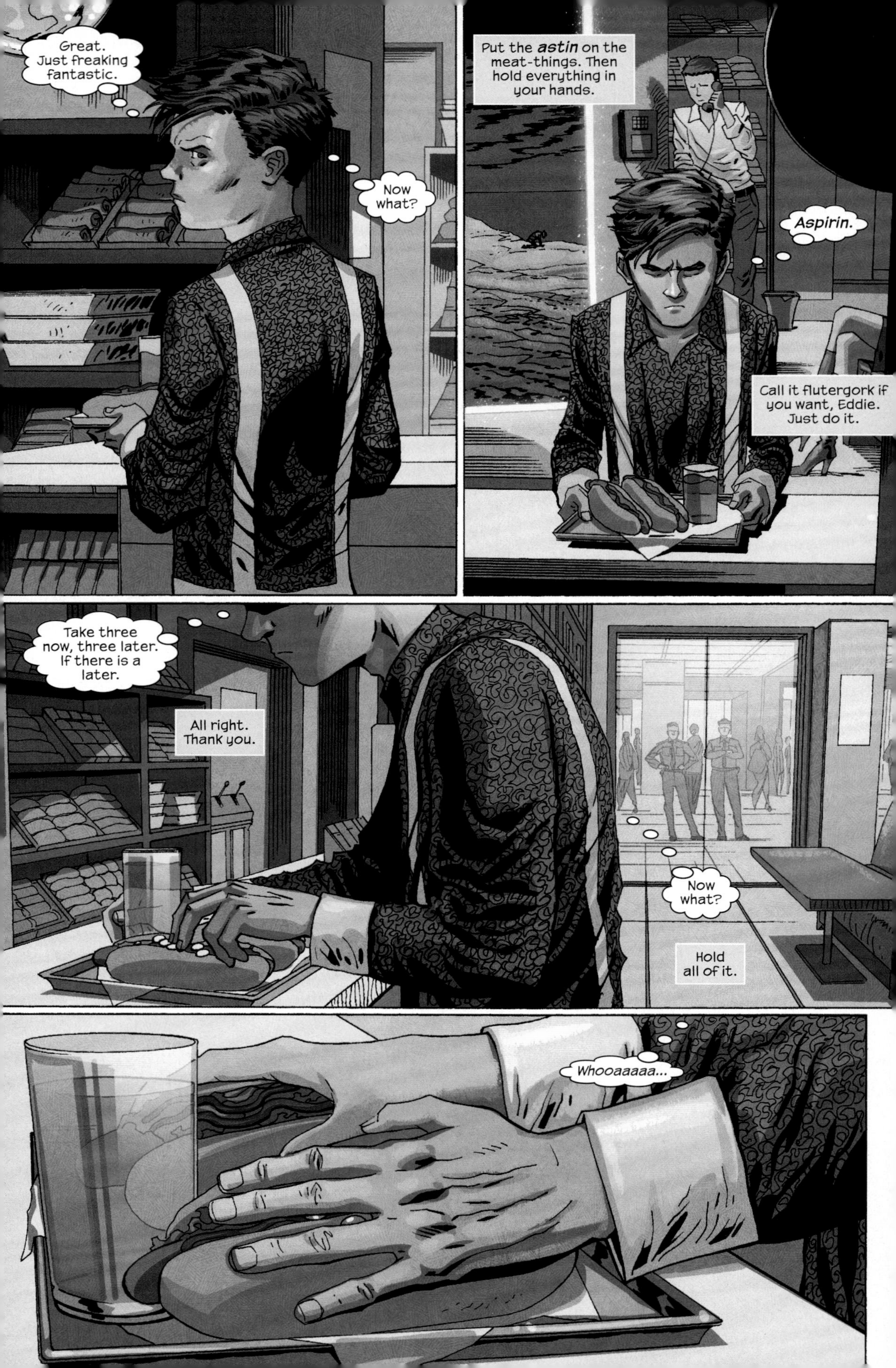

Great. Just freaking fantastic.
Now what?
Put the *astin* on the meat-things. Then hold everything in your hands.
*Aspirin.*
Call it flutergork if you want, Eddie. Just do it.
Take three now, three later. If there is a later.
All right. Thank you.
Now what?
Hold all of it.
Whooaaaaa...

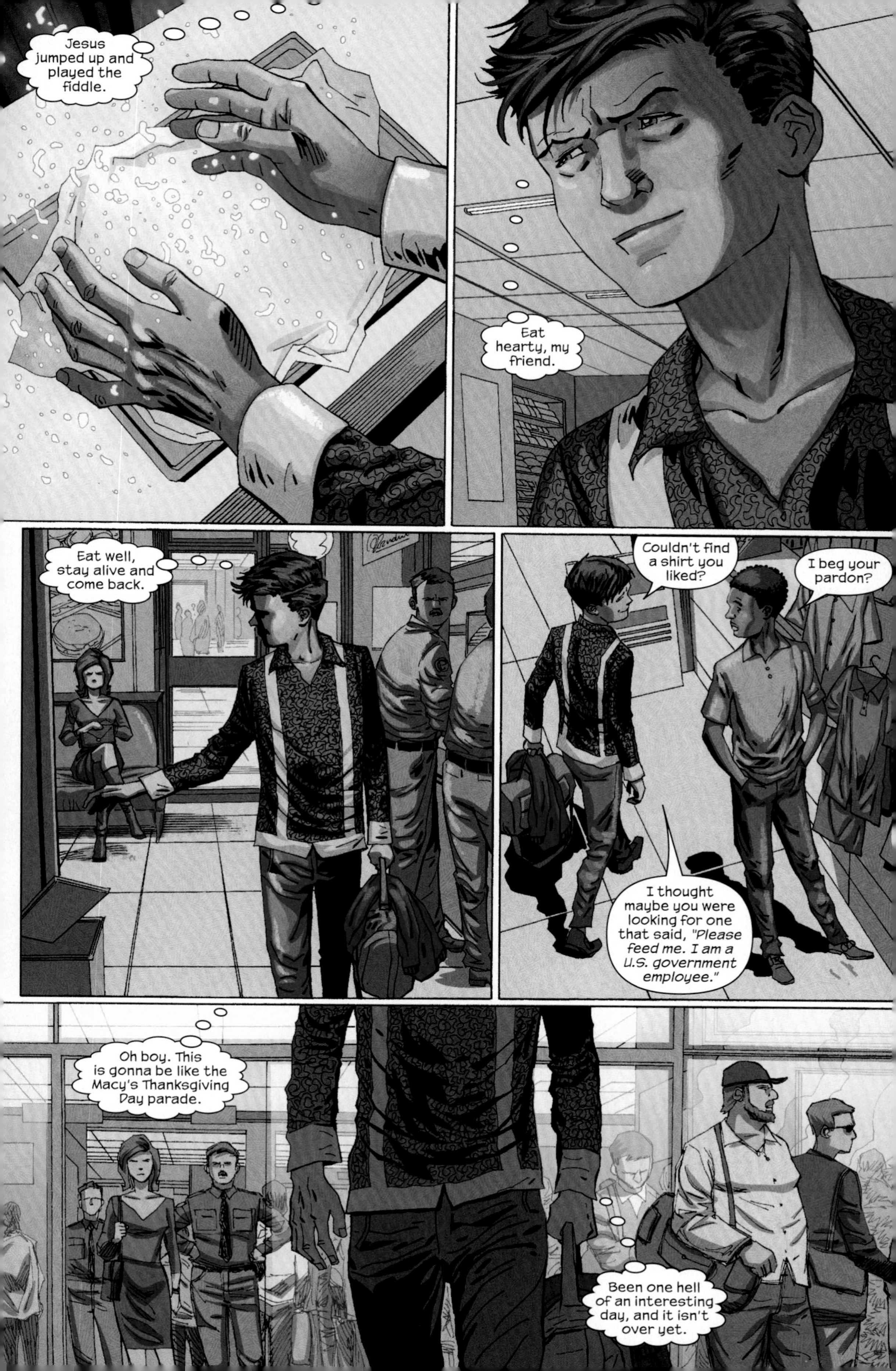
Jesus jumped up and played the fiddle.
Eat hearty, my friend.
Eat well, stay alive and come back.
Couldn't find a shirt you liked?
I beg your pardon?
I thought maybe you were looking for one that said, *"Please feed me. I am a U.S. government employee."*
Oh boy. This is gonna be like the Macy's Thanksgiving Day parade.
Been one hell of an interesting day, and it isn't over yet.

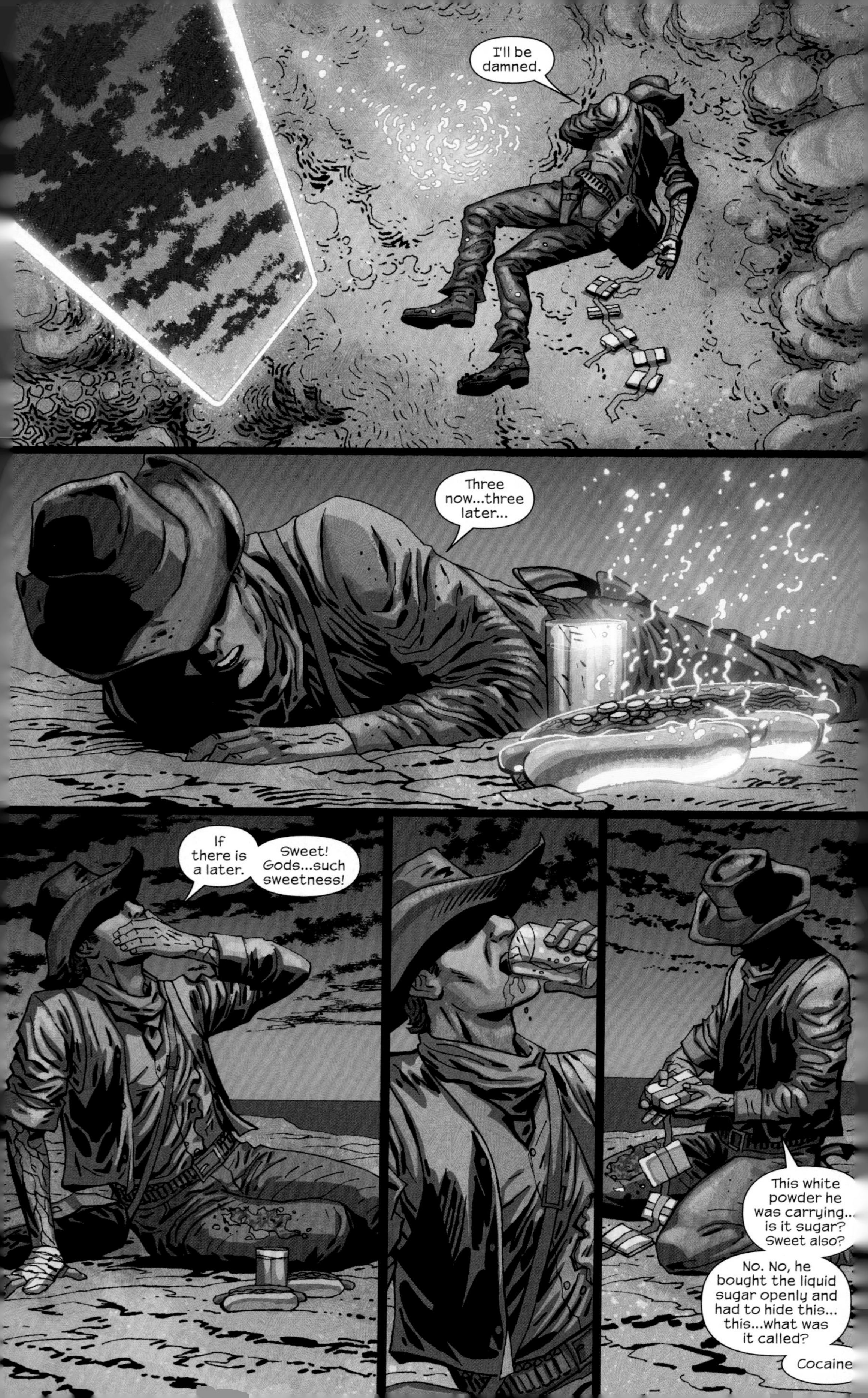
I'll be damned.
Three now...three later...
If there is a later.
Sweet! Gods...such sweetness!
This white powder he was carrying... is it sugar? Sweet also?
No. No, he bought the liquid sugar openly and had to hide this... this...what was it called?
Cocaine

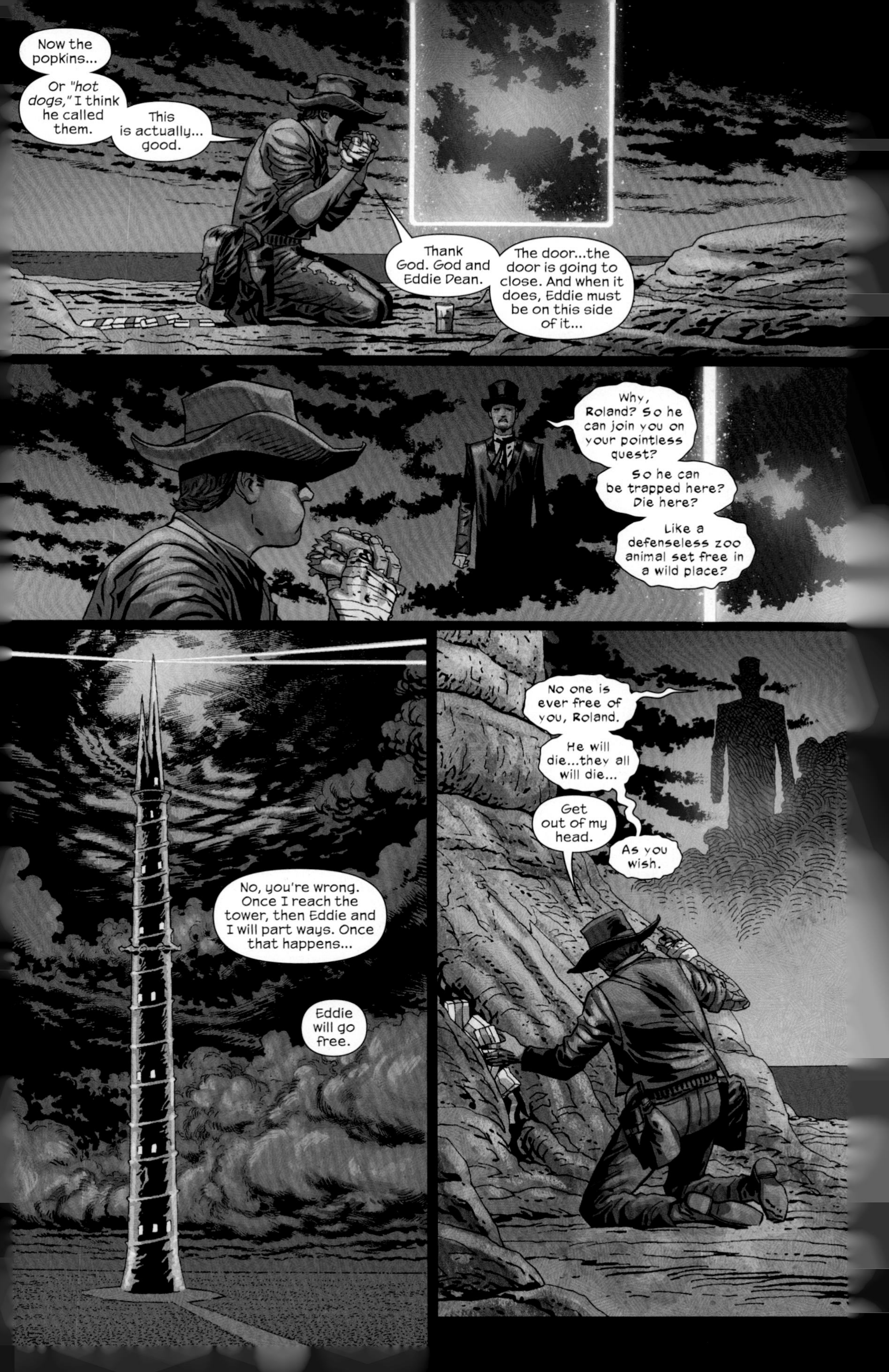

Now the popkins...
Or "hot dogs," I think he called them.
This is actually... good.
Thank God. God and Eddie Dean.
The door...the door is going to close. And when it does, Eddie must be on this side of it...
Why, Roland? So he can join you on your pointless quest?
So he can be trapped here? Die here?
Like a defenseless zoo animal set free in a wild place?
No, you're wrong. Once I reach the tower, then Eddie and I will part ways. Once that happens...
Eddie will go free.
No one is ever free of you, Roland.
He will die...they all will die...
Get out of my head.
As you wish.

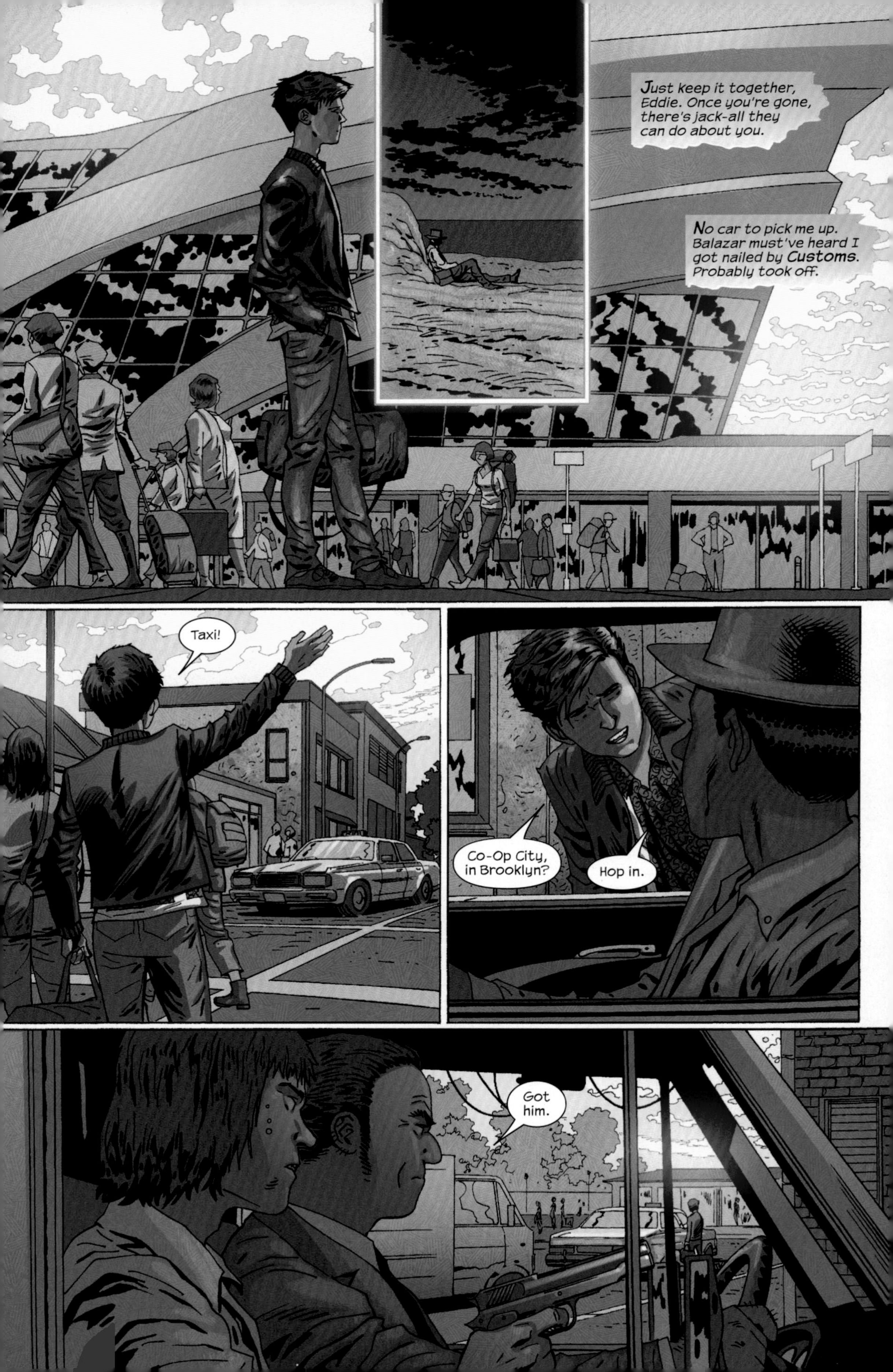

Just keep it together, Eddie. Once you're gone, there's jack-all they can do about you.
No car to pick me up. Balazar must've heard I got nailed by Customs. Probably took off.
Taxi!
Co-Op City, in Brooklyn?
Hop in.
Got him.

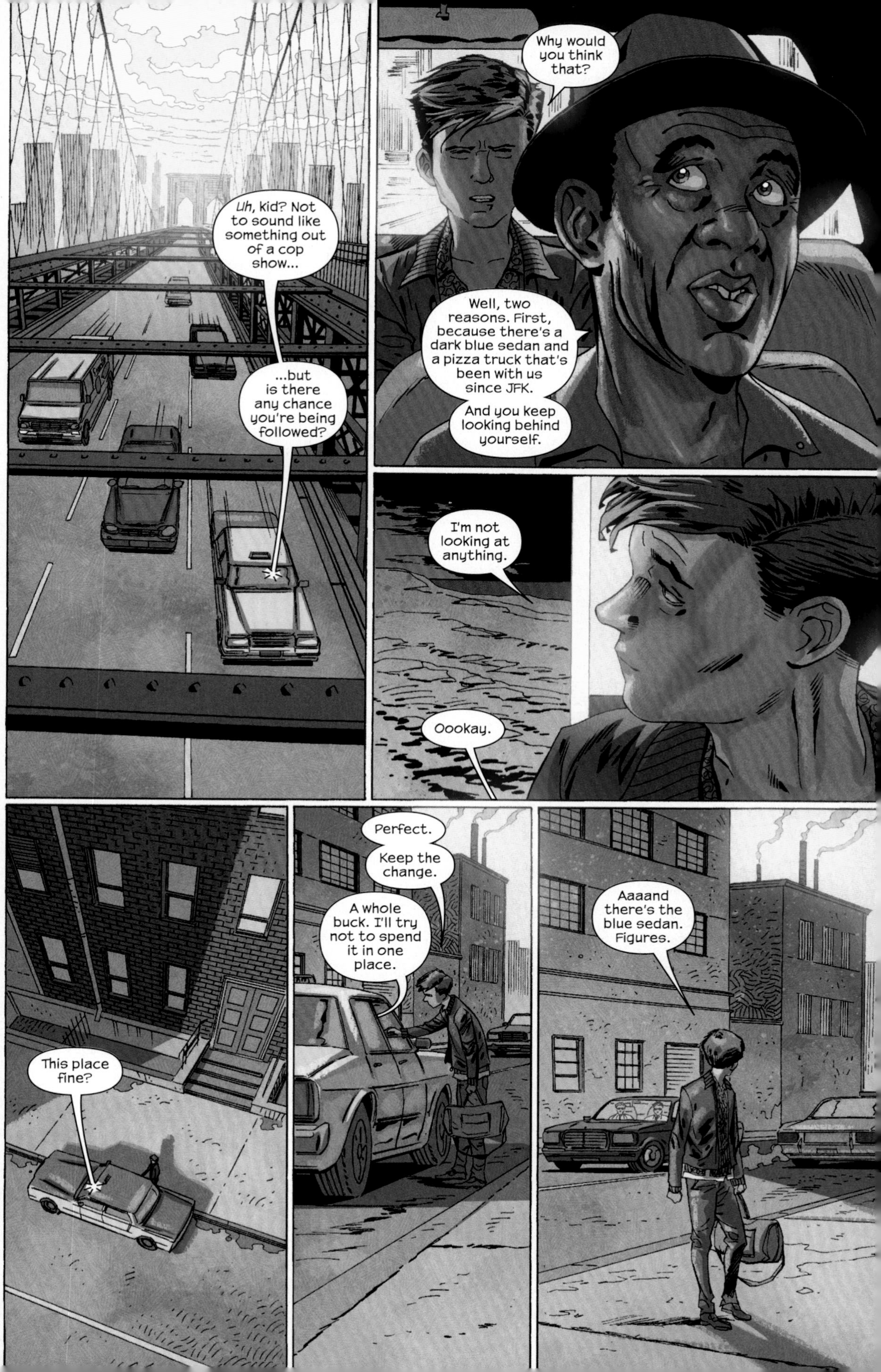

Uh, kid? Not to sound like something out of a cop show...
...but is there any chance you're being followed?
Why would you think that?
Well, two reasons. First, because there's a dark blue sedan and a pizza truck that's been with us since JFK.
And you keep looking behind yourself.
I'm not looking at anything.
Oookay.
This place fine?
Perfect.
Keep the change.
A whole buck. I'll try not to spend it in one place.
Aaaand there's the blue sedan. Figures.

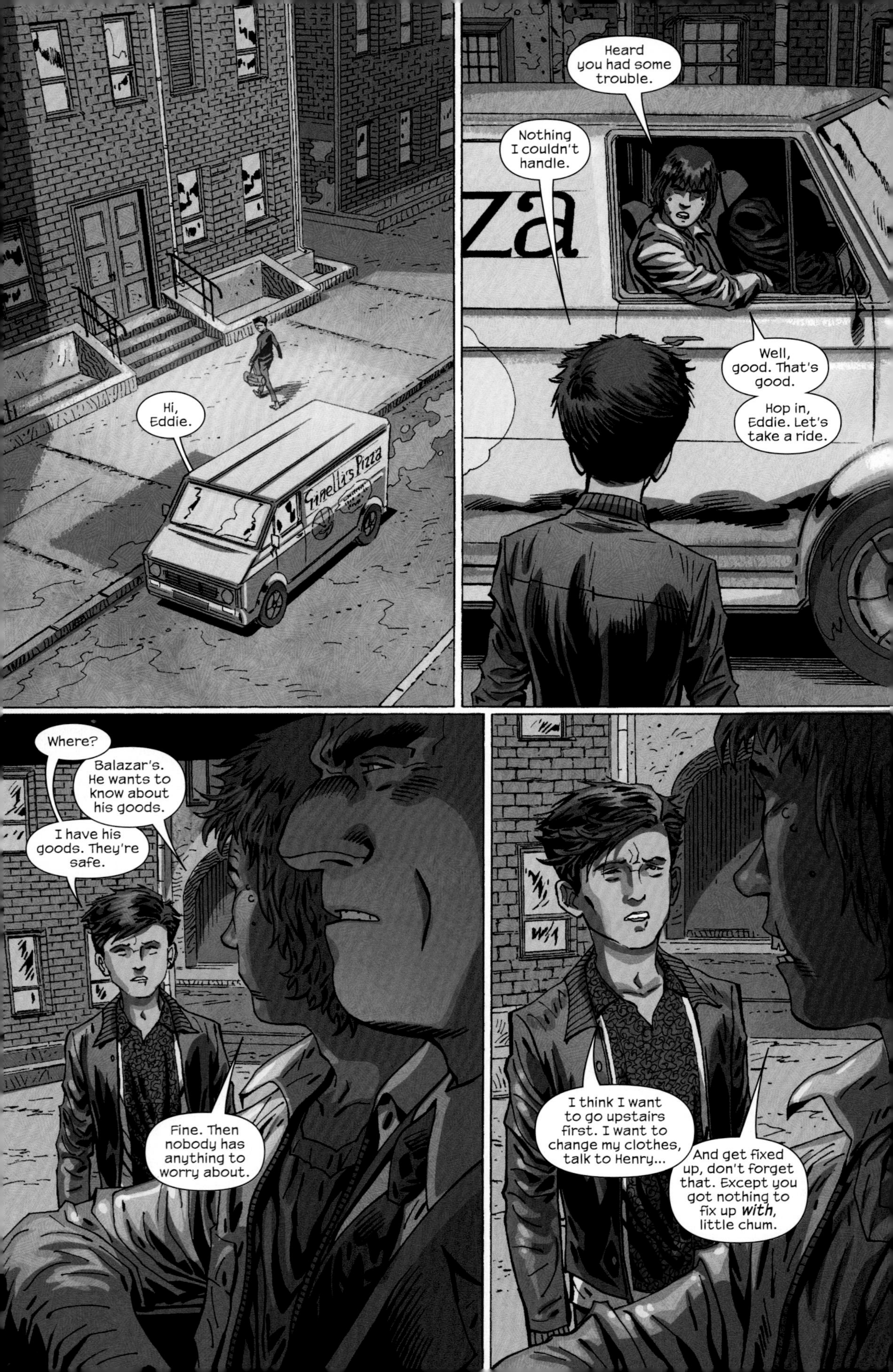
Hi, Eddie.
Fineli's Pizza
Heard you had some trouble.
Nothing I couldn't handle.
za
Well, good. That's good.
Hop in, Eddie. Let's take a ride.
Where?
Balazar's. He wants to know about his goods.
I have his goods. They're safe.
Fine. Then nobody has anything to worry about.
I think I want to go upstairs first. I want to change my clothes, talk to Henry...
And get fixed up, don't forget that. Except you got nothing to fix up *with*, little chum.

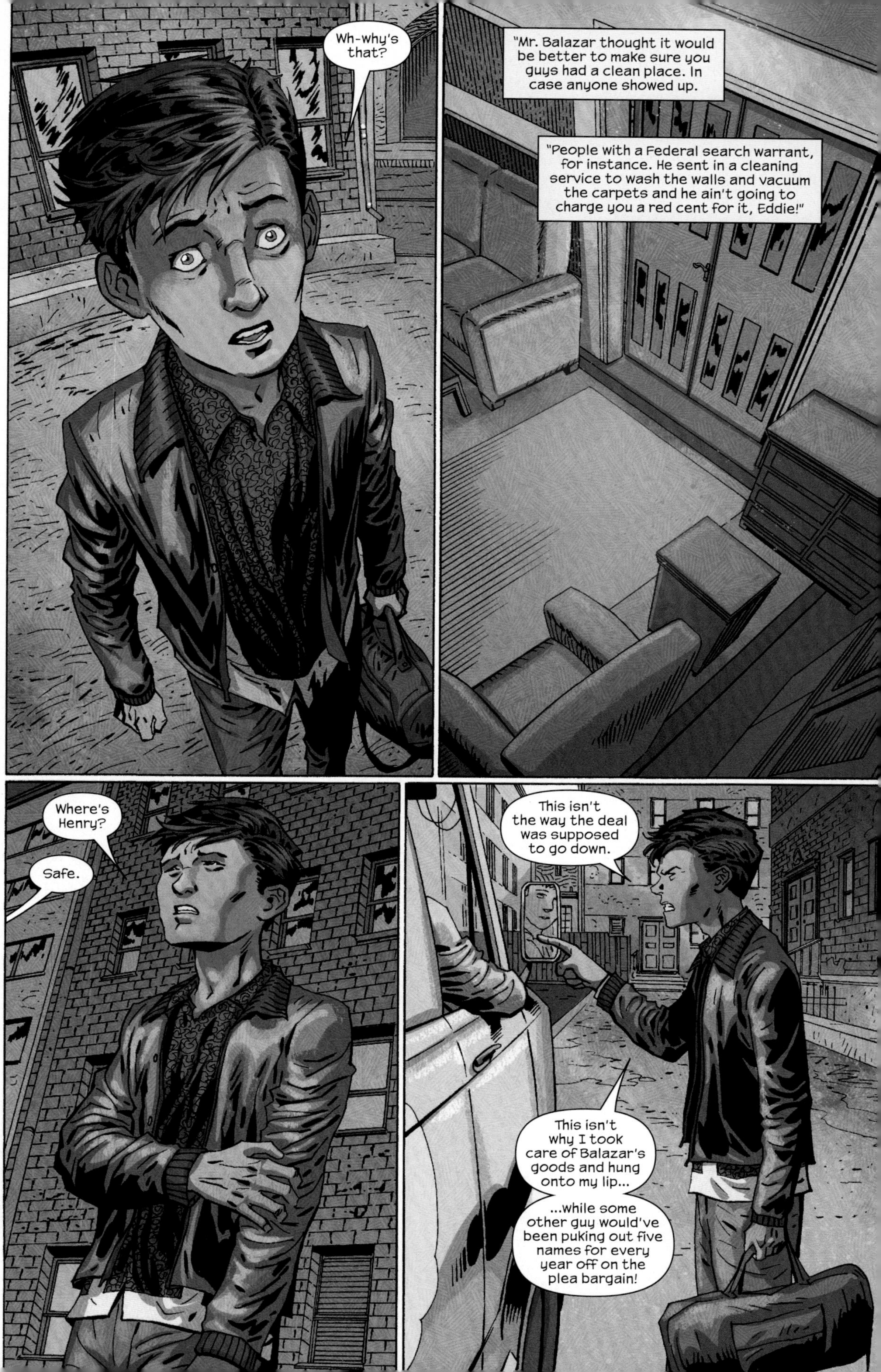

Wh-why's that?
"Mr. Balazar thought it would be better to make sure you guys had a clean place. In case anyone showed up.
"People with a Federal search warrant, for instance. He sent in a cleaning service to wash the walls and vacuum the carpets and he ain't going to charge you a red cent for it, Eddie!"
Where's Henry?
Safe.
This isn't the way the deal was supposed to go down.
This isn't why I took care of Balazar's goods and hung onto my lip...
...while some other guy would've been puking out five names for every year off on the plea bargain!

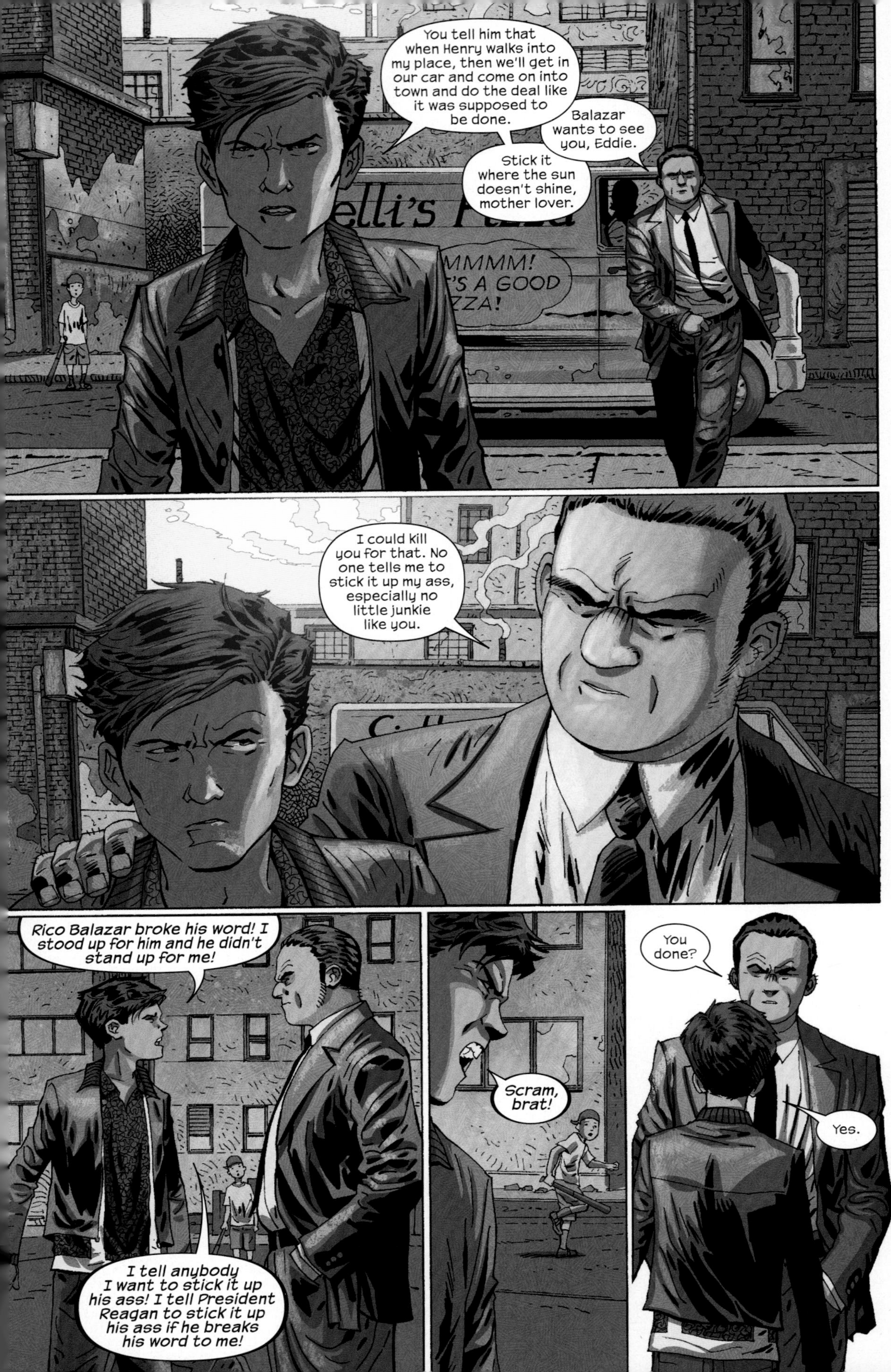
You tell him that when Henry walks into my place, then we'll get in our car and come on into town and do the deal like it was supposed to be done.
Balazar wants to see you, Eddie.
Stick it where the sun doesn't shine, mother lover.
I could kill you for that. No one tells me to stick it up my ass, especially no little junkie like you.
Rico Balazar broke his word! I stood up for him and he didn't stand up for me!
I tell anybody I want to stick it up his ass! I tell President Reagan to stick it up his ass if he breaks his word to me!
Scram, brat!
You done?
Yes.

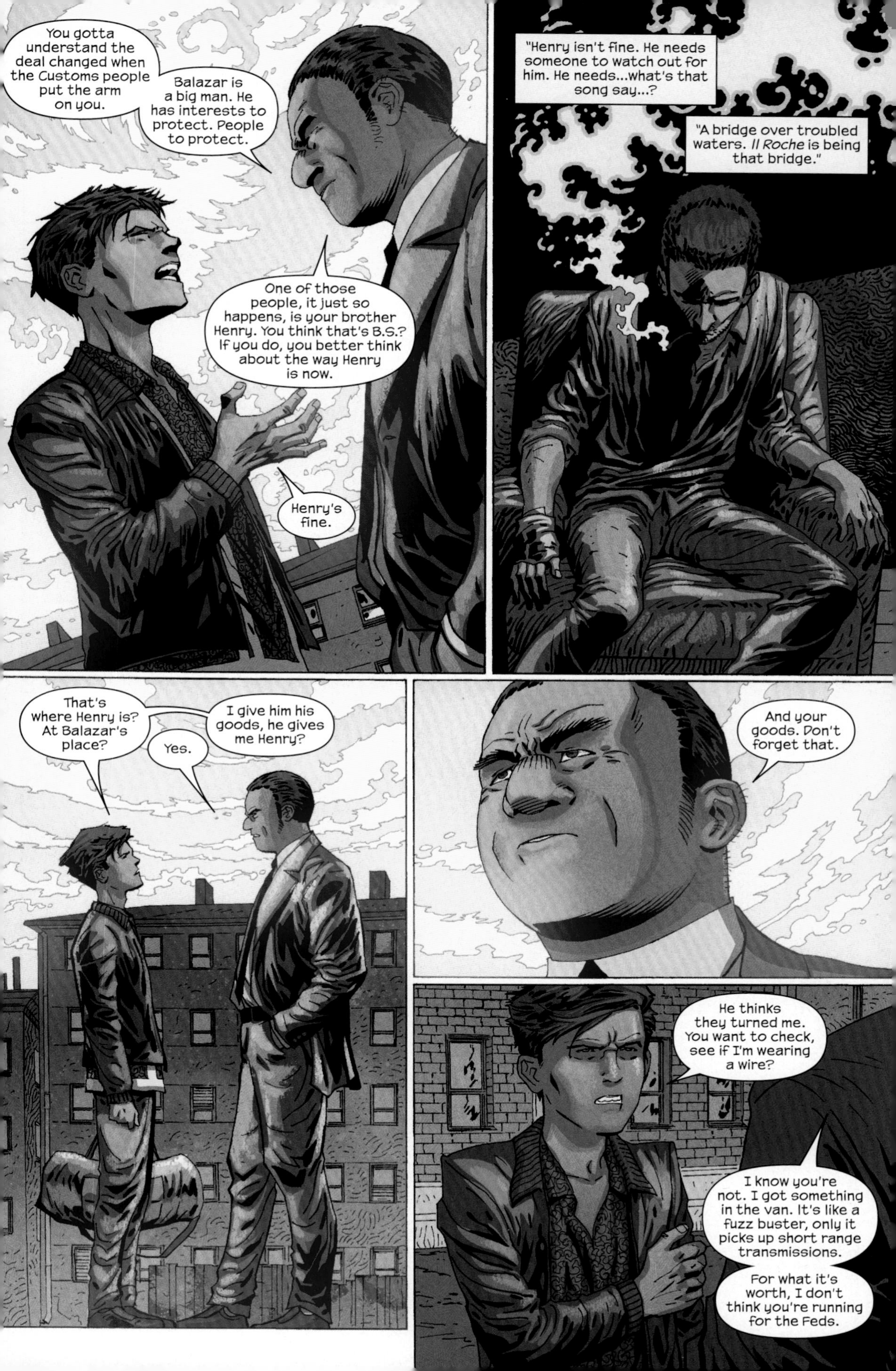
You gotta understand the deal changed when the Customs people put the arm on you.
Balazar is a big man. He has interests to protect. People to protect.
One of those people, it just so happens, is your brother Henry. You think that's B.S.? If you do, you better think about the way Henry is now.
Henry's fine.
"Henry isn't fine. He needs someone to watch out for him. He needs...what's that song say...?
"A bridge over troubled waters. *Il Roche* is being that bridge."
That's where Henry is? At Balazar's place?
Yes.
I give him his goods, he gives me Henry?
And your goods. Don't forget that.
He thinks they turned me. You want to check, see if I'm wearing a wire?
I know you're not. I got something in the van. It's like a fuzz buster, only it picks up short range transmissions.
For what it's worth, I don't think you're running for the Feds.

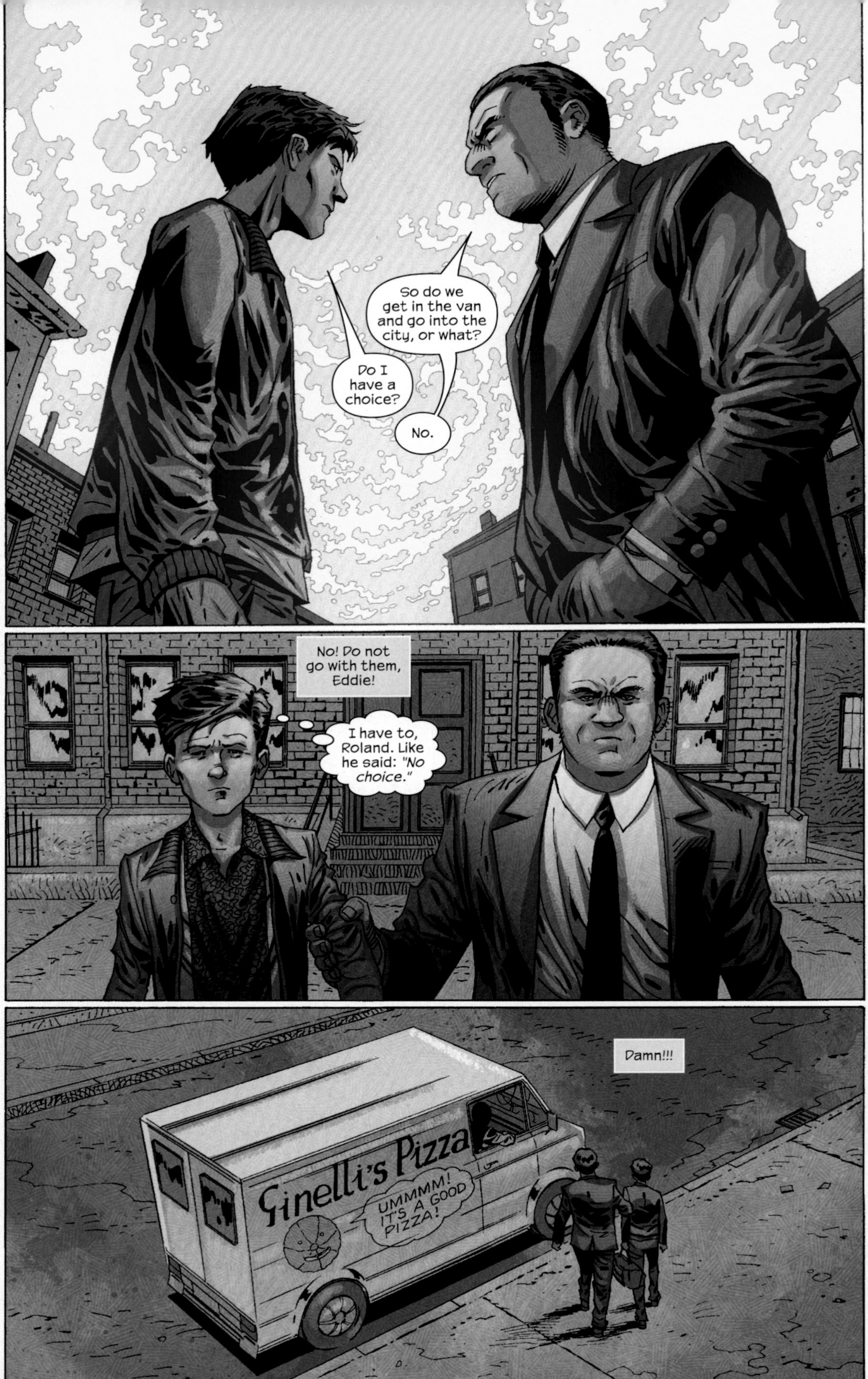
So do we get in the van and go into the city, or what?
Do I have a choice?
No.
No! Do not go with them, Eddie!
I have to, Roland. Like he said: "No choice."
Damn!!!
Ginelli's Pizza
UMMMM! IT'S A GOOD PIZZA!

# THE DARK TOWER
# THE DRAWING OF THE THREE
## STEPHEN KING

# HOUSE OF CARDS
## CHAPTER THREE

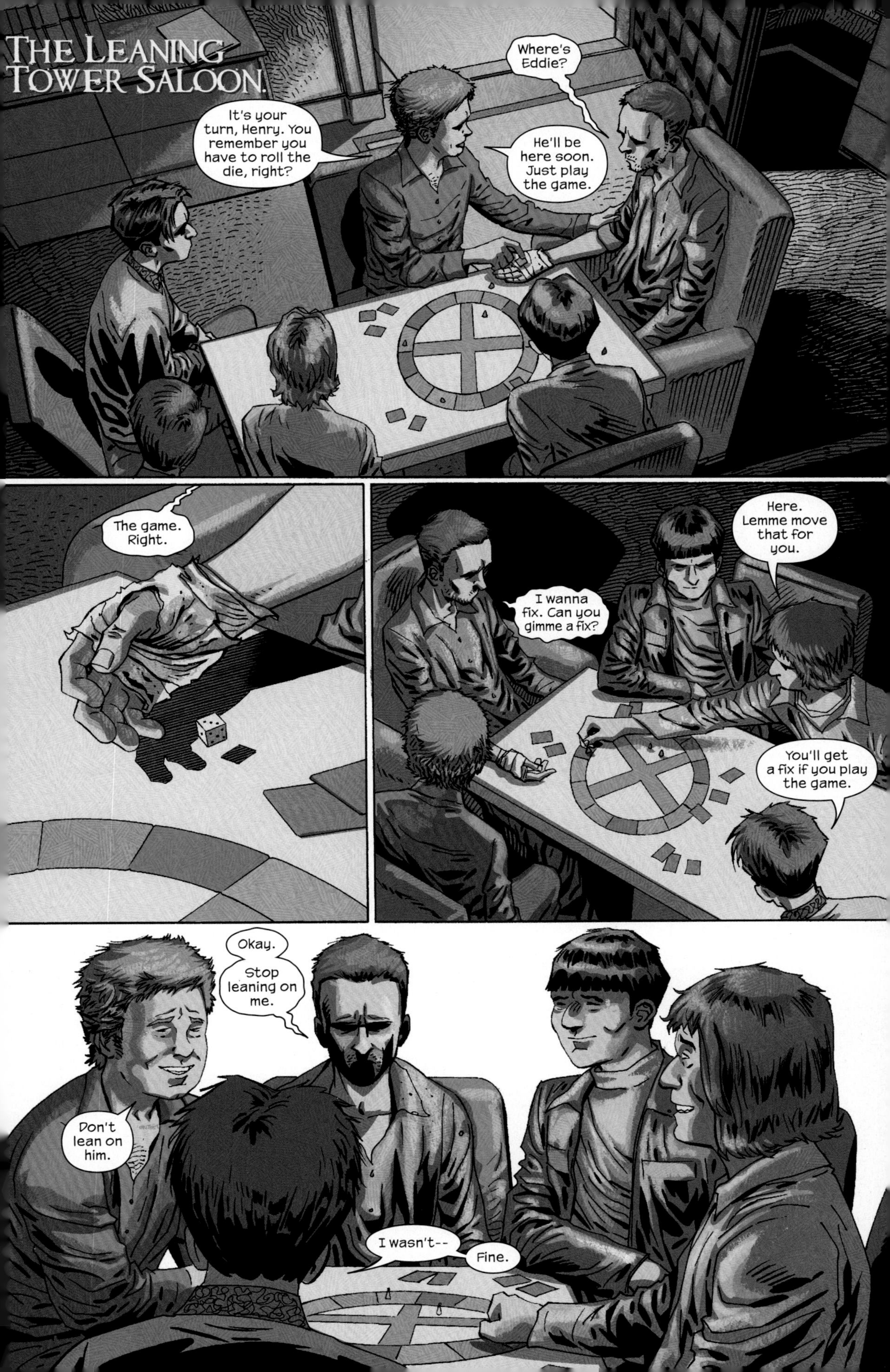
THE LEANING TOWER SALOON.
Where's Eddie?
It's your turn, Henry. You remember you have to roll the die, right?
He'll be here soon. Just play the game.
The game. Right.
Here. Lemme move that for you.
I wanna fix. Can you gimme a fix?
You'll get a fix if you play the game.
Okay.
Stop leaning on me.
Don't lean on him.
I wasn't--
Fine.

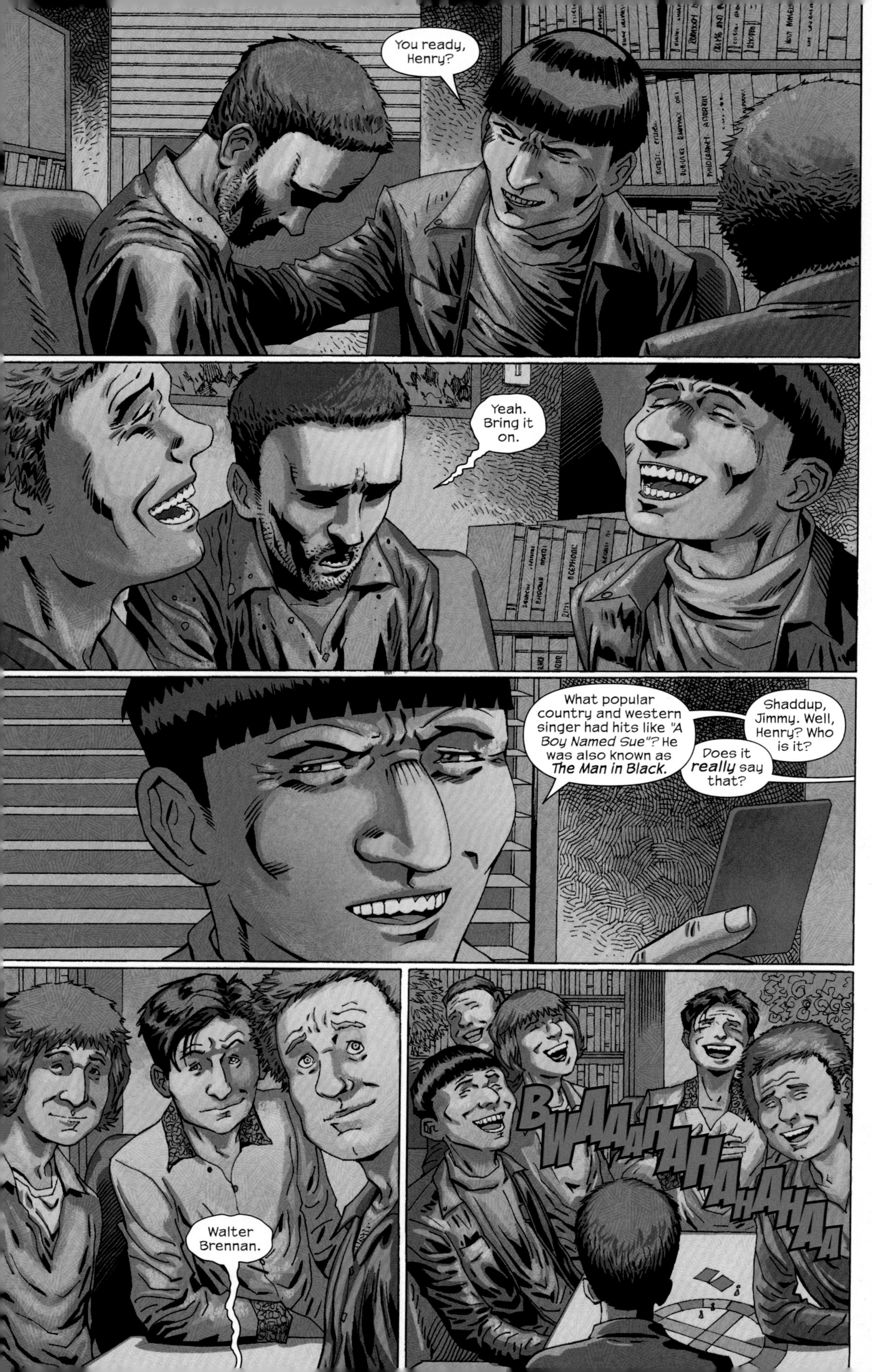
You ready, Henry?
Yeah. Bring it on.
What popular country and western singer had hits like "A Boy Named Sue"? He was also known as The Man in Black.
Does it really say that?
Shaddup, Jimmy. Well, Henry? Who is it?
Walter Brennan.
BWAAAHAHAHAHAHAA

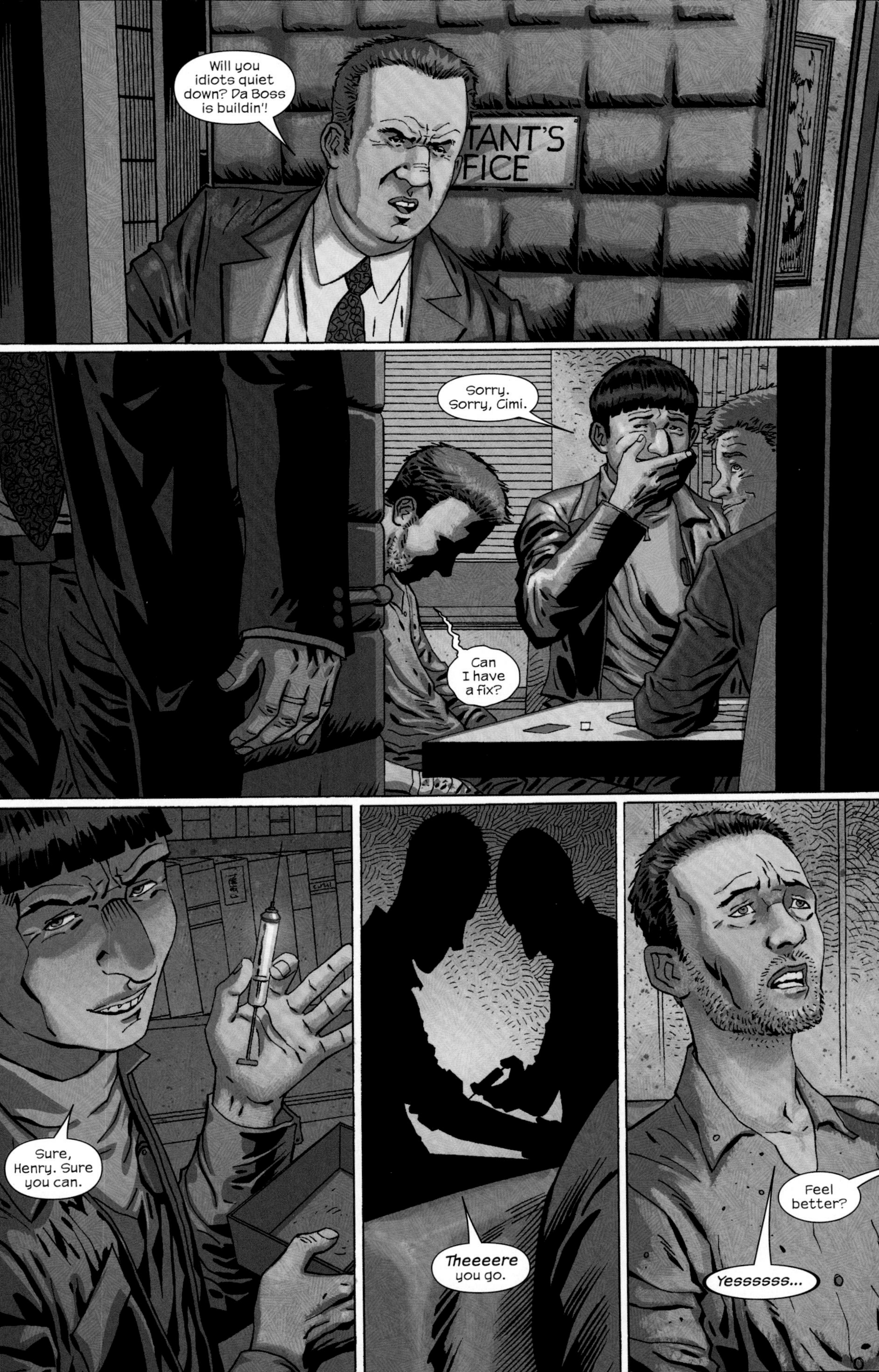
Will you idiots quiet down? Da Boss is buildin'!
TANT'S
FICE
Sorry. Sorry, Cimi.
Can I have a fix?
Sure, Henry. Sure you can.
Theeeere you go.
Feel better?
Yessssss...

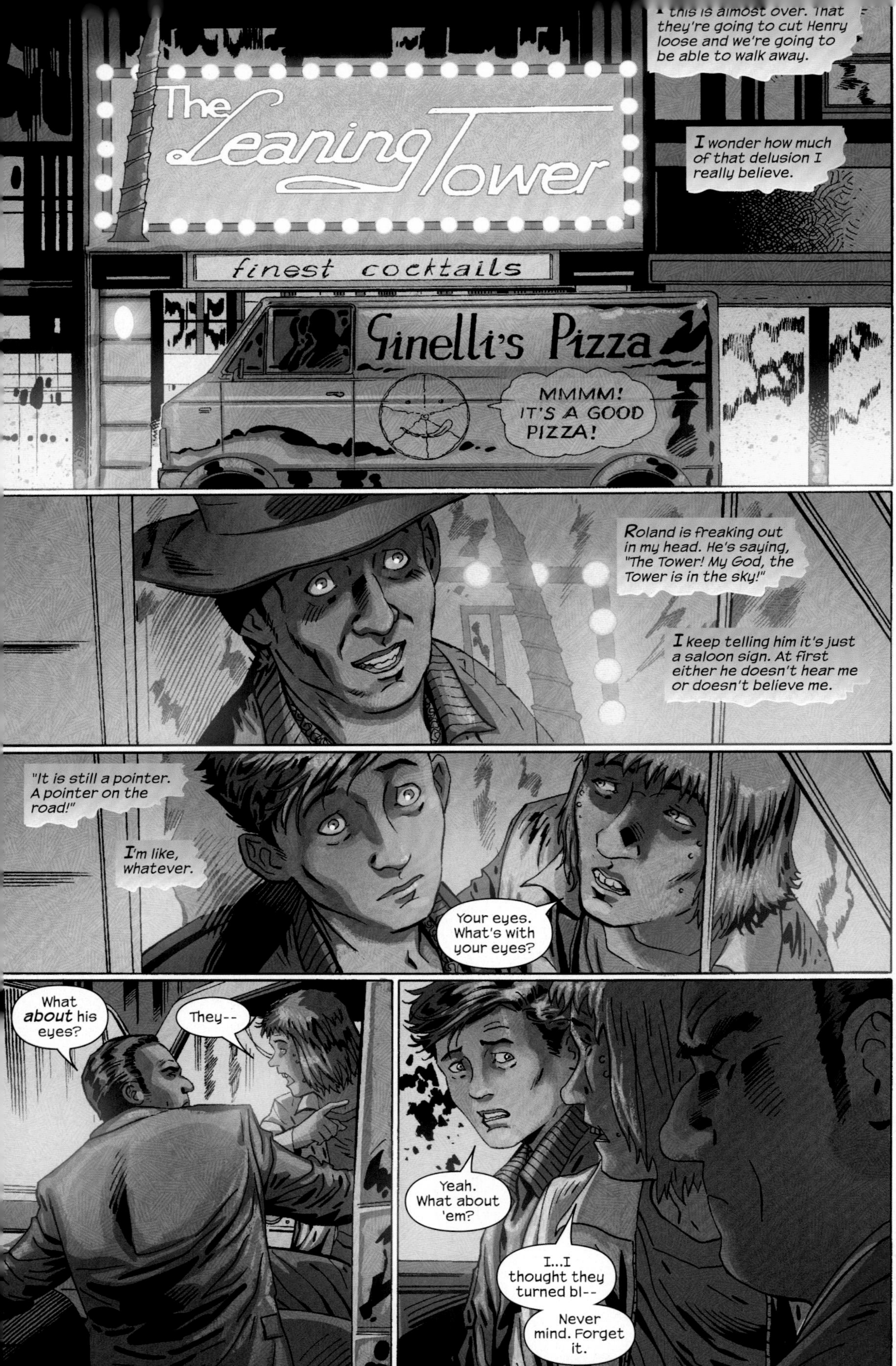

this is almost over. That they're going to cut Henry loose and we're going to be able to walk away.
The Leaning Tower
I wonder how much of that delusion I really believe.
finest cocktails
Ginelli's Pizza
MMMM! IT'S A GOOD PIZZA!
Roland is freaking out in my head. He's saying, "The Tower! My God, the Tower is in the sky!"
I keep telling him it's just a saloon sign. At first either he doesn't hear me or doesn't believe me.
"It is still a pointer. A pointer on the road!"
I'm like, whatever.
Your eyes. What's with your eyes?
What about his eyes?
They--
Yeah. What about 'em?
I...I thought they turned bl--
Never mind. Forget it.

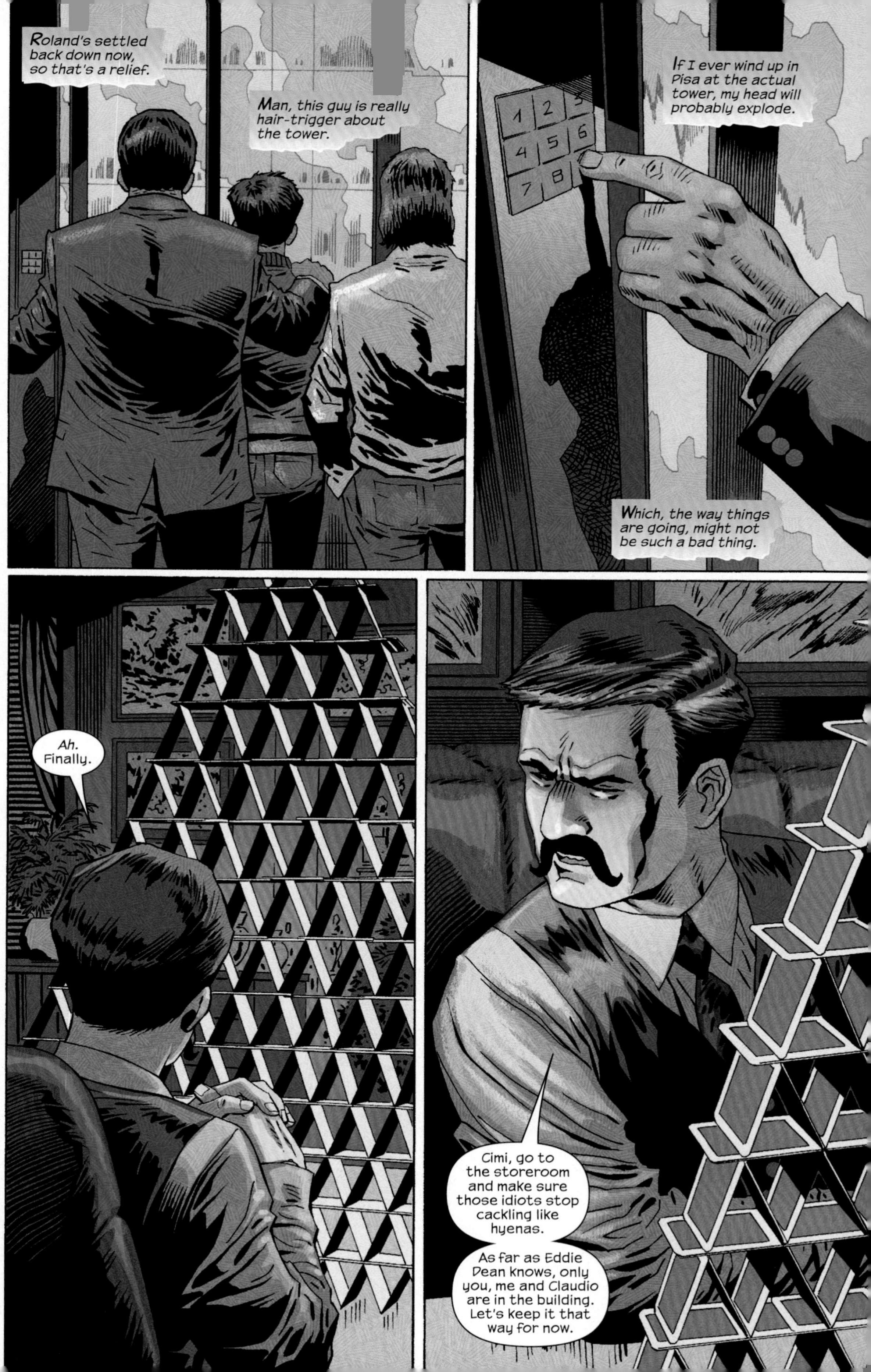
Roland's settled back down now, so that's a relief.
Man, this guy is really hair-trigger about the tower.
If I ever wind up in Pisa at the actual tower, my head will probably explode.
Which, the way things are going, might not be such a bad thing.
Ah. Finally.
Cimi, go to the storeroom and make sure those idiots stop cackling like hyenas.
As far as Eddie Dean knows, only you, me and Claudio are in the building. Let's keep it that way for now.

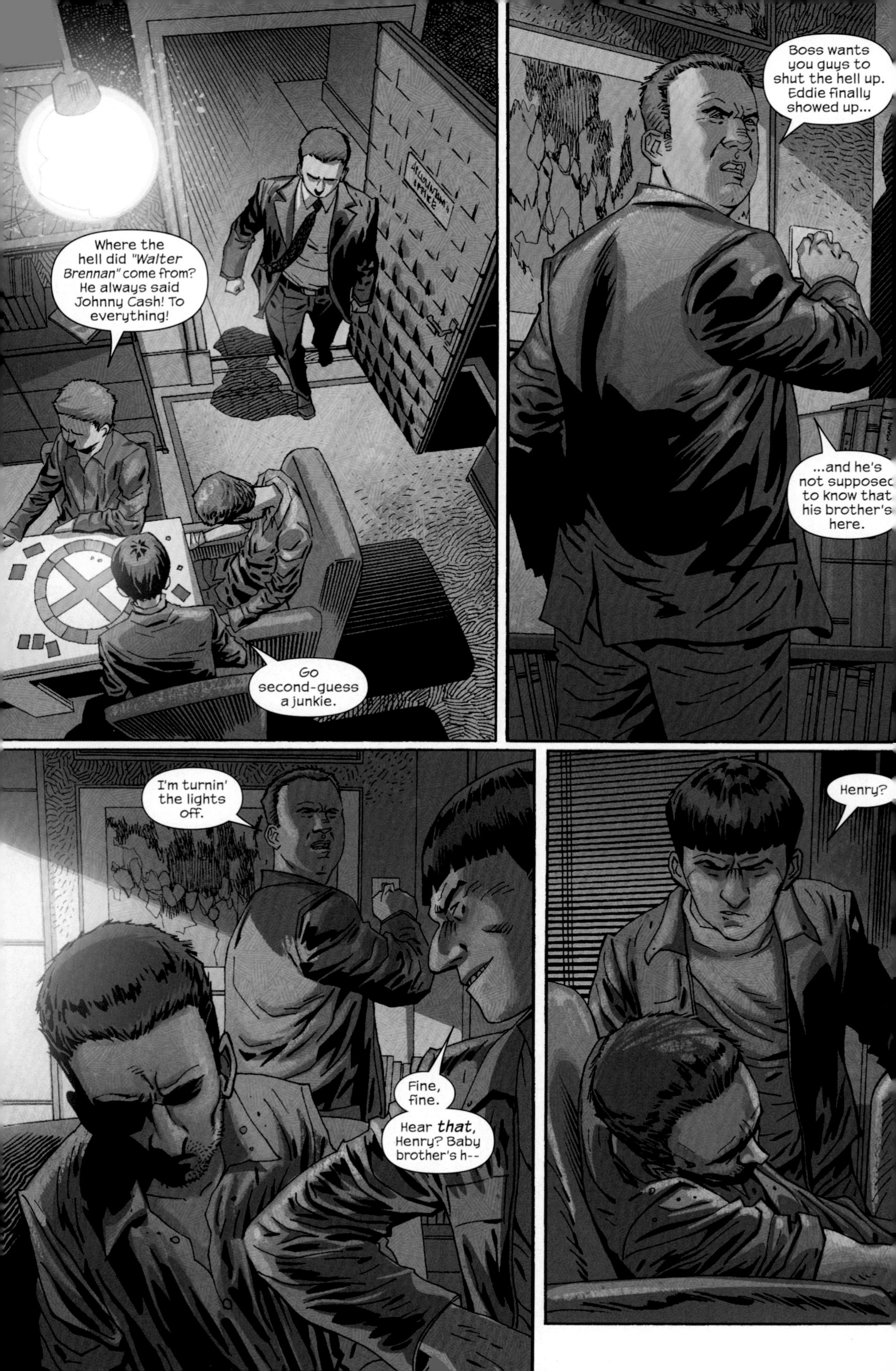
Where the hell did "Walter Brennan" come from? He always said Johnny Cash! To everything!
Go second-guess a junkie.
Boss wants you guys to shut the hell up. Eddie finally showed up...
...and he's not supposed to know that his brother's here.
I'm turnin' the lights off.
Fine, fine.
Hear *that*, Henry? Baby brother's h--
Henry?

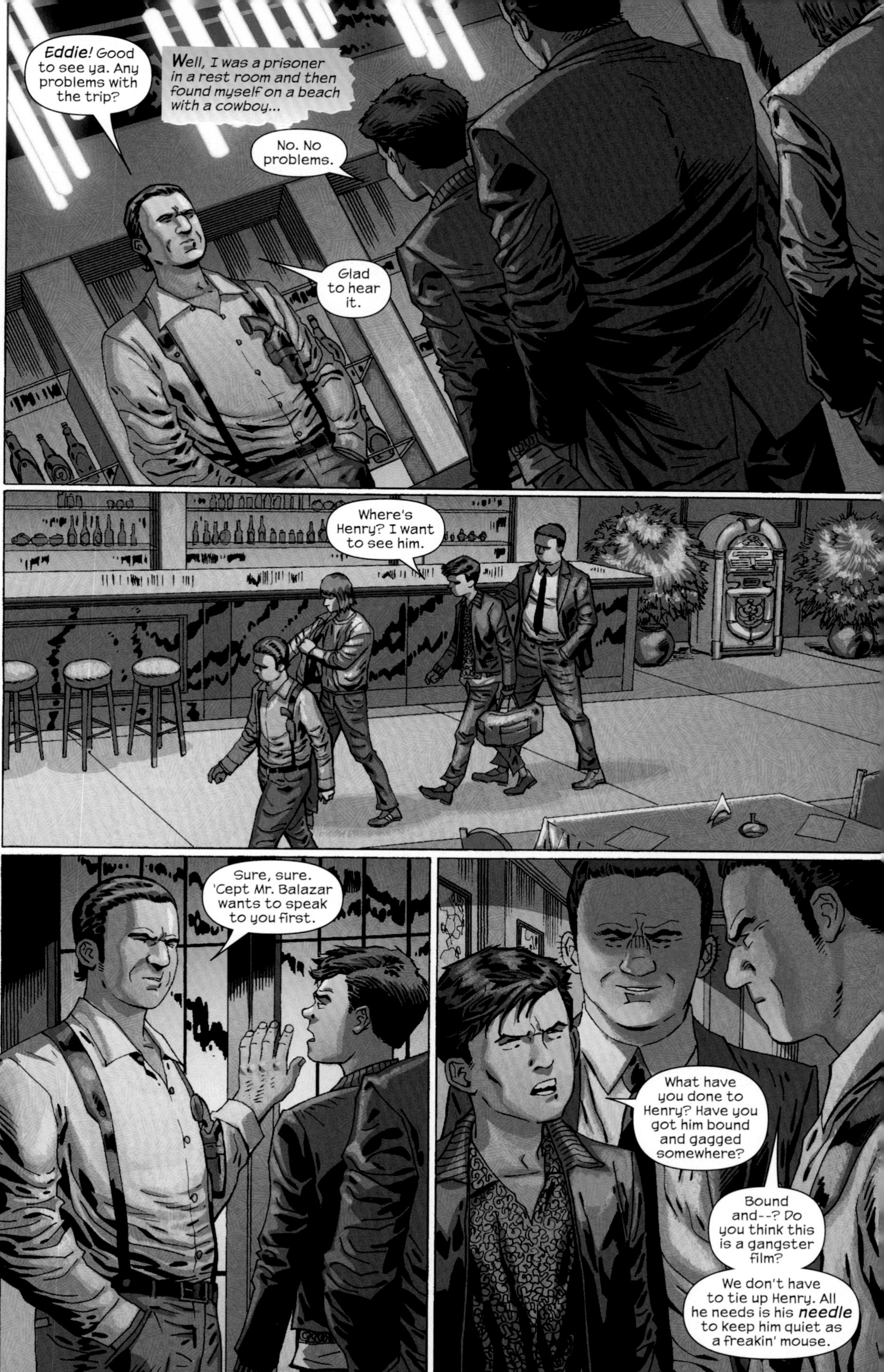
Eddie! Good to see ya. Any problems with the trip?
Well, I was a prisoner in a rest room and then found myself on a beach with a cowboy...
No. No problems.
Glad to hear it.
Where's Henry? I want to see him.
Sure, sure. 'Cept Mr. Balazar wants to speak to you first.
What have you done to Henry? Have you got him bound and gagged somewhere?
Bound and--? Do you think this is a gangster film?
We don't have to tie up Henry. All he needs is his needle to keep him quiet as a freakin' mouse.

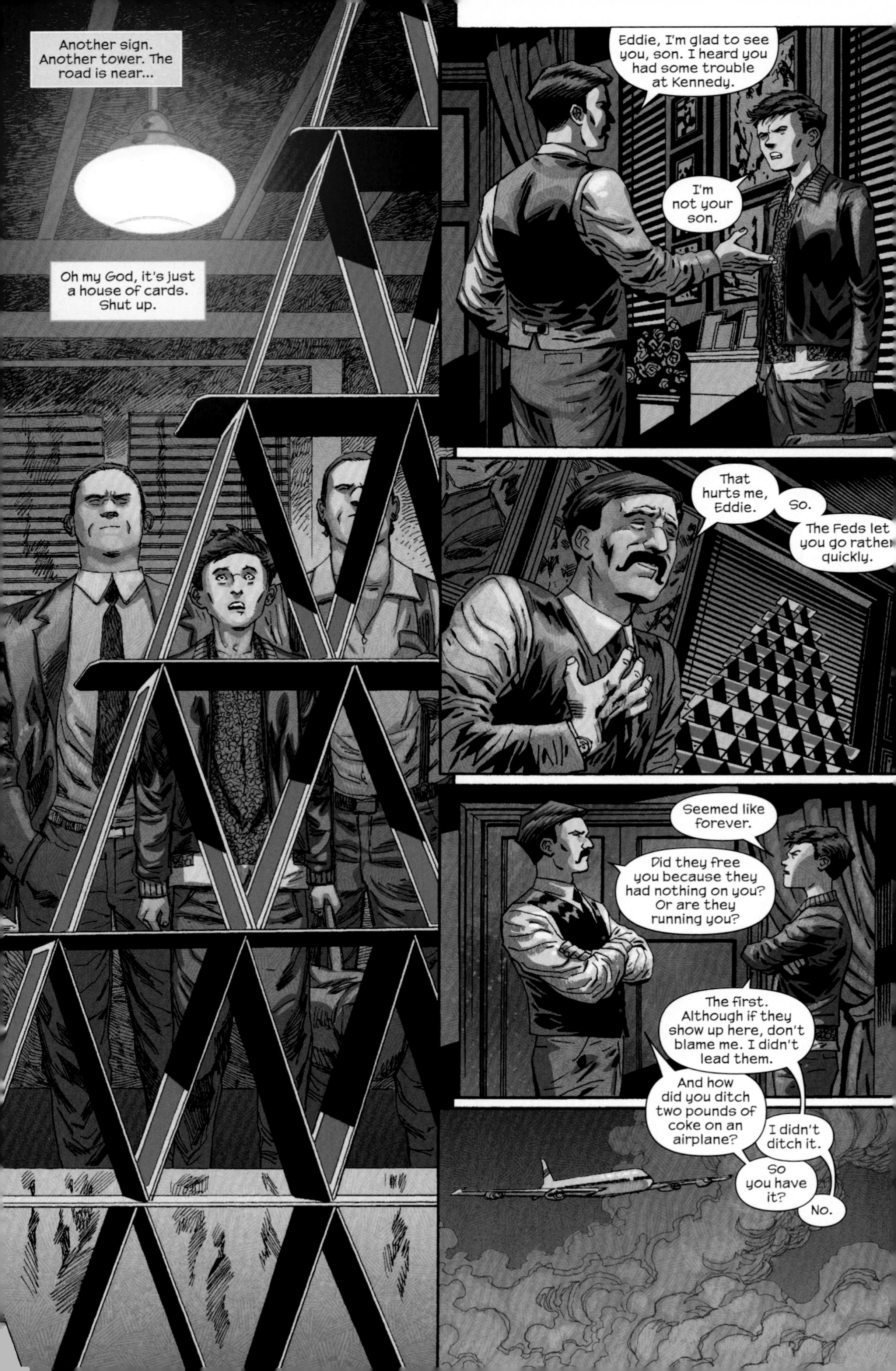
Another sign. Another tower. The road is near...
Oh my God, it's just a house of cards. Shut up.
Eddie, I'm glad to see you, son. I heard you had some trouble at Kennedy.
I'm not your son.
That hurts me, Eddie.
So.
The Feds let you go rather quickly.
Seemed like forever.
Did they free you because they had nothing on you? Or are they running you?
The first. Although if they show up here, don't blame me. I didn't lead them.
And how did you ditch two pounds of coke on an airplane?
I didn't ditch it.
So you have it?
No.

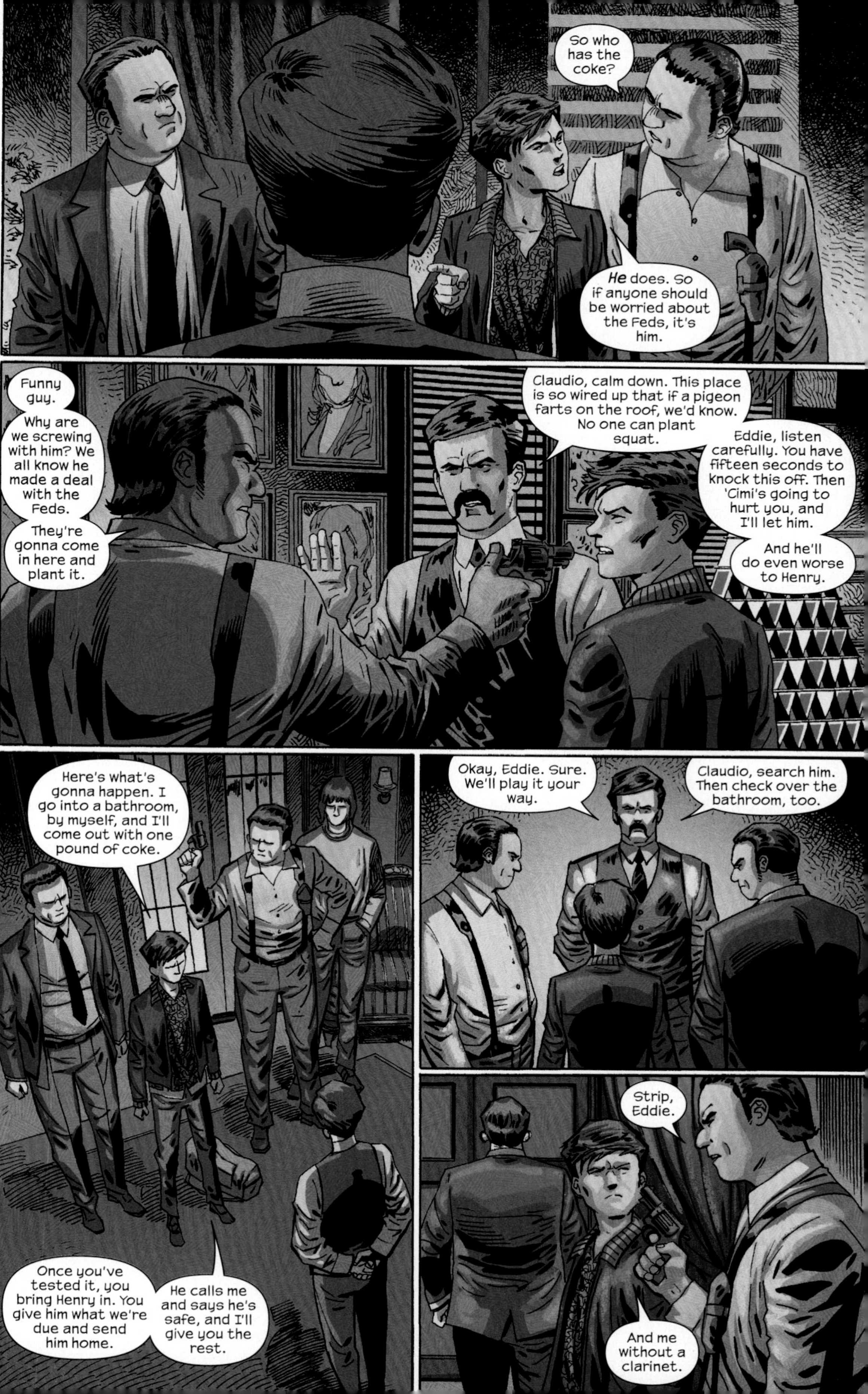

So who has the coke?
He does. So if anyone should be worried about the Feds, it's him.
Funny guy.
Why are we screwing with him? We all know he made a deal with the Feds.
They're gonna come in here and plant it.
Claudio, calm down. This place is so wired up that if a pigeon farts on the roof, we'd know. No one can plant squat.
Eddie, listen carefully. You have fifteen seconds to knock this off. Then 'Cimi's going to hurt you, and I'll let him.
And he'll do even worse to Henry.
Here's what's gonna happen. I go into a bathroom, by myself, and I'll come out with one pound of coke.
Once you've tested it, you bring Henry in. You give him what we're due and send him home.
He calls me and says he's safe, and I'll give you the rest.
Okay, Eddie. Sure. We'll play it your way.
Claudio, search him. Then check over the bathroom, too.
Strip, Eddie.
And me without a clarinet.

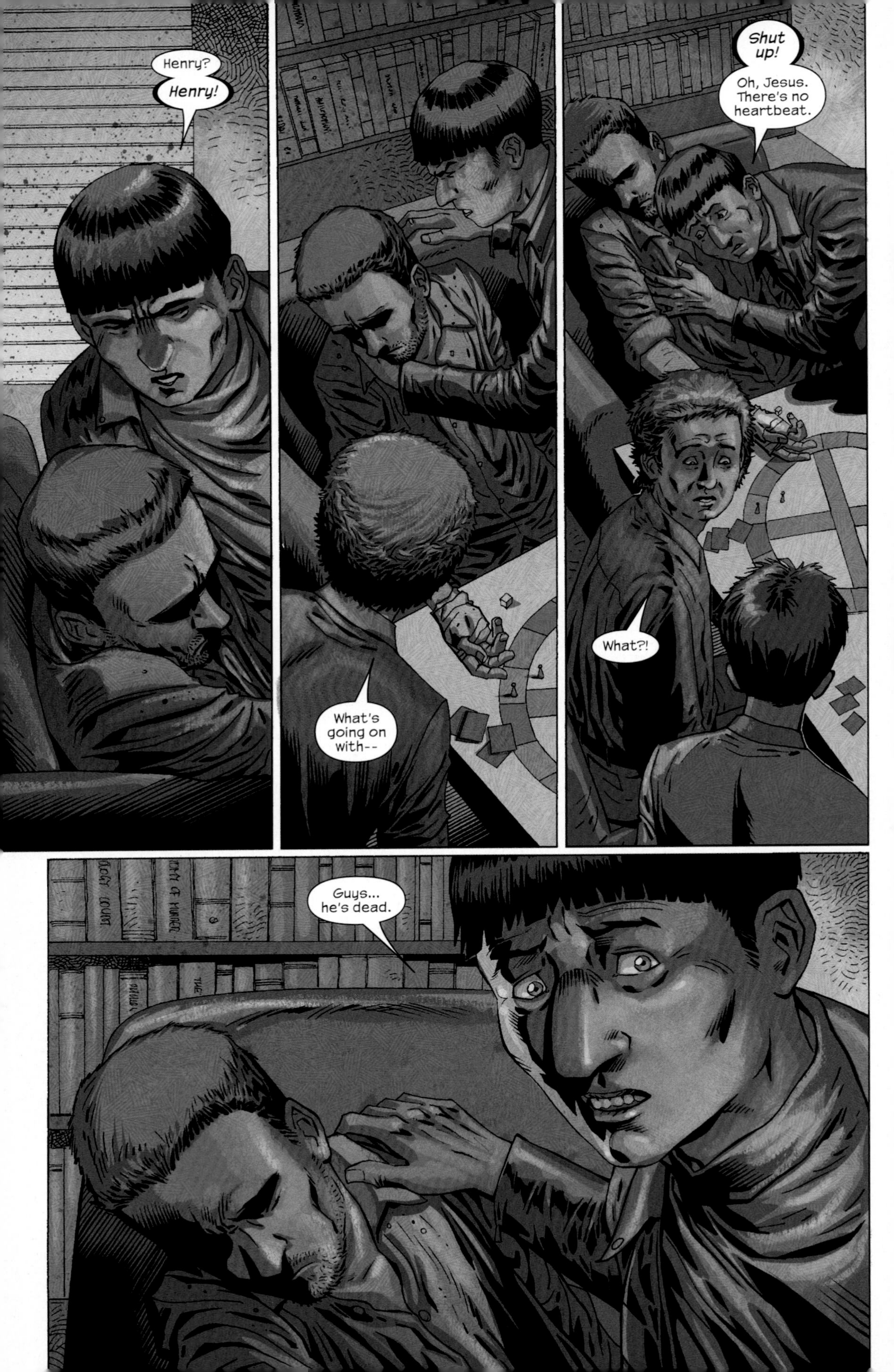
Henry?
Henry!
What's going on with--
Shut up!
Oh, Jesus. There's no heartbeat.
What?!
Guys... he's dead.

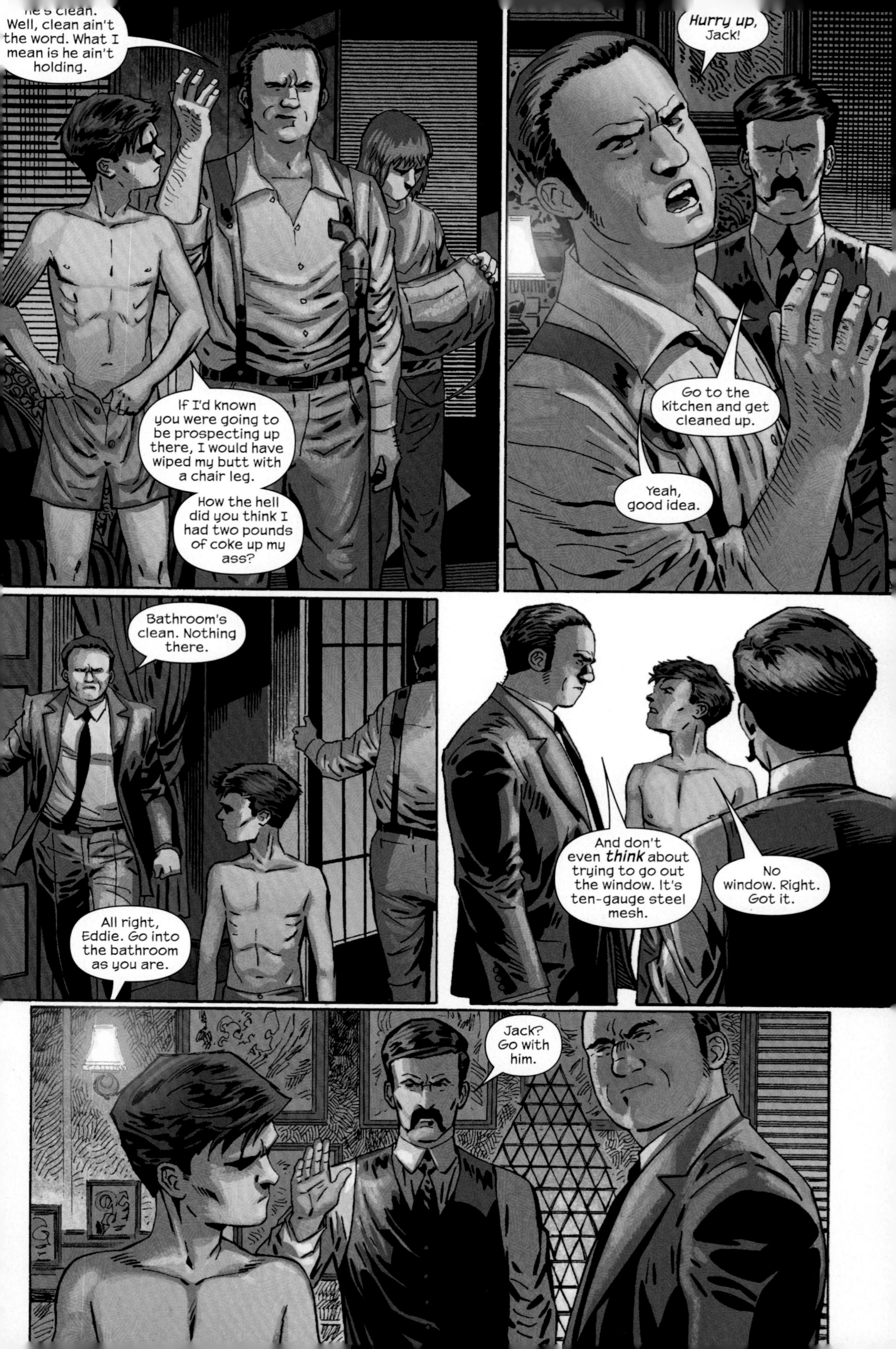
he's clean. Well, clean ain't the word. What I mean is he ain't holding.
If I'd known you were going to be prospecting up there, I would have wiped my butt with a chair leg.
How the hell did you think I had two pounds of coke up my ass?
*Hurry up,* Jack!
Go to the kitchen and get cleaned up.
Yeah, good idea.
Bathroom's clean. Nothing there.
All right, Eddie. Go into the bathroom as you are.
And don't even **think** about trying to go out the window. It's ten-gauge steel mesh.
No window. Right. Got it.
Jack? Go with him.

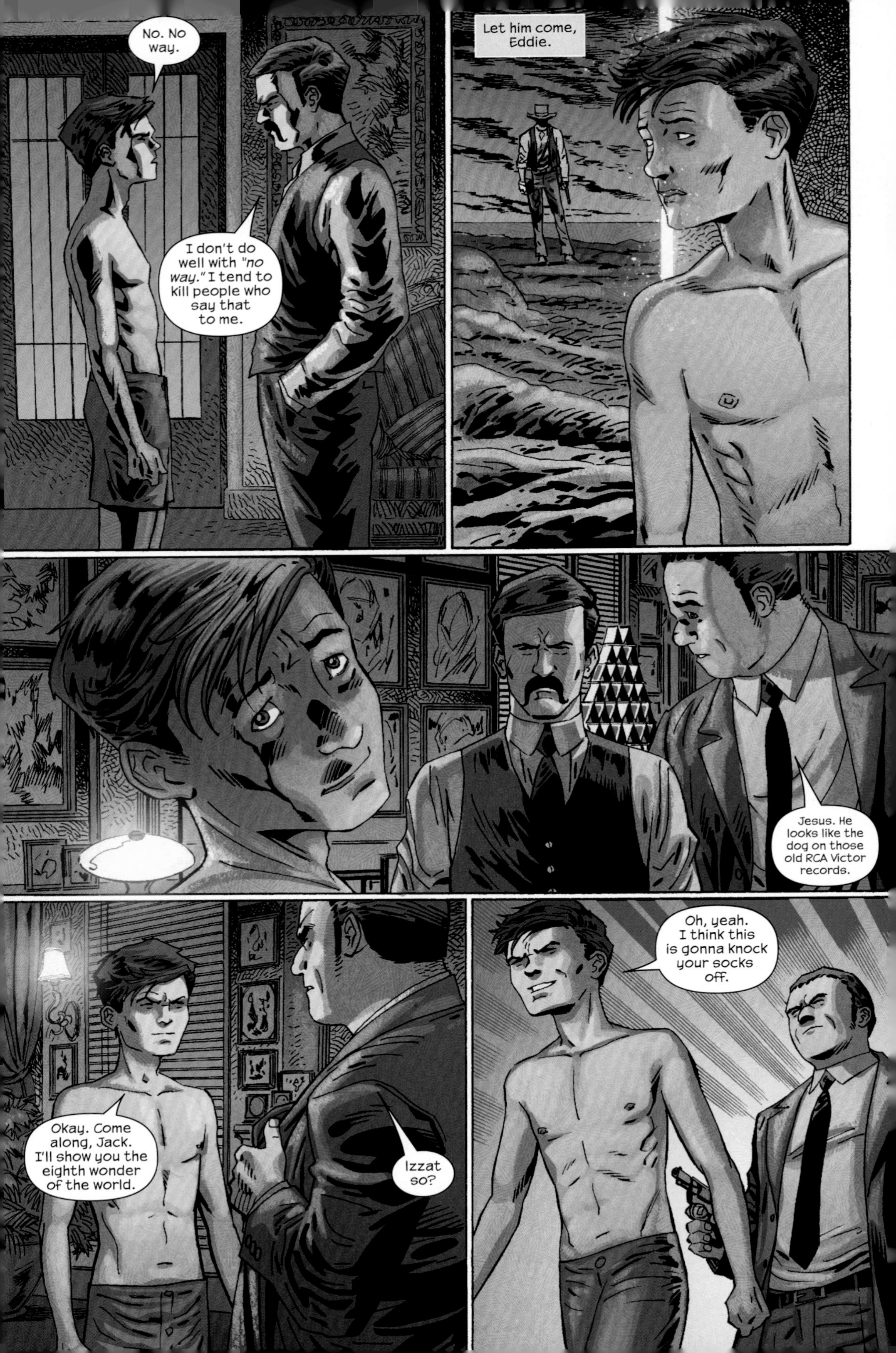
No. No way.
I don't do well with "no way." I tend to kill people who say that to me.
Let him come, Eddie.
Jesus. He looks like the dog on those old RCA Victor records.
Okay. Come along, Jack. I'll show you the eighth wonder of the world.
Izzat so?
Oh, yeah. I think this is gonna knock your socks off.

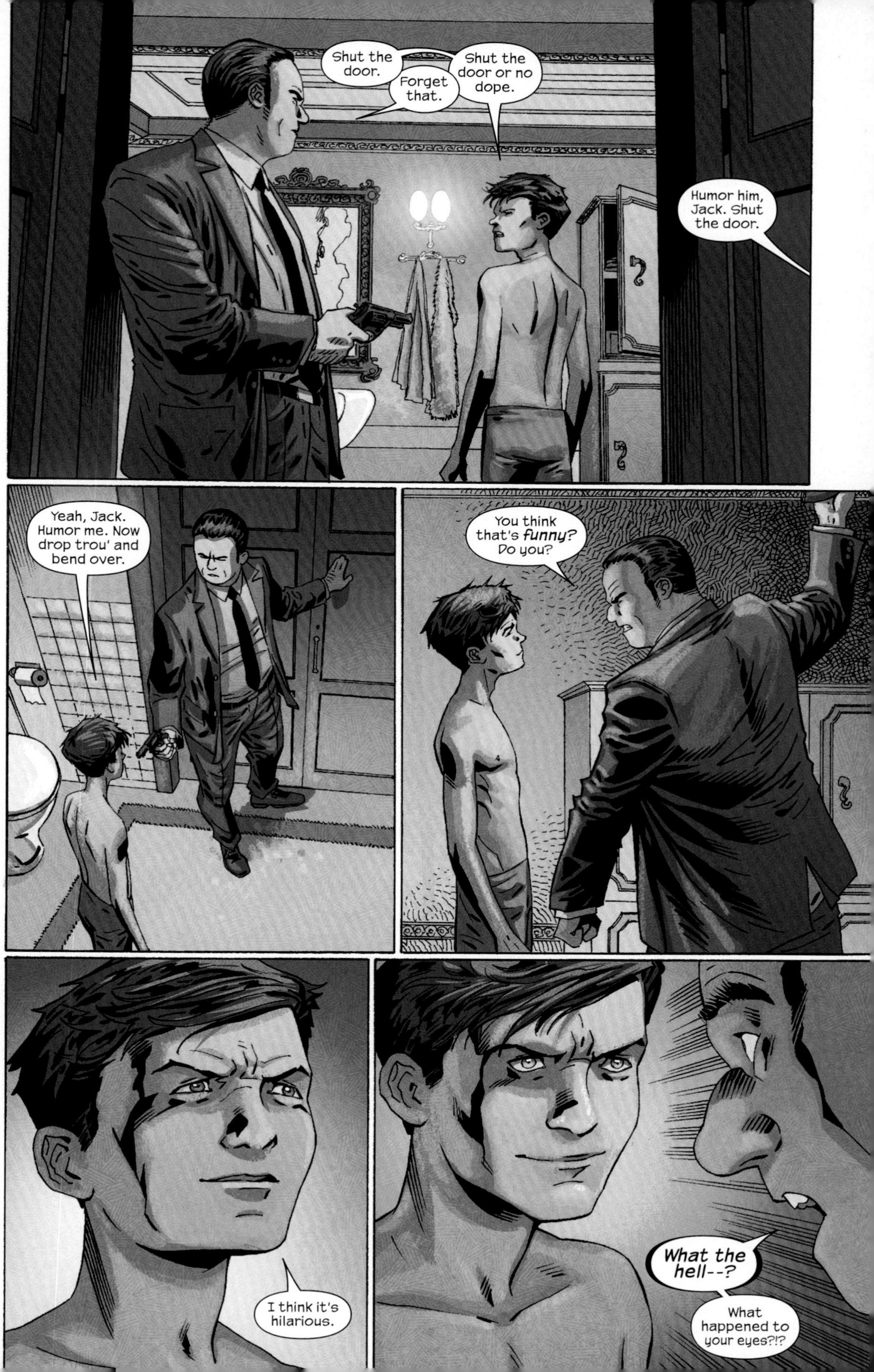

Shut the door.
Forget that.
Shut the door or no dope.
Humor him, Jack. Shut the door.
Yeah, Jack. Humor me. Now drop trou' and bend over.
You think that's *funny?* Do you?
I think it's hilarious.
*What the hell--?*
What happened to your eyes?!?

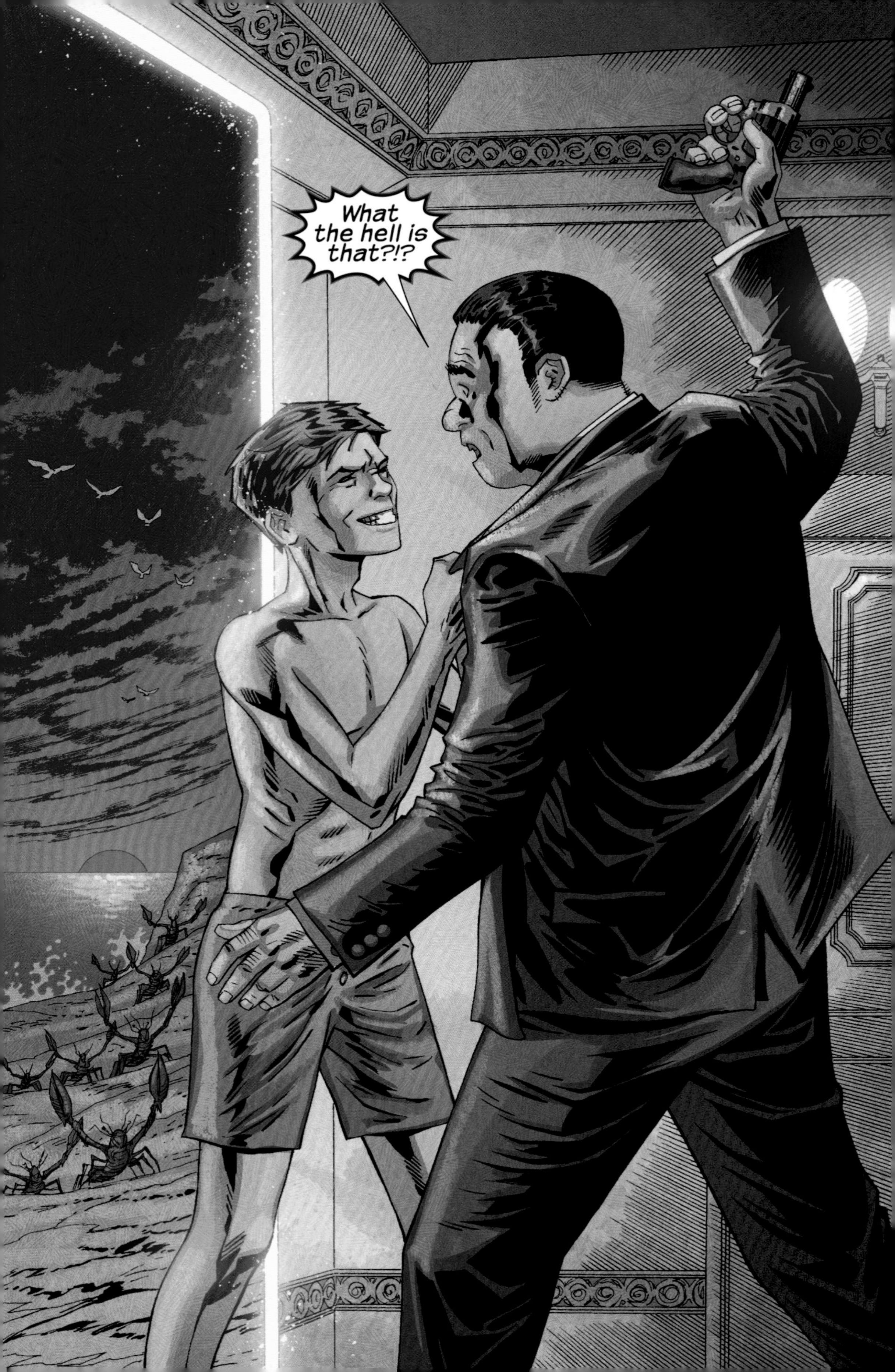
What the hell is that?!?

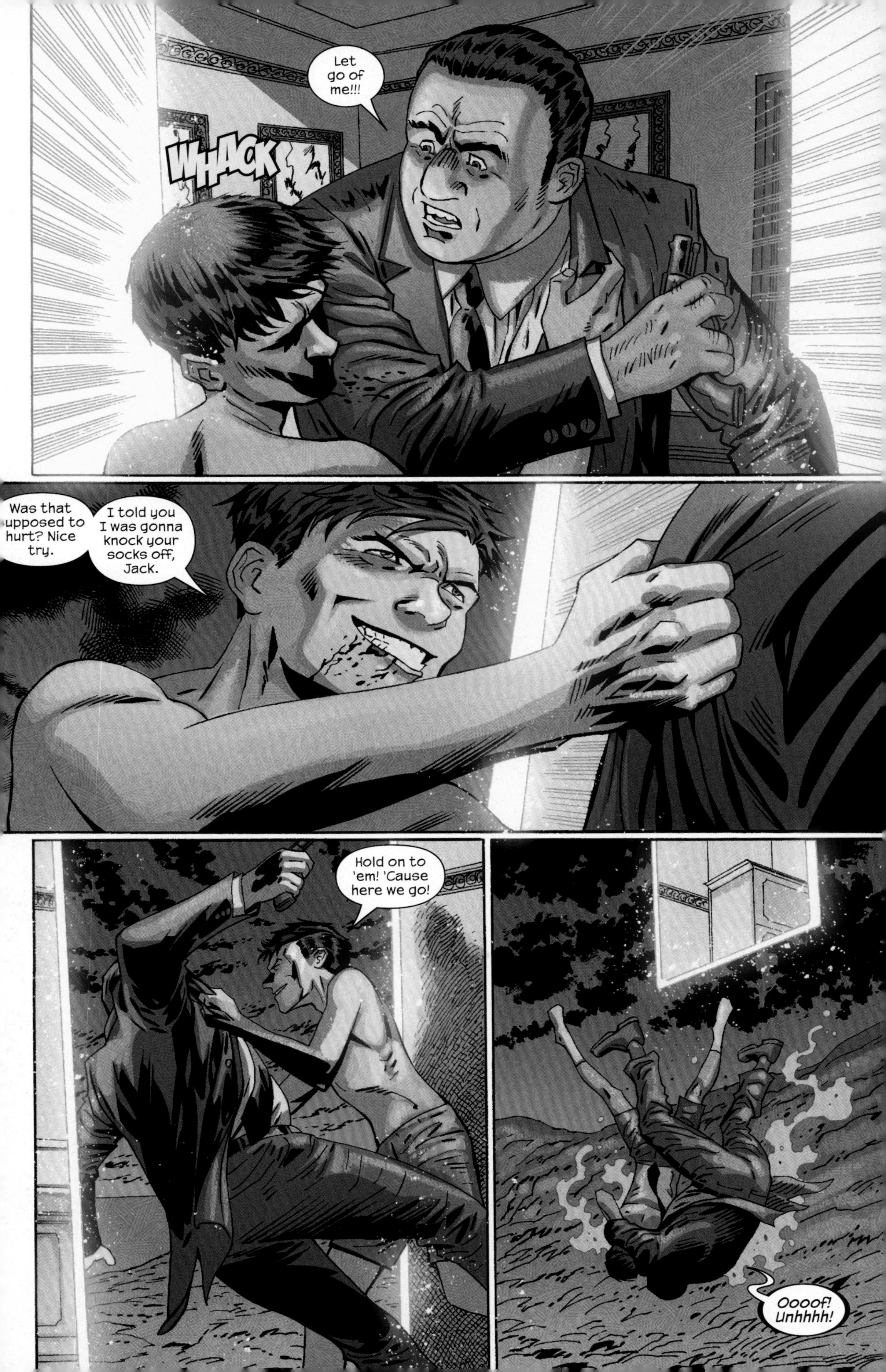
Let go of me!!!
WHACK
Was that supposed to hurt? Nice try.
I told you I was gonna knock your socks off, Jack.
Hold on to 'em! 'Cause here we go!
Oooof! Unhhhh!

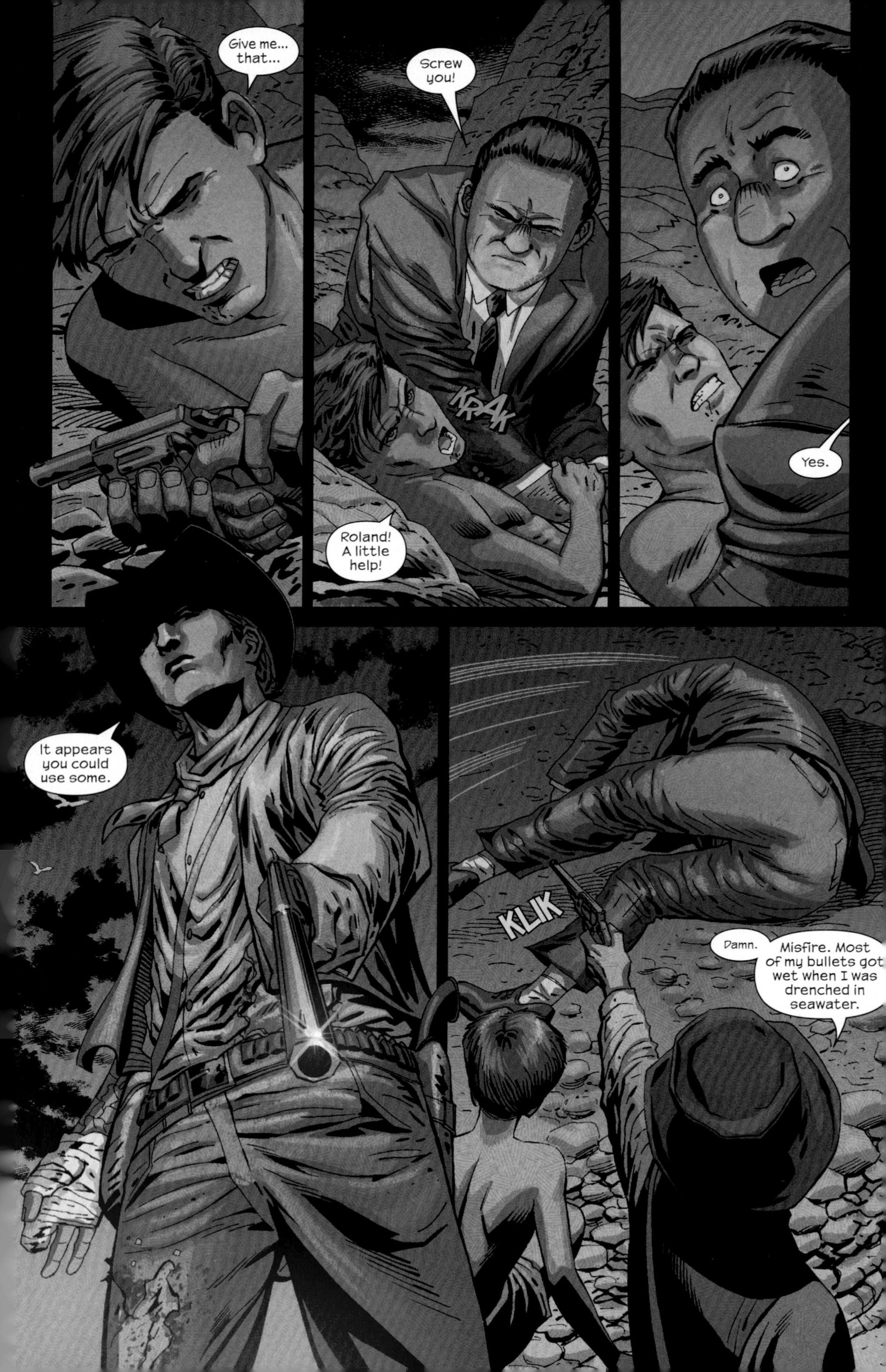
Give me... that...
Screw you!
KRAK
Roland! A little help!
Yes.
It appears you could use some.
KLIK
Damn.
Misfire. Most of my bullets got wet when I was drenched in seawater.

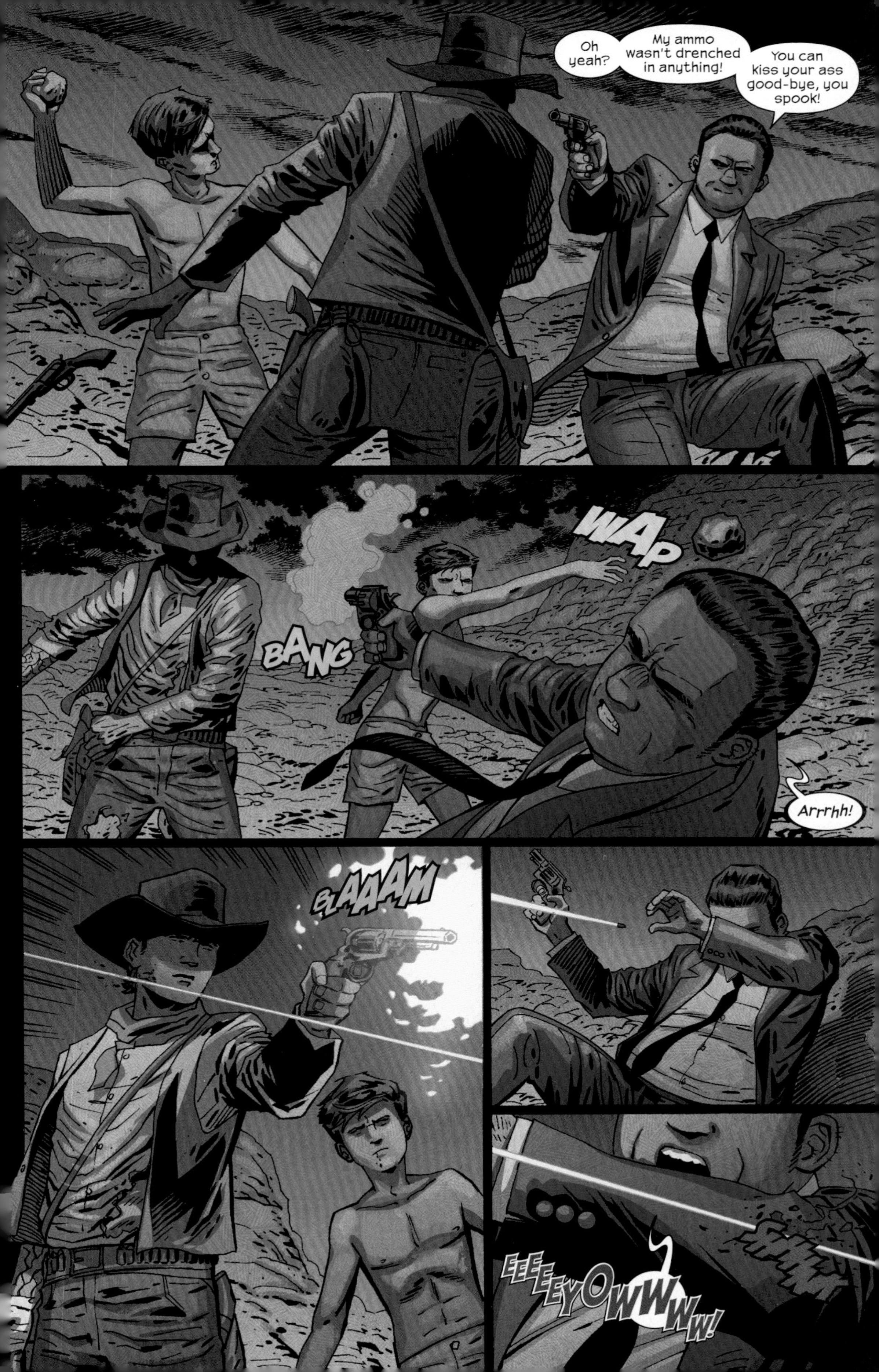
Oh yeah?
My ammo wasn't drenched in anything!
You can kiss your ass good-bye, you spook!
WAP
BANG
Arrrhh!
BLAAAM
EEEEEYOWWWWW!

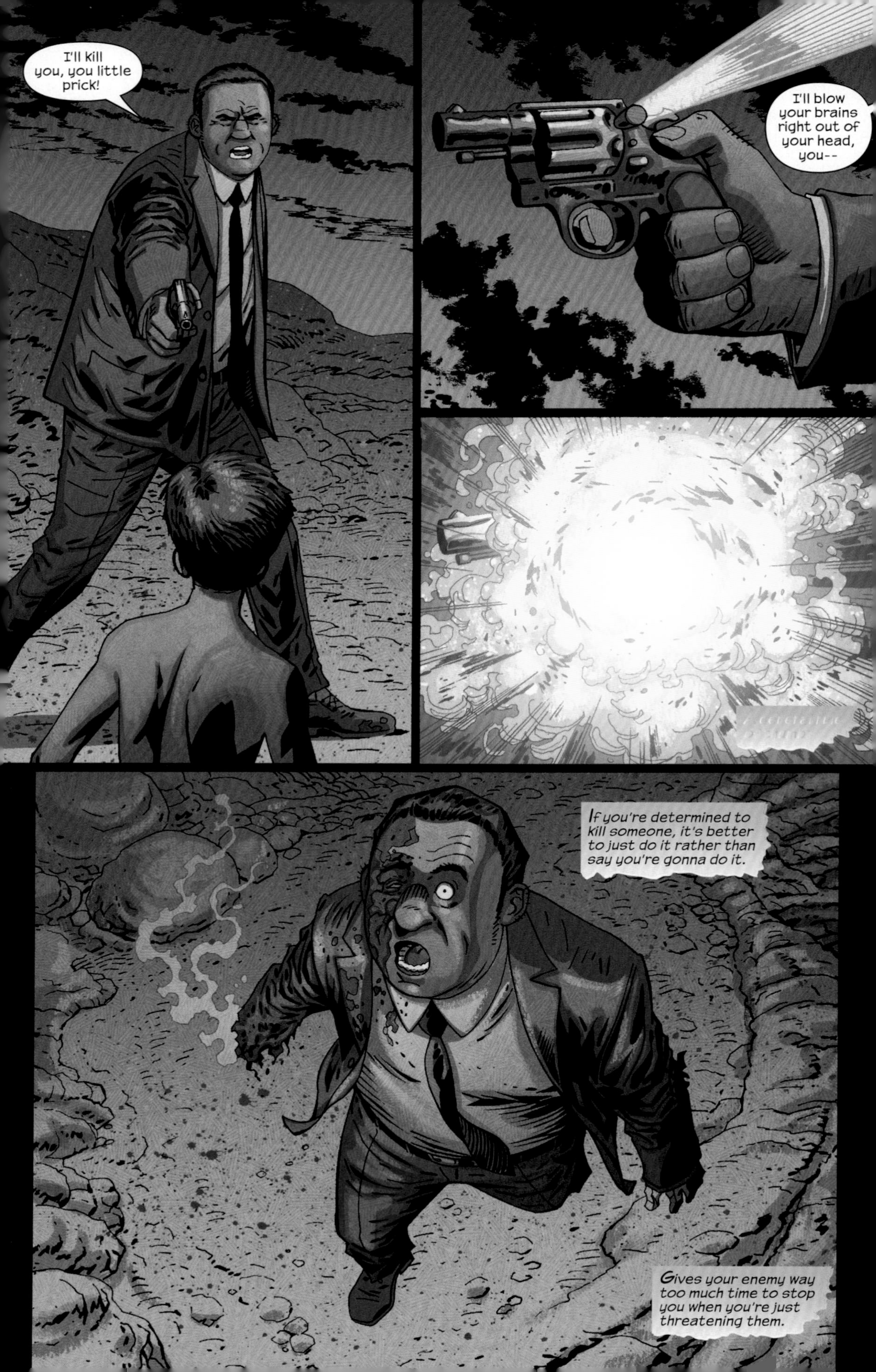
I'll kill you, you little prick!
I'll blow your brains right out of your head, you--
If you're determined to kill someone, it's better to just do it rather than say you're gonna do it.
Gives your enemy way too much time to stop you when you're just threatening them.

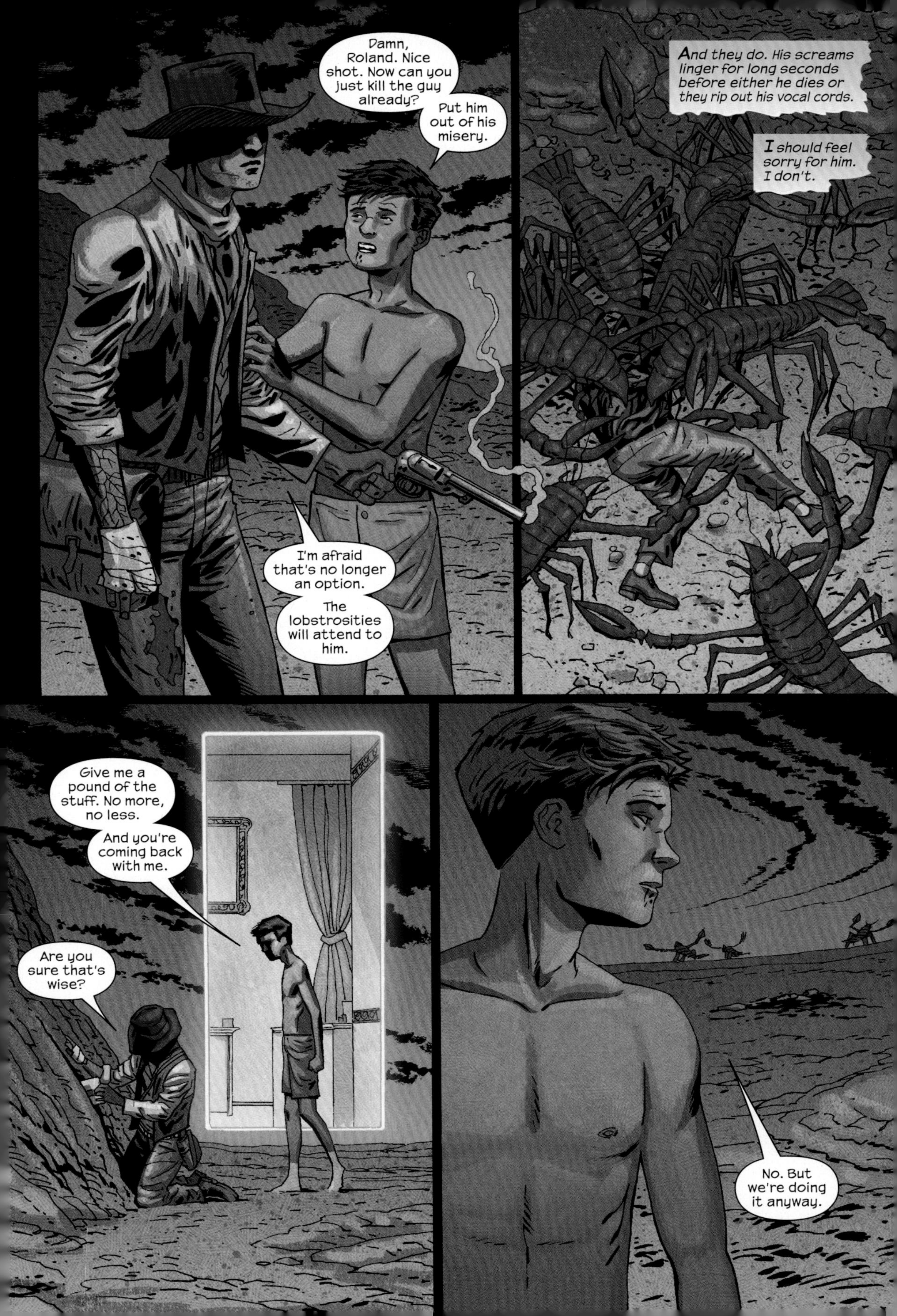
Damn, Roland. Nice shot. Now can you just kill the guy already?
Put him out of his misery.
I'm afraid that's no longer an option.
The lobstrosities will attend to him.
And they do. His screams linger for long seconds before either he dies or they rip out his vocal cords.
I should feel sorry for him. I don't.
Give me a pound of the stuff. No more, no less.
And you're coming back with me.
Are you sure that's wise?
No. But we're doing it anyway.

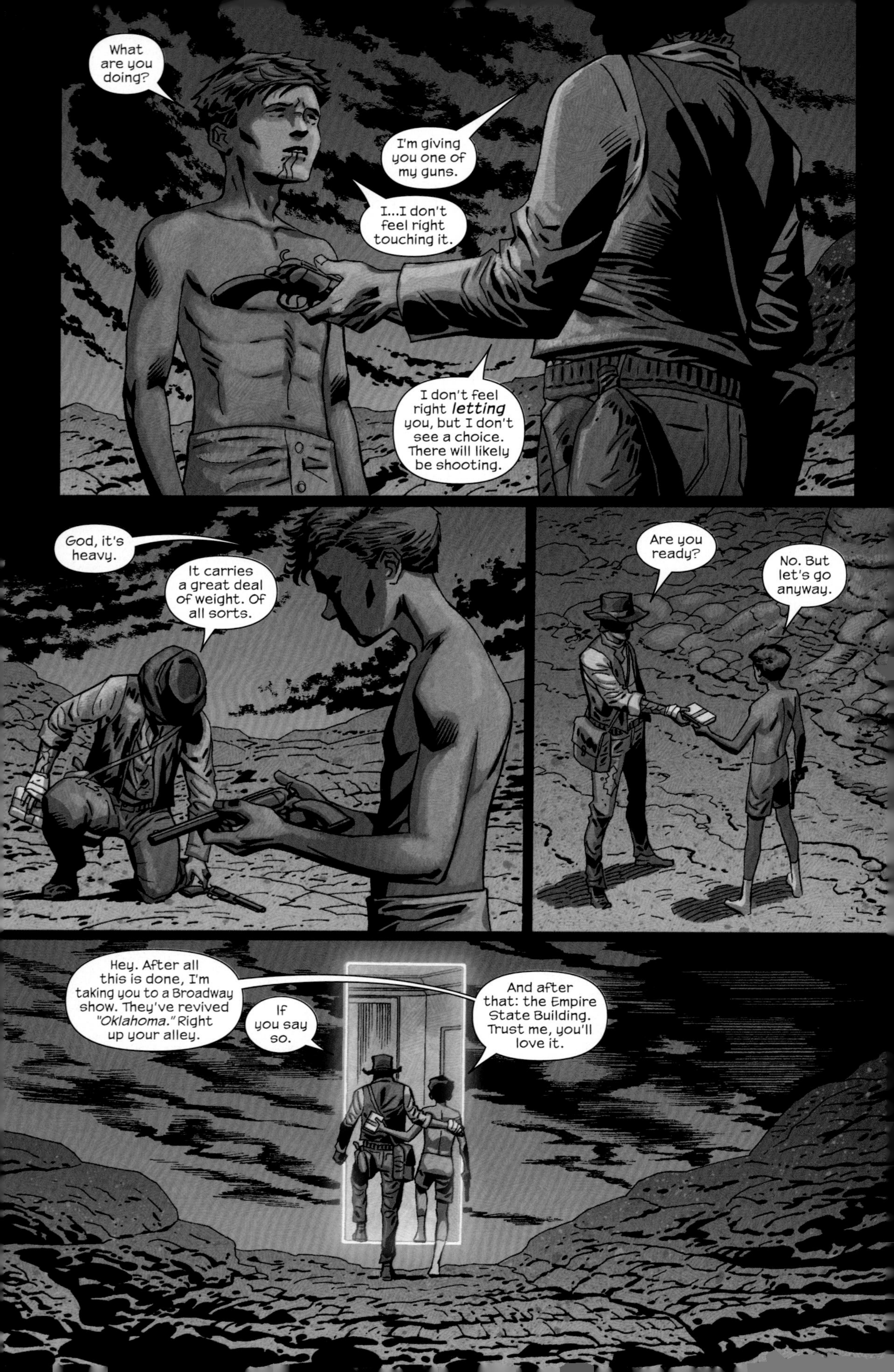
What are you doing?
I'm giving you one of my guns.
I...I don't feel right touching it.
I don't feel right *letting* you, but I don't see a choice. There will likely be shooting.
God, it's heavy.
It carries a great deal of weight. Of all sorts.
Are you ready?
No. But let's go anyway.
Hey. After all this is done, I'm taking you to a Broadway show. They've revived *"Oklahoma."* Right up your alley.
If you say so.
And after that: the Empire State Building. Trust me, you'll love it.

# THE DARK TOWER
# THE DRAWING OF THE THREE
## STEPHEN KING

# HOUSE OF CARDS
## CHAPTER FOUR

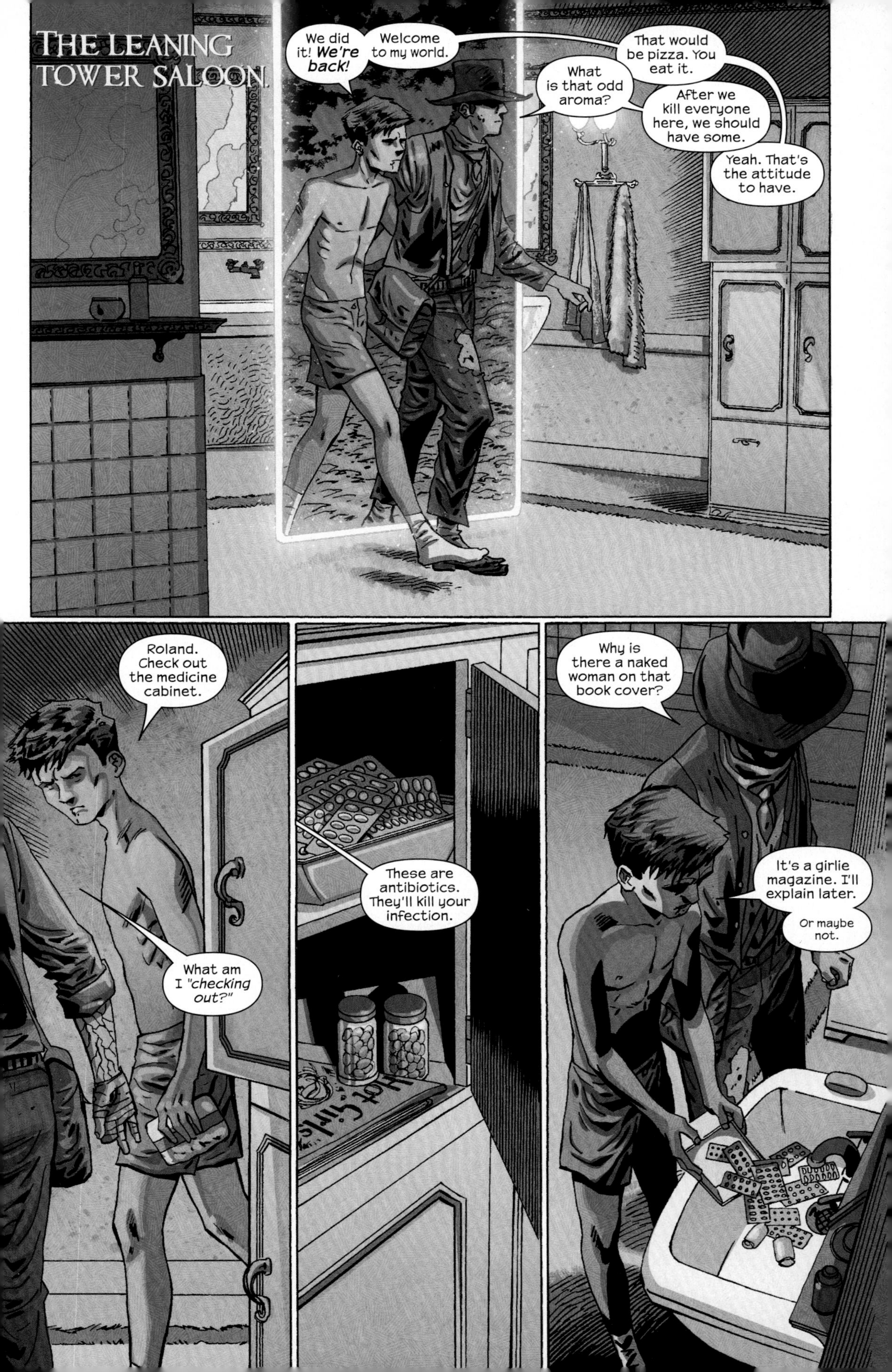
THE LEANING TOWER SALOON.
We did it! *We're back!*
Welcome to my world.
What is that odd aroma?
That would be pizza. You eat it.
After we kill everyone here, we should have some.
Yeah. That's the attitude to have.
Roland. Check out the medicine cabinet.
What am I *"checking out?"*
These are antibiotics. They'll kill your infection.
Why is there a naked woman on that book cover?
It's a girlie magazine. I'll explain later.
Or maybe not.

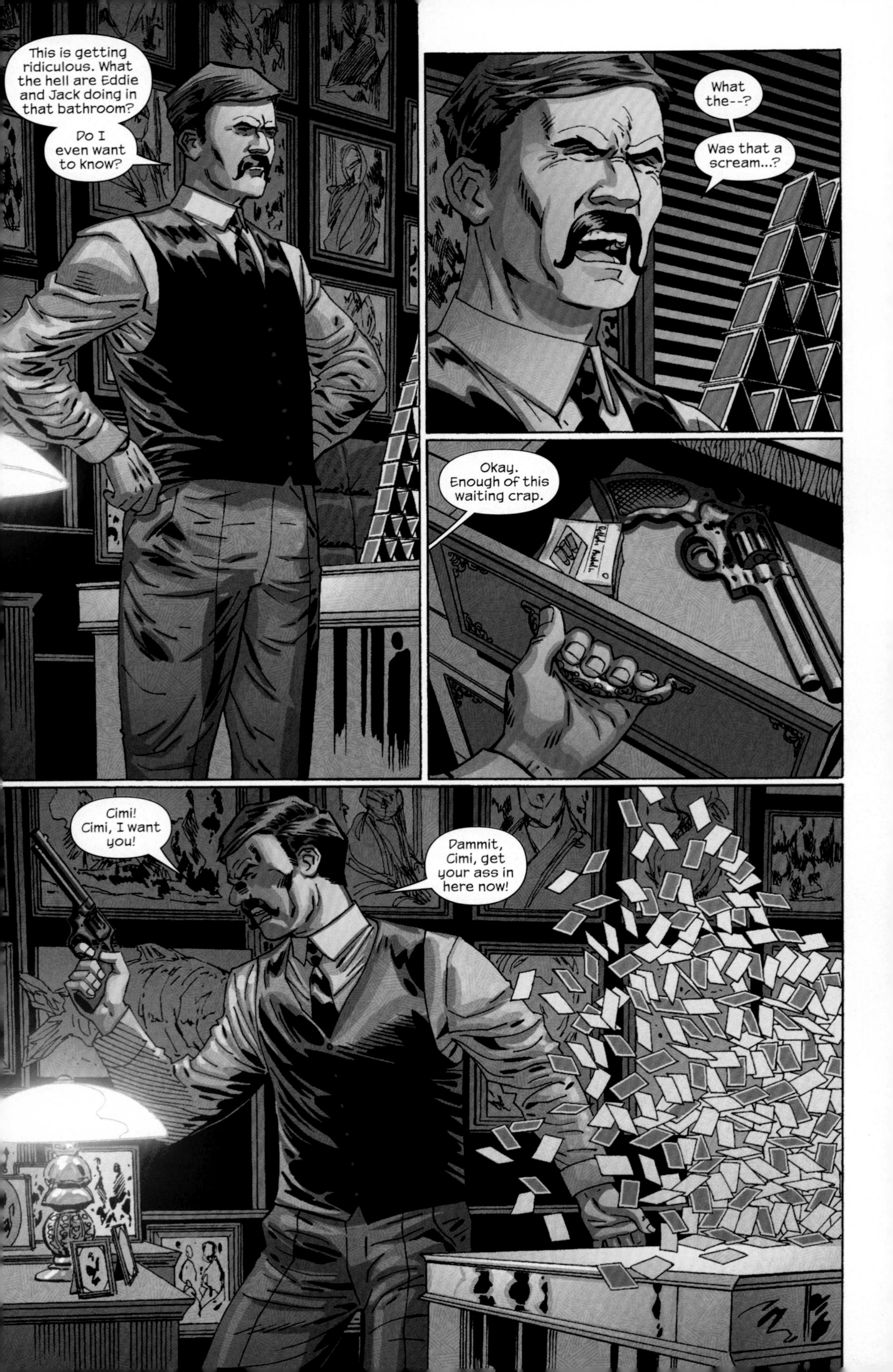
This is getting ridiculous. What the hell are Eddie and Jack doing in that bathroom?
Do I even want to know?
What the--?
Was that a scream...?
Okay. Enough of this waiting crap.
Cimi! Cimi, I want you!
Dammit, Cimi, get your ass in here now!

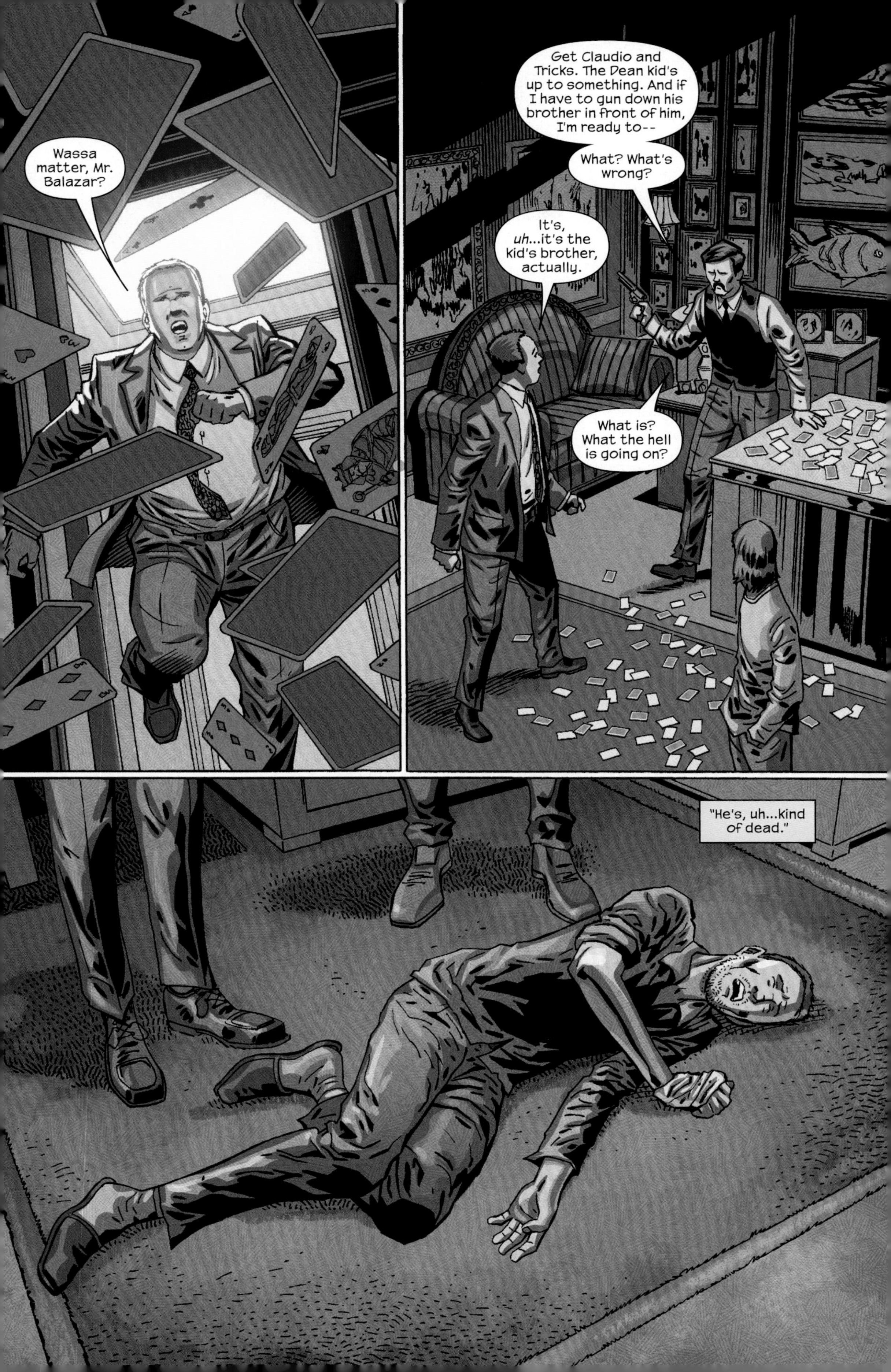
Wassa matter, Mr. Balazar?
Get Claudio and Tricks. The Dean kid's up to something. And if I have to gun down his brother in front of him, I'm ready to--
What? What's wrong?
It's, *uh*...it's the kid's brother, actually.
What is? What the hell is going on?
"He's, uh...kind of dead."

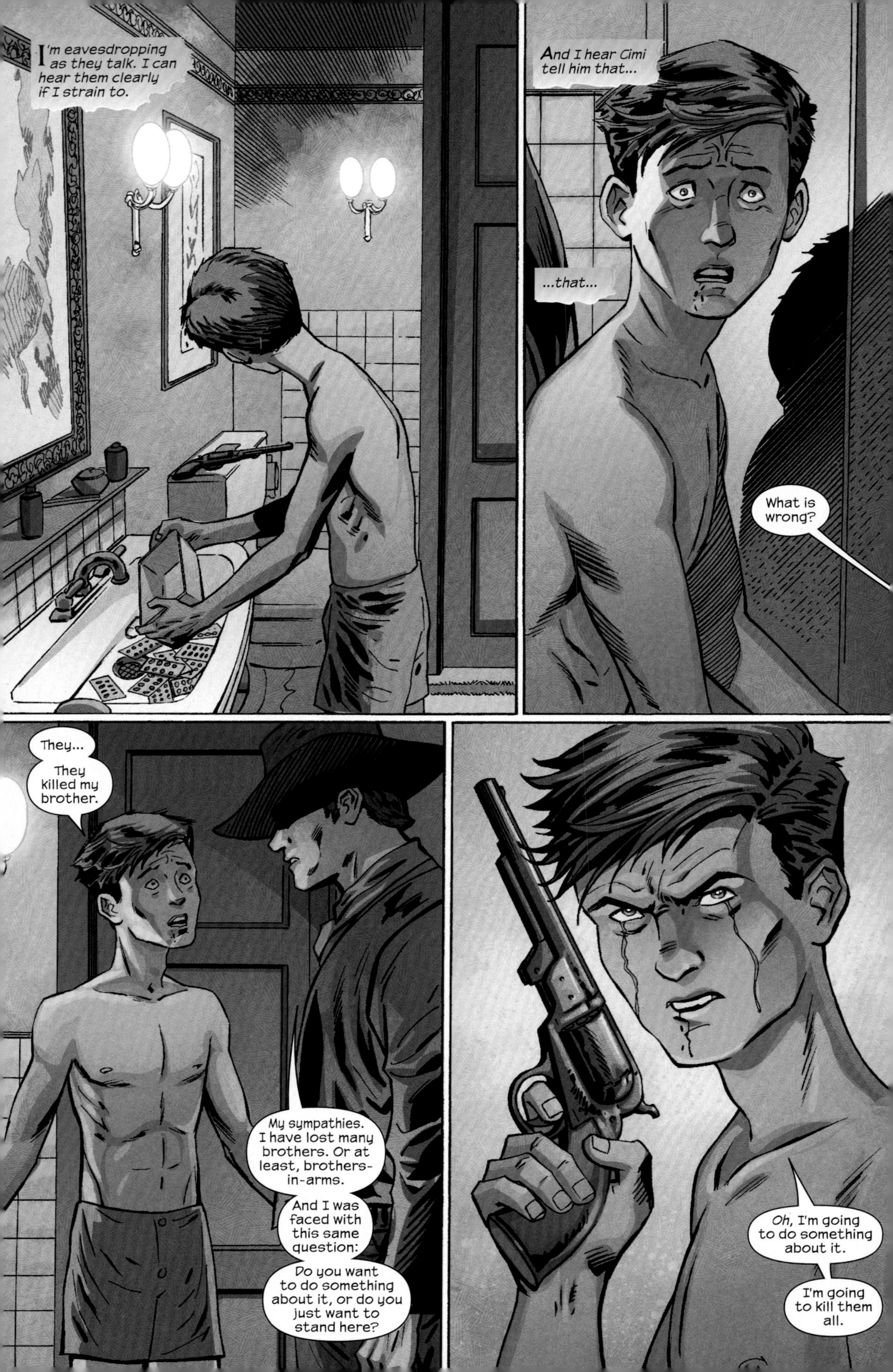
I'm eavesdropping as they talk. I can hear them clearly if I strain to.
And I hear Cimi tell him that...
...that...
What is wrong?
They...
They killed my brother.
My sympathies. I have lost many brothers. Or at least, brothers-in-arms.
And I was faced with this same question:
Do you want to do something about it, or do you just want to stand here?
Oh, I'm going to do something about it.
I'm going to kill them all.

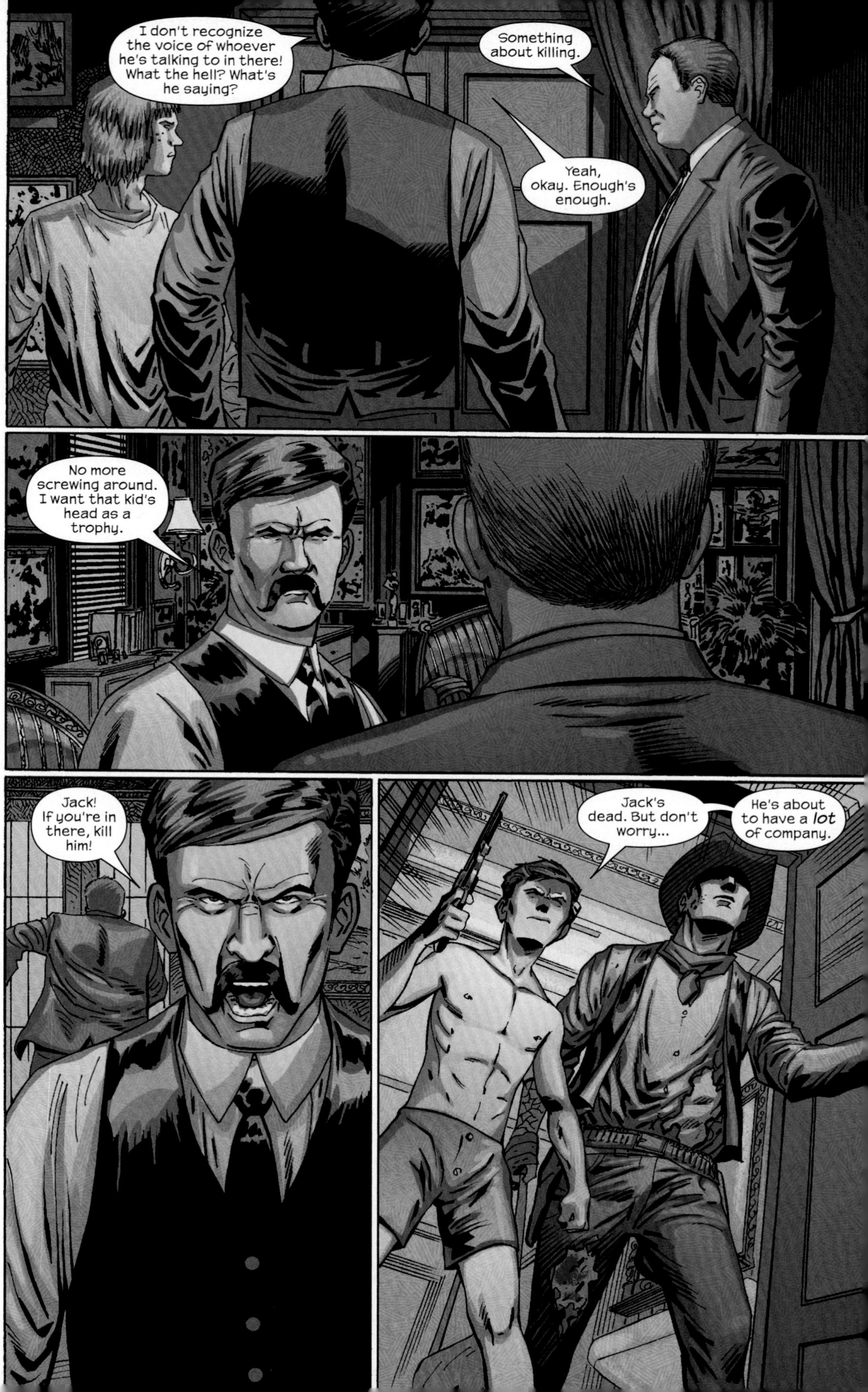
I don't recognize the voice of whoever he's talking to in there! What the hell? What's he saying?
Something about killing.
Yeah, okay. Enough's enough.
No more screwing around. I want that kid's head as a trophy.
Jack! If you're in there, kill him!
Jack's dead. But don't worry...
He's about to have a *lot* of company.

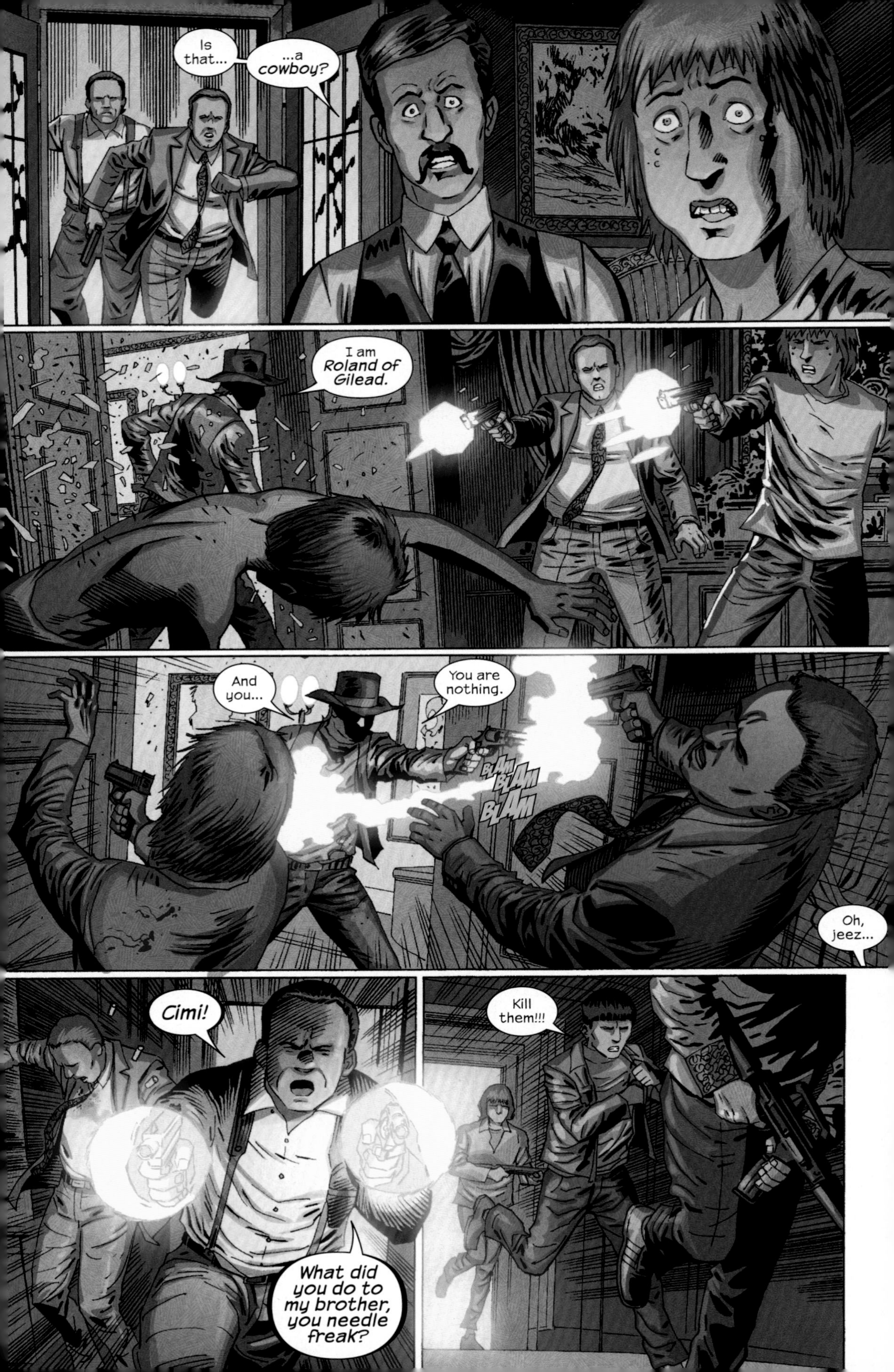
Is that...
...a cowboy?
I am Roland of Gilead.
And you...
You are nothing.
BLAM BLAM BLAM
Oh, jeez...
Cimi!
What did you do to my brother, you needle freak?
Kill them!!!

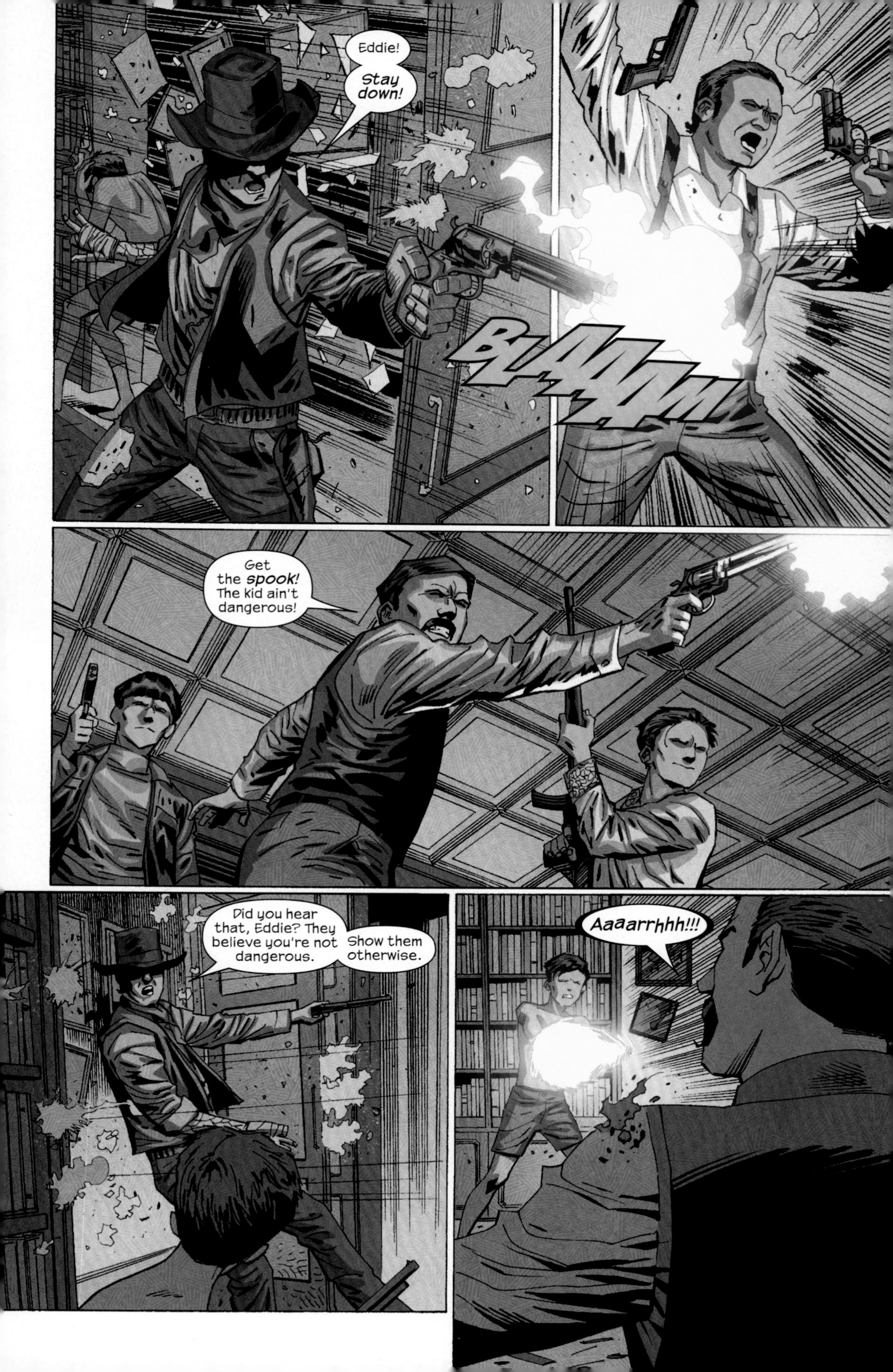
Eddie!
Stay down!
BLAAAM
Get the spook! The kid ain't dangerous!
Did you hear that, Eddie? They believe you're not dangerous.
Show them otherwise.
Aaaarrhhh!!!

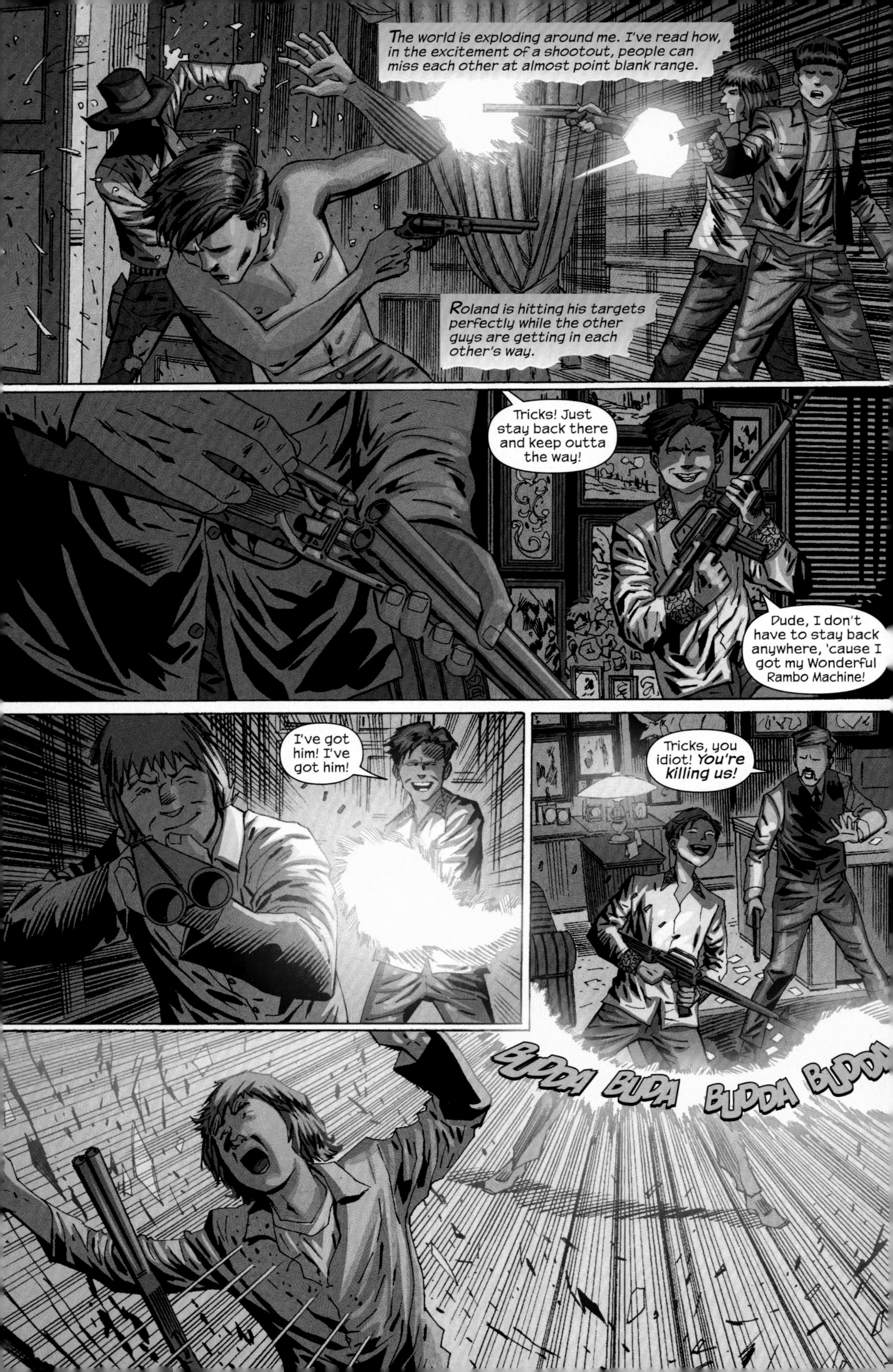
The world is exploding around me. I've read how, in the excitement of a shootout, people can miss each other at almost point blank range.
Roland is hitting his targets perfectly while the other guys are getting in each other's way.
Tricks! Just stay back there and keep outta the way!
Dude, I don't have to stay back anywhere, 'cause I got my Wonderful Rambo Machine!
I've got him! I've got him!
Tricks, you idiot! You're killing us!
BUDDA BUDA BUDDA BUDDA

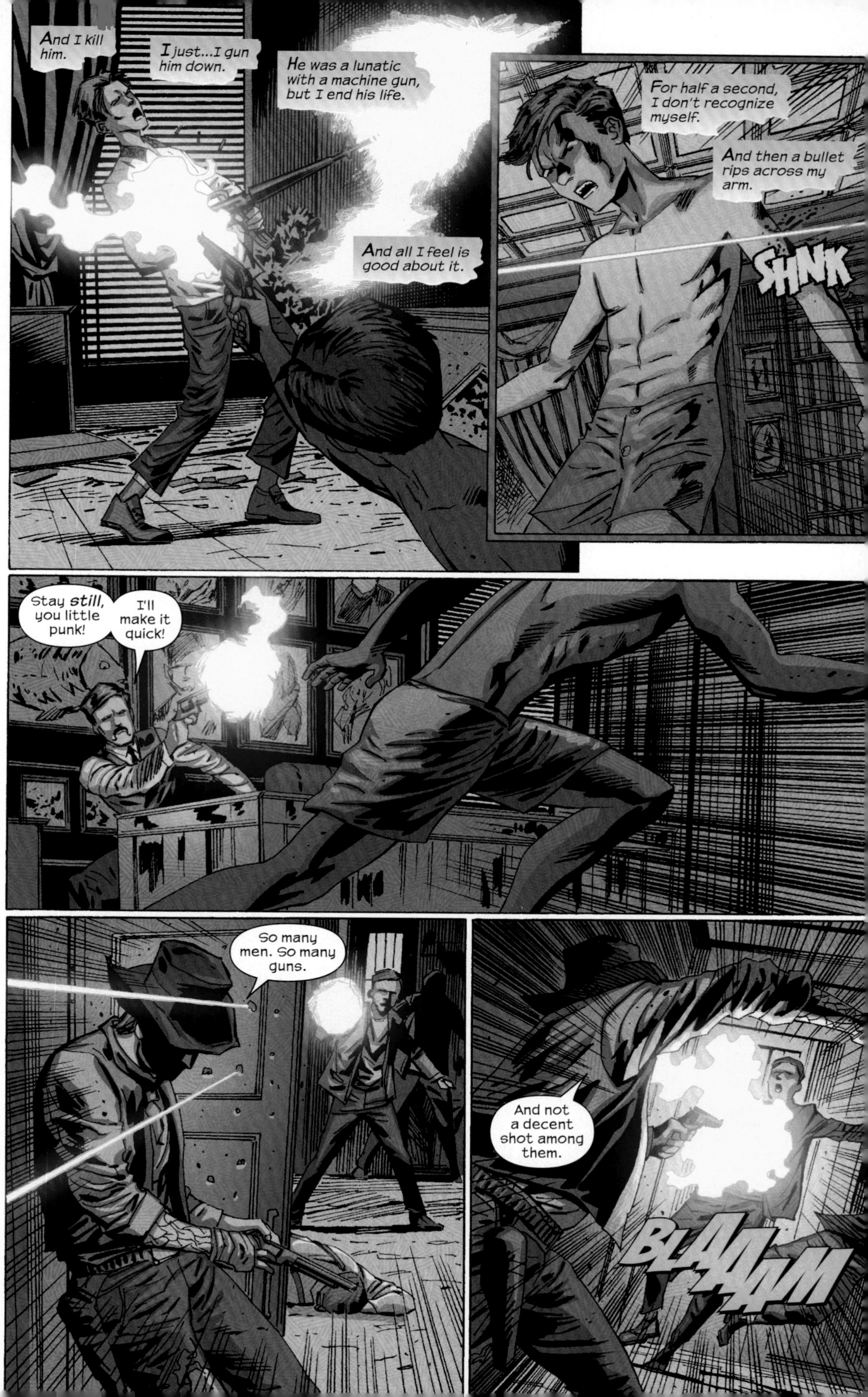

And I kill him.
I just...I gun him down.
He was a lunatic with a machine gun, but I end his life.
And all I feel is good about it.
For half a second, I don't recognize myself.
And then a bullet rips across my arm.
SHNK
Stay still, you little punk!
I'll make it quick!
So many men. So many guns.
And not a decent shot among them.
BLAAAM

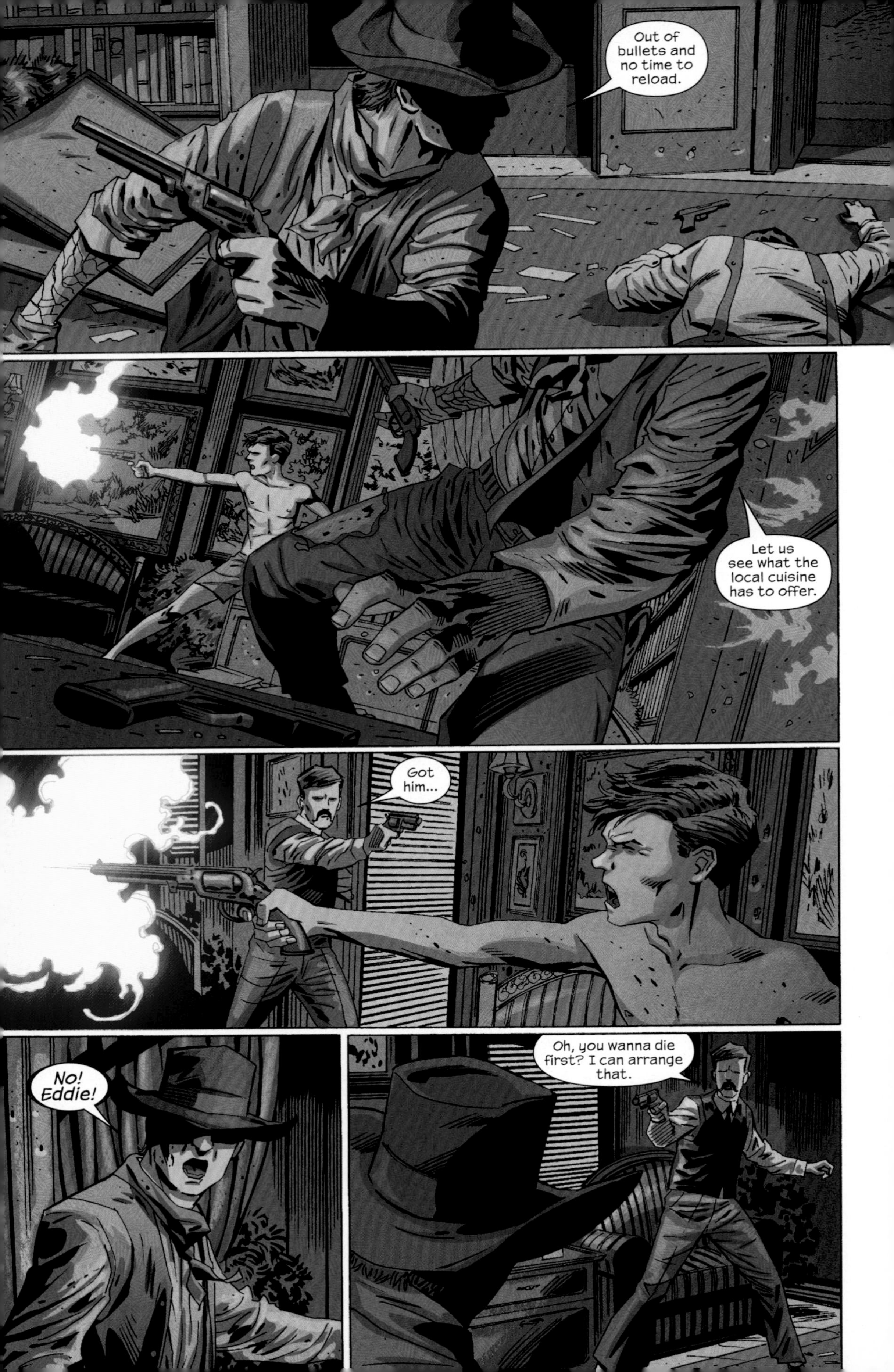

Out of bullets and no time to reload.
Let us see what the local cuisine has to offer.
Got him...
No! Eddie!
Oh, you wanna die first? I can arrange that.

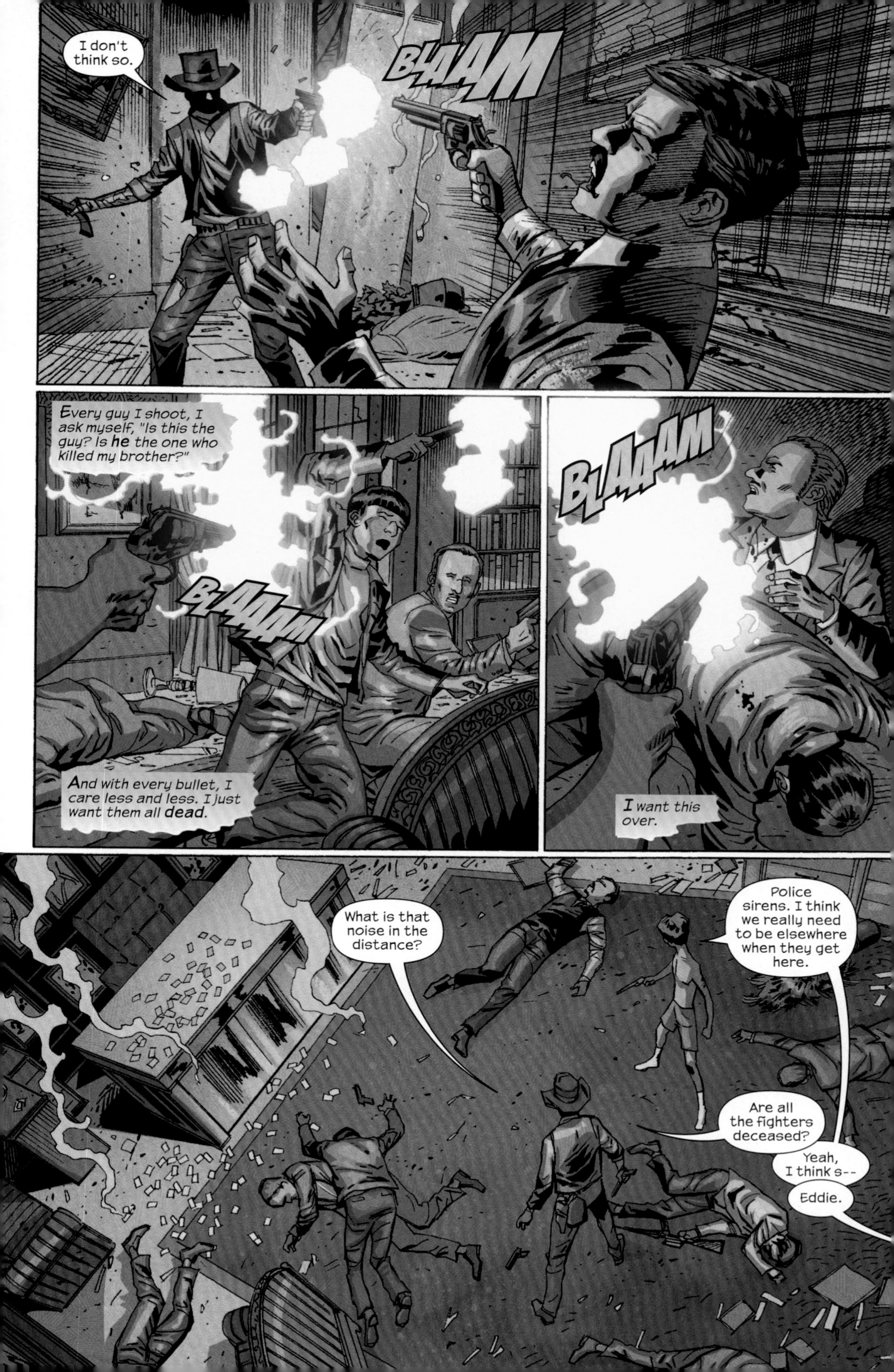
I don't think so.
BLAAM
Every guy I shoot, I ask myself, "Is this the guy? Is he the one who killed my brother?"
BLAAAM
And with every bullet, I care less and less. I just want them all dead.
BLAAAM
I want this over.
What is that noise in the distance?
Police sirens. I think we really need to be elsewhere when they get here.
Are all the fighters deceased?
Yeah, I think s--
Eddie.

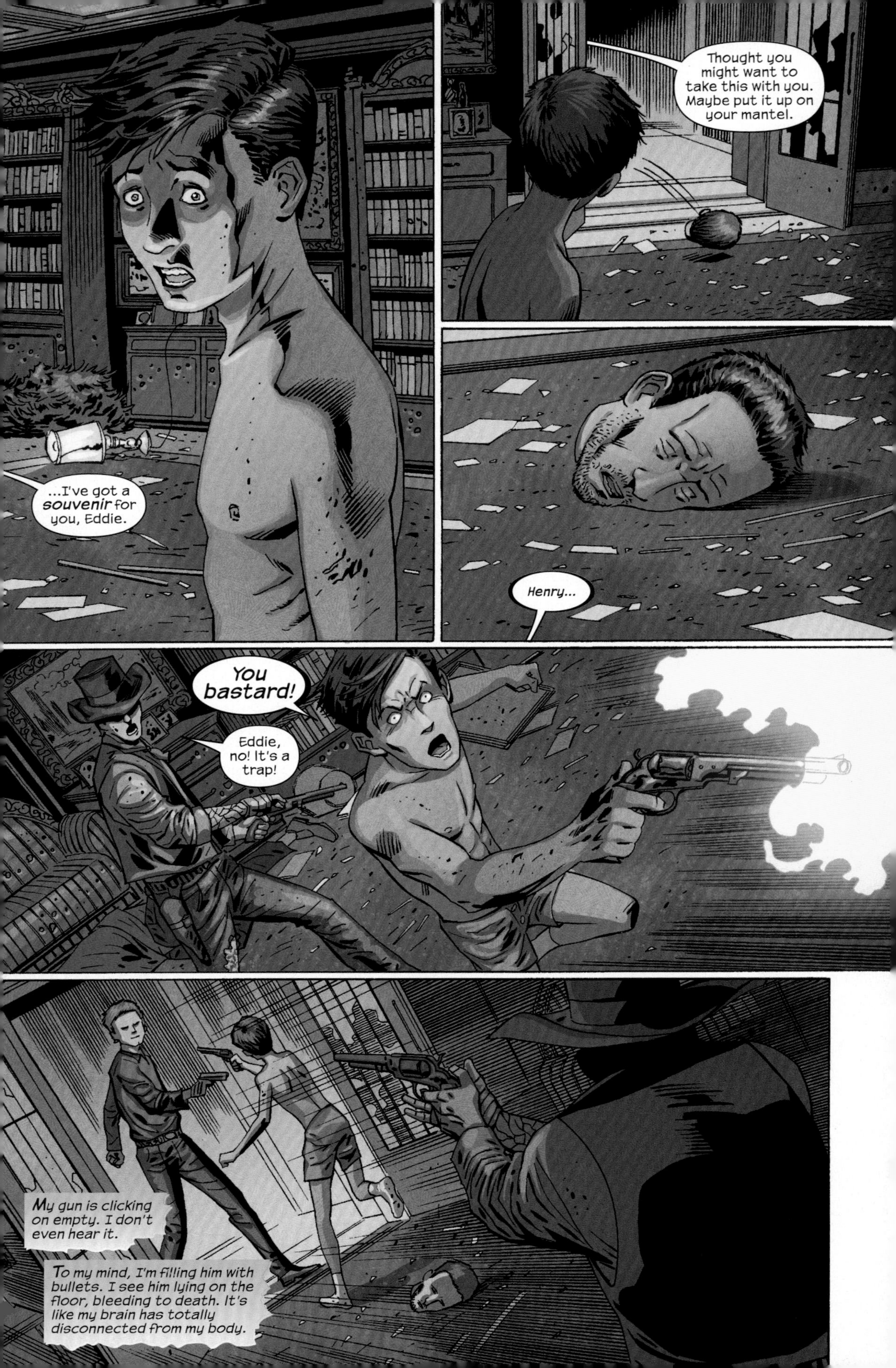
...I've got a souvenir for you, Eddie.
Thought you might want to take this with you. Maybe put it up on your mantel.
Henry...
You bastard!
Eddie, no! It's a trap!
My gun is clicking on empty. I don't even hear it.
To my mind, I'm filling him with bullets. I see him lying on the floor, bleeding to death. It's like my brain has totally disconnected from my body.

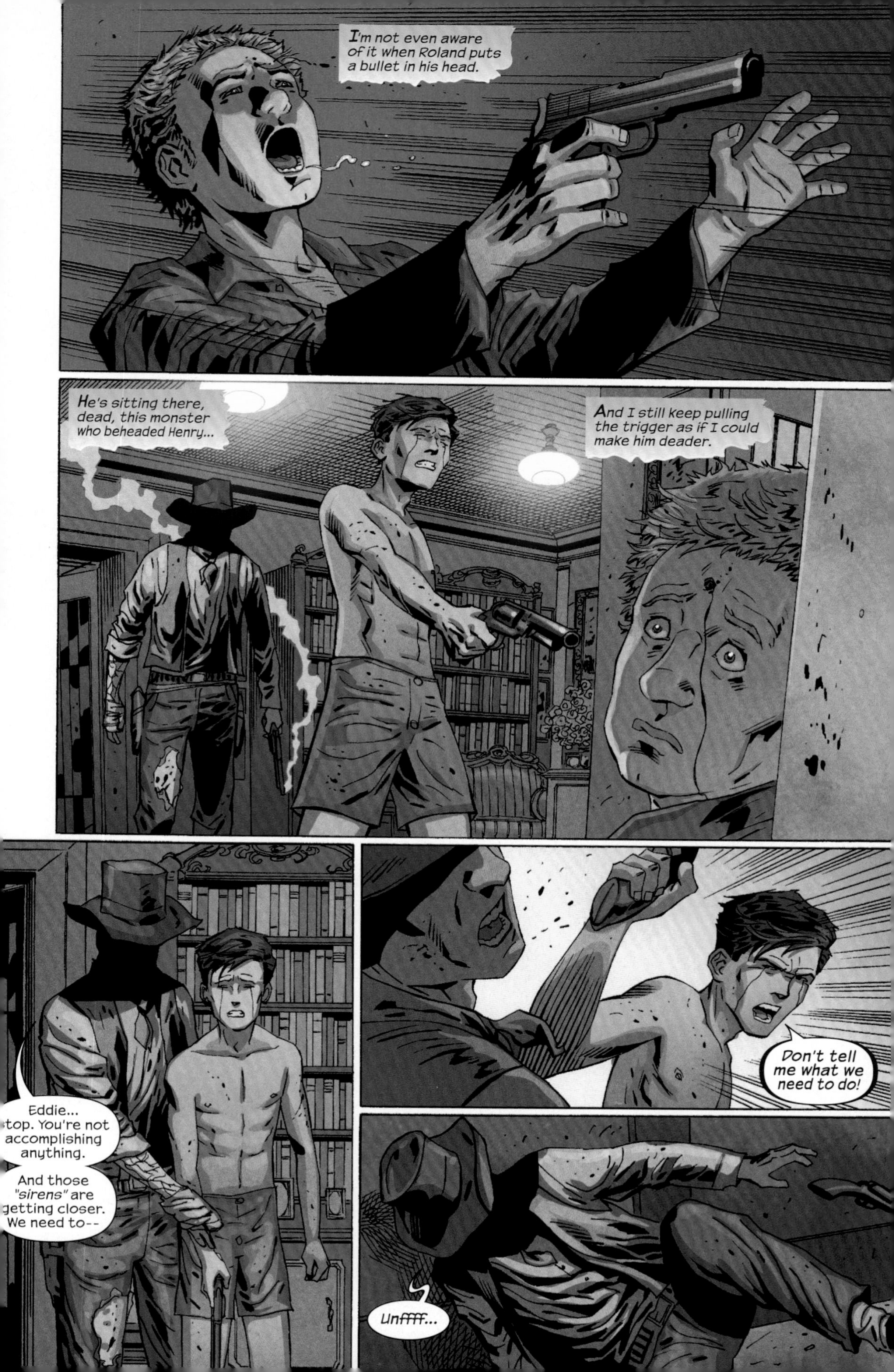
I'm not even aware of it when Roland puts a bullet in his head.
He's sitting there, dead, this monster who beheaded Henry...
And I still keep pulling the trigger as if I could make him deader.
Eddie... stop. You're not accomplishing anything.
And those "sirens" are getting closer. We need to--
Don't tell me what we need to do!
Unffff...

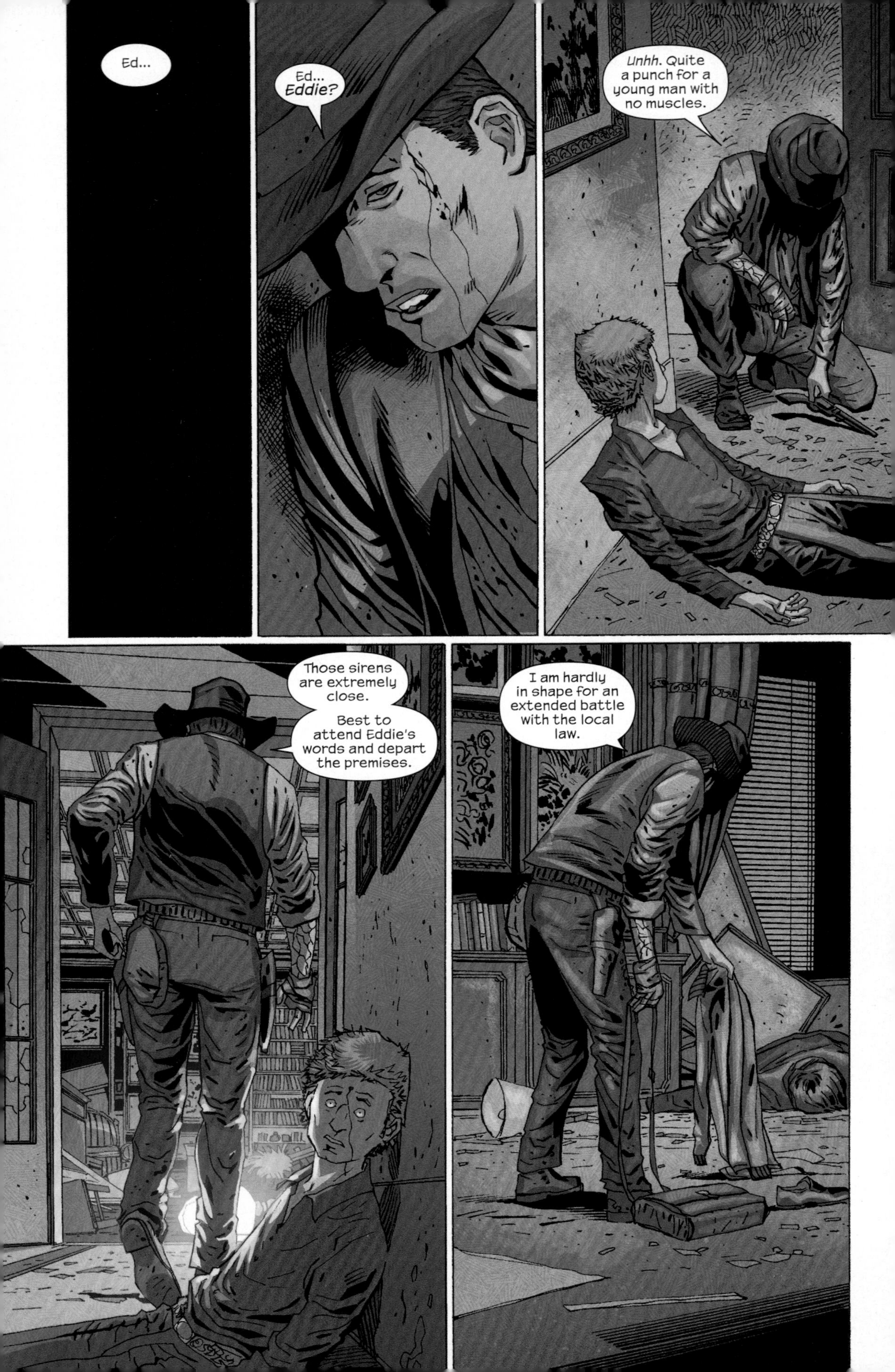
Ed...
Ed... *Eddie?*
*Unhh.* Quite a punch for a young man with no muscles.
Those sirens are extremely close.
Best to attend Eddie's words and depart the premises.
I am hardly in shape for an extended battle with the local law.

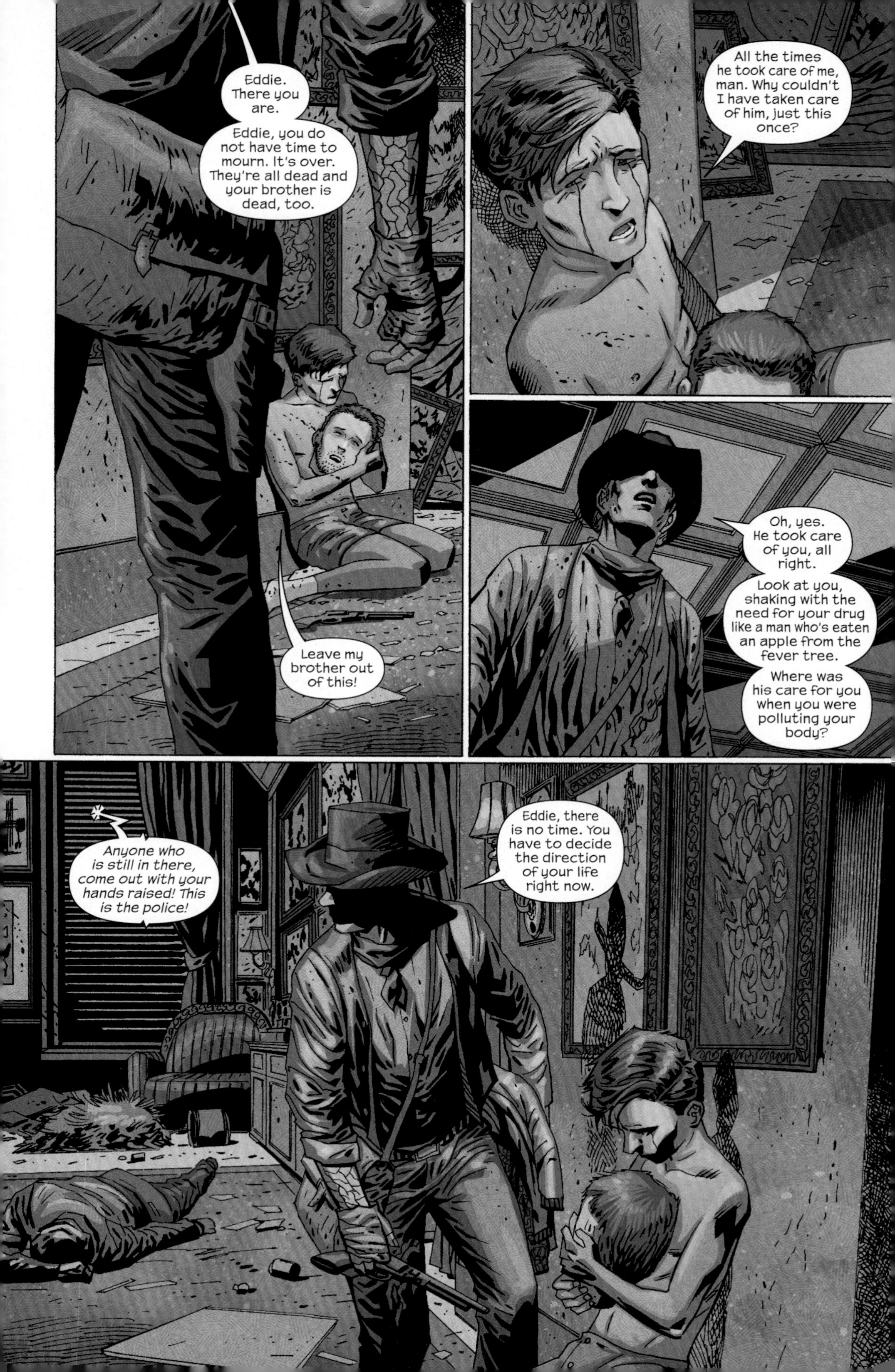
Eddie. There you are.
Eddie, you do not have time to mourn. It's over. They're all dead and your brother is dead, too.
Leave my brother out of this!
All the times he took care of me, man. Why couldn't I have taken care of him, just this once?
Oh, yes. He took care of you, all right.
Look at you, shaking with the need for your drug like a man who's eaten an apple from the fever tree.
Where was his care for you when you were polluting your body?
Anyone who is still in there, come out with your hands raised! This is the police!
Eddie, there is no time. You have to decide the direction of your life right now.

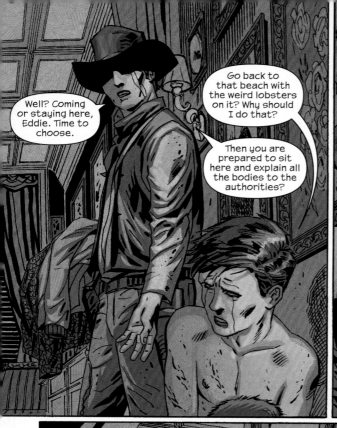

Well? Coming or staying here, Eddie. Time to choose.

Go back to that beach with the weird lobsters on it? Why should I do that?

Then you are prepared to sit here and explain all the bodies to the authorities?

I don't care. Nothing matters without Henry.

Maybe it doesn't matter to you, but there are others involved, prisoner.

Don't call me that!

I'll call you a prisoner until you show me you can walk out of the cell you're in! Throw that rotten piece of meat away and stop *puling!*

I'll *pule* all I want!

...What's puling?

Whining.

Talk normal!

The S.W.A.T. squad has arrived! I repeat, the S.W.A.T. squad has arrived!

Come out with your hands up!

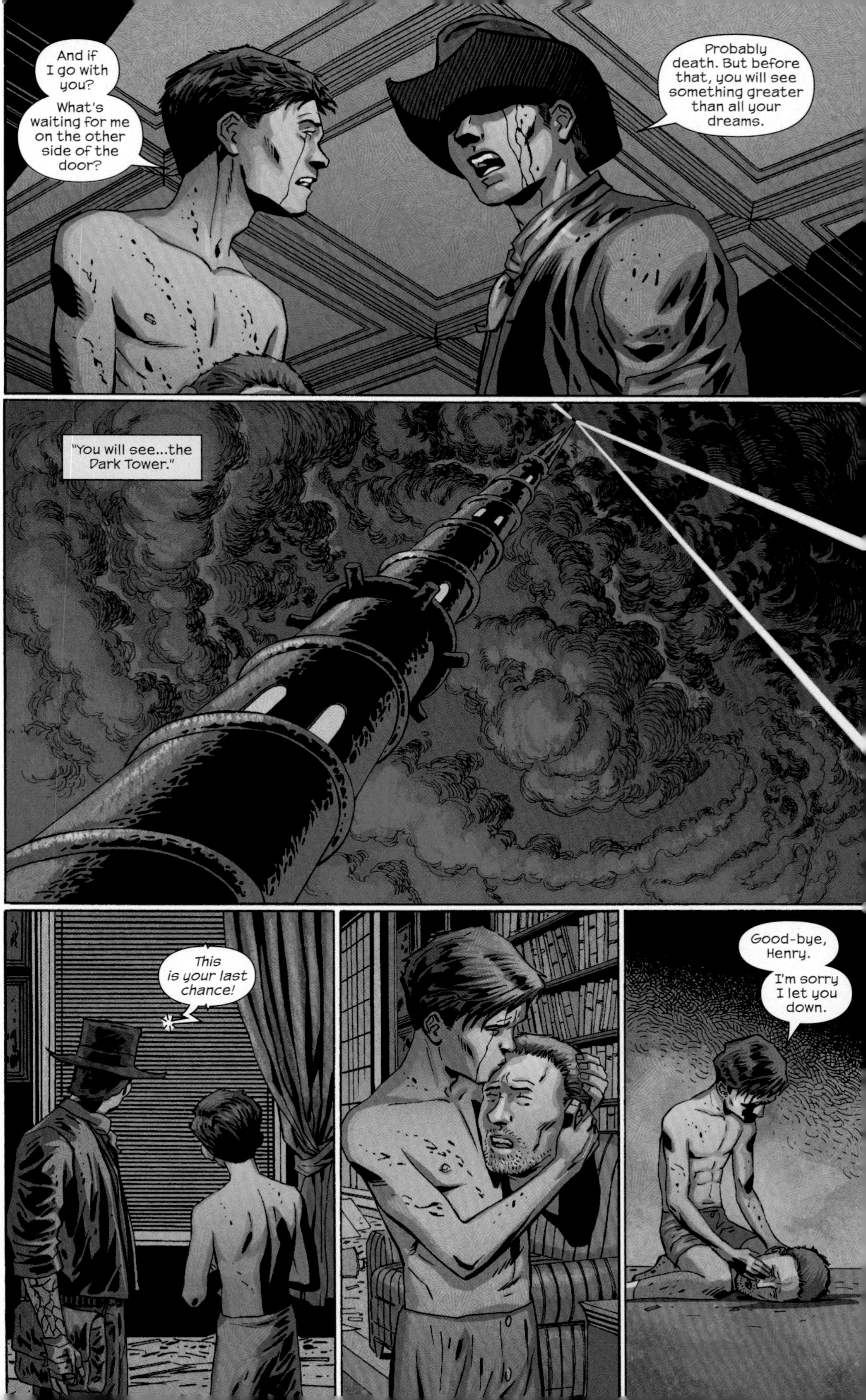

And if I go with you?
What's waiting for me on the other side of the door?
Probably death. But before that, you will see something greater than all your dreams.
"You will see...the Dark Tower."
This is your last chance!
Good-bye, Henry.
I'm sorry I let you down.

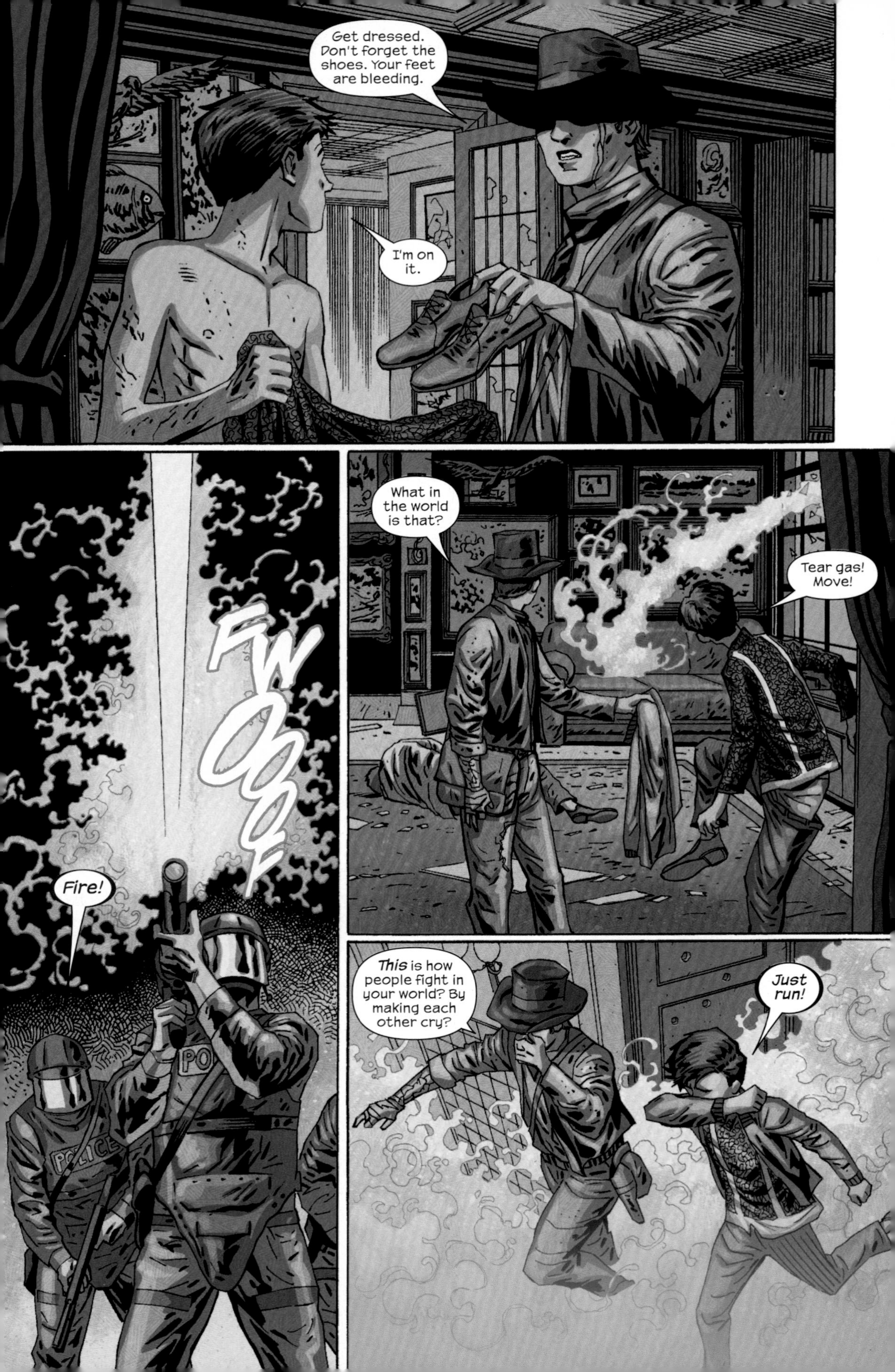

Get dressed. Don't forget the shoes. Your feet are bleeding.
I'm on it.
FWOOOF
Fire!
What in the world is that?
Tear gas! Move!
This is how people fight in your world? By making each other cry?
Just run!

Grab the antibiotics! Hurry!

Are you ready?

Anything but.

I will accept that.

*Body's starting to shake. With the adrenaline wearing off, my need for drugs is starting to kick in. And I don't think I've ever needed them so bad.*

Well done...

What is wrong?

Ohhh... nothing. Just, y'know... *heroin withdrawal.* No big thing.

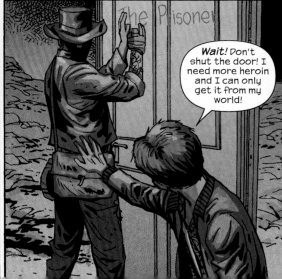

The Prisoner

*Wait!* Don't shut the door! I need more heroin and I can only get it from my world!

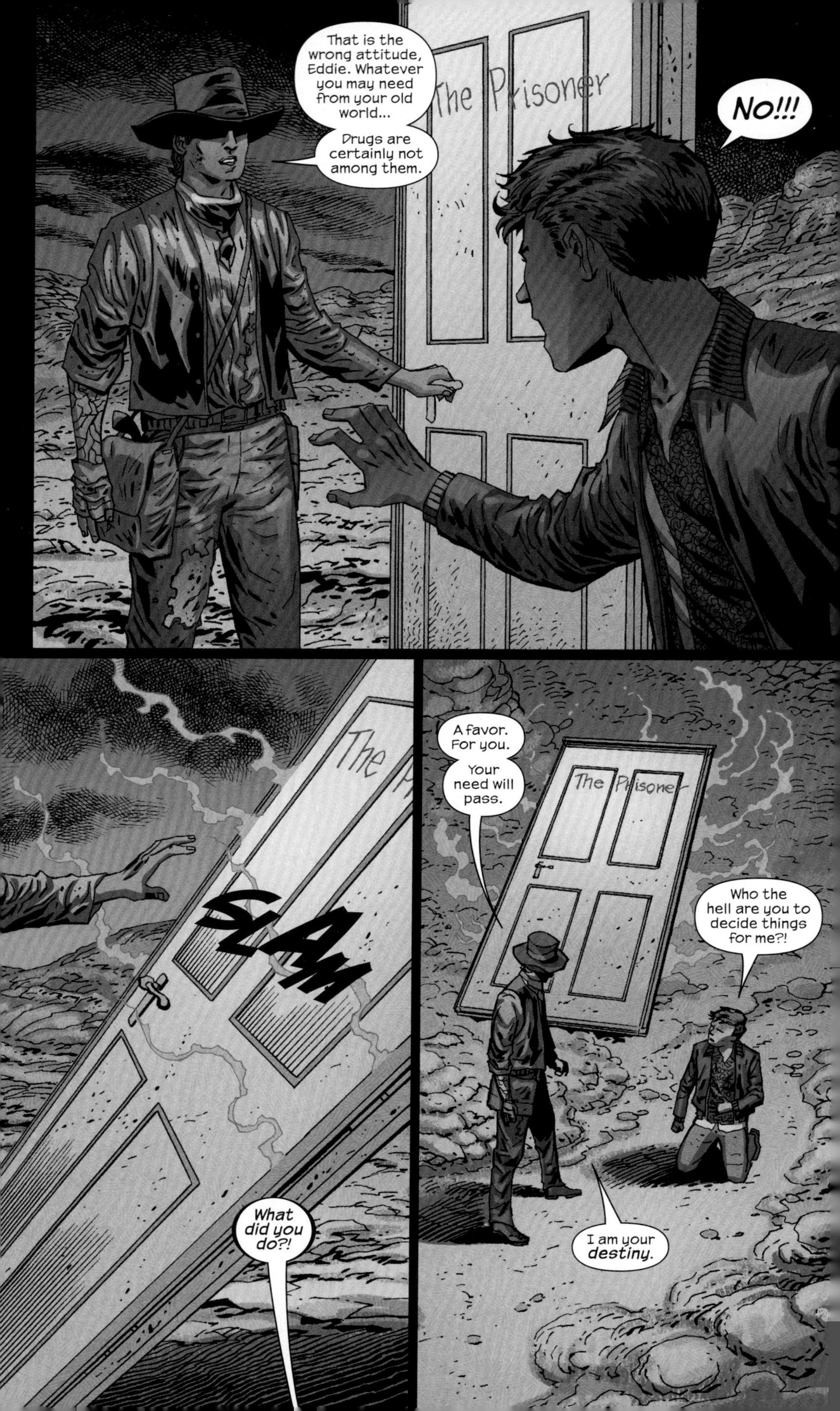
The Prisoner
That is the wrong attitude, Eddie. Whatever you may need from your old world...
Drugs are certainly not among them.
NO!!!
The
SLAM
What did you do?!
A favor. For you.
Your need will pass.
The Prisoner
Who the hell are you to decide things for me?!
I am your *destiny*.

# THE DARK TOWER

## THE DRAWING OF THE THREE

### OF THE

### STEPHEN KING

# USE OF CARDS

## CHAPTER FIVE

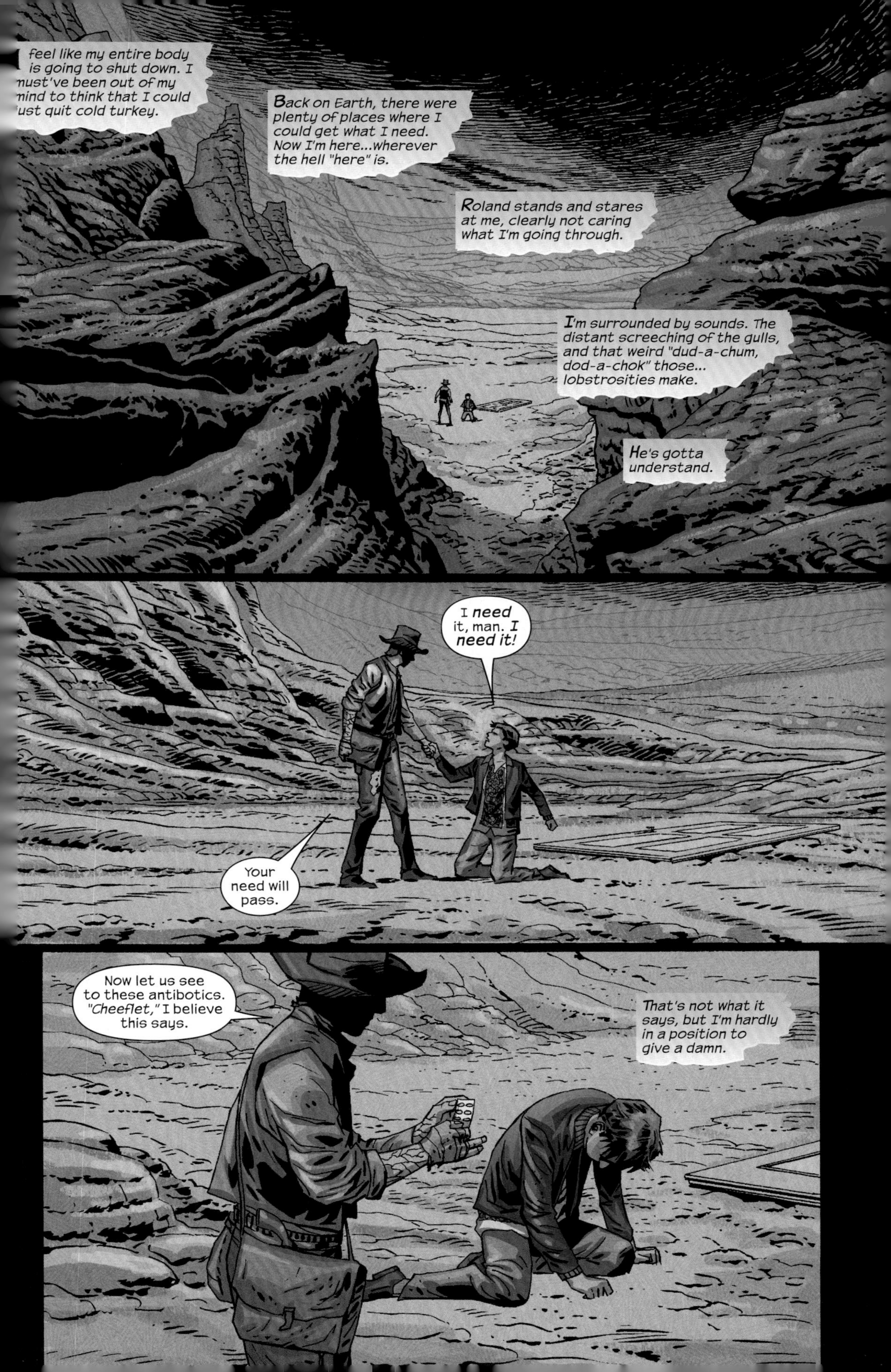
I feel like my entire body is going to shut down. I must've been out of my mind to think that I could just quit cold turkey.
Back on Earth, there were plenty of places where I could get what I need. Now I'm here...wherever the hell "here" is.
Roland stands and stares at me, clearly not caring what I'm going through.
I'm surrounded by sounds. The distant screeching of the gulls, and that weird "dud-a-chum, dod-a-chok" those... lobstrosities make.
He's gotta understand.
I need it, man. I need it!
Your need will pass.
Now let us see to these antibotics. "Cheeflet," I believe this says.
That's not what it says, but I'm hardly in a position to give a damn.

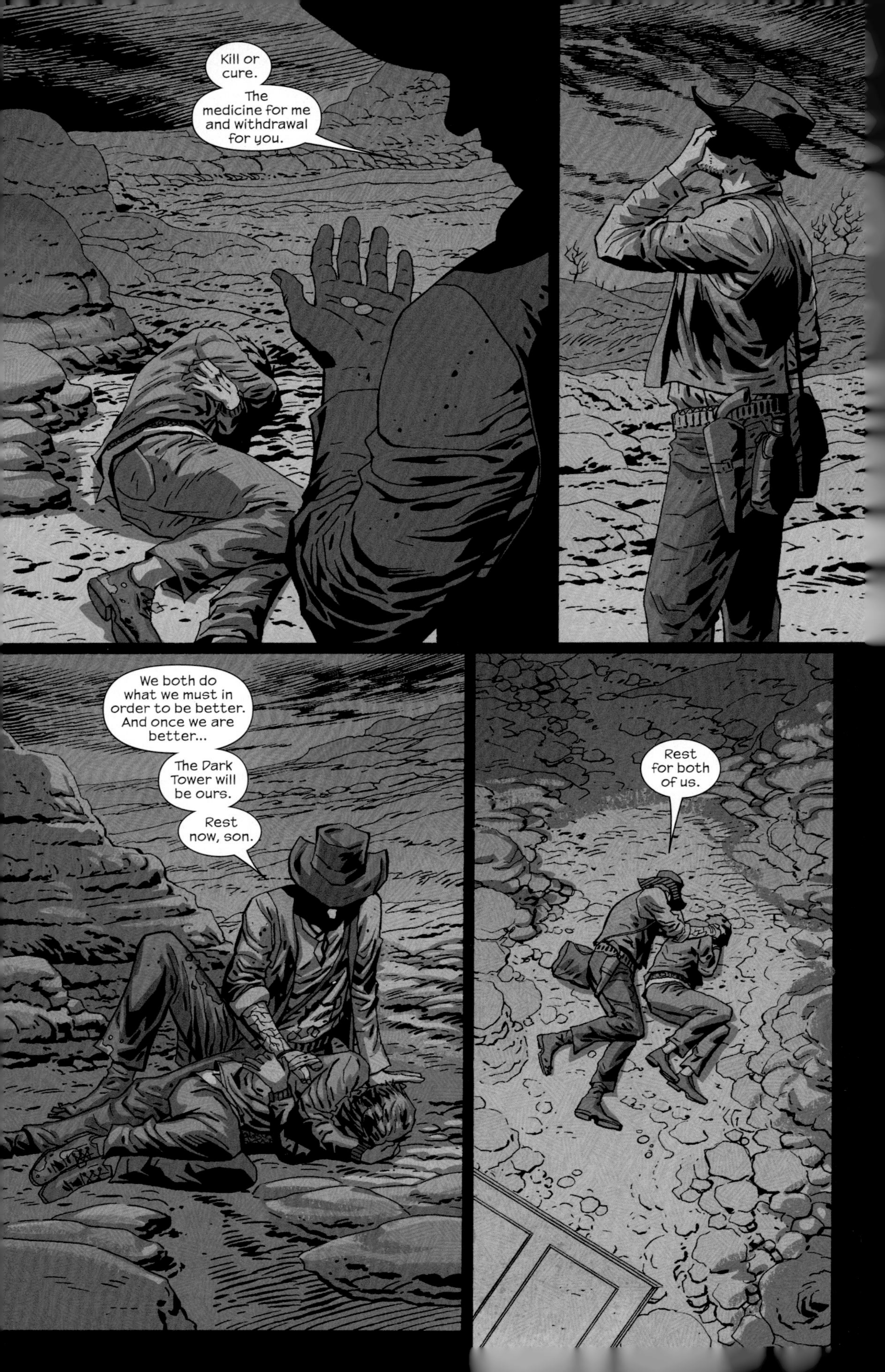
Kill or cure.
The medicine for me and withdrawal for you.
We both do what we must in order to be better. And once we are better...
The Dark Tower will be ours.
Rest now, son.
Rest for both of us.

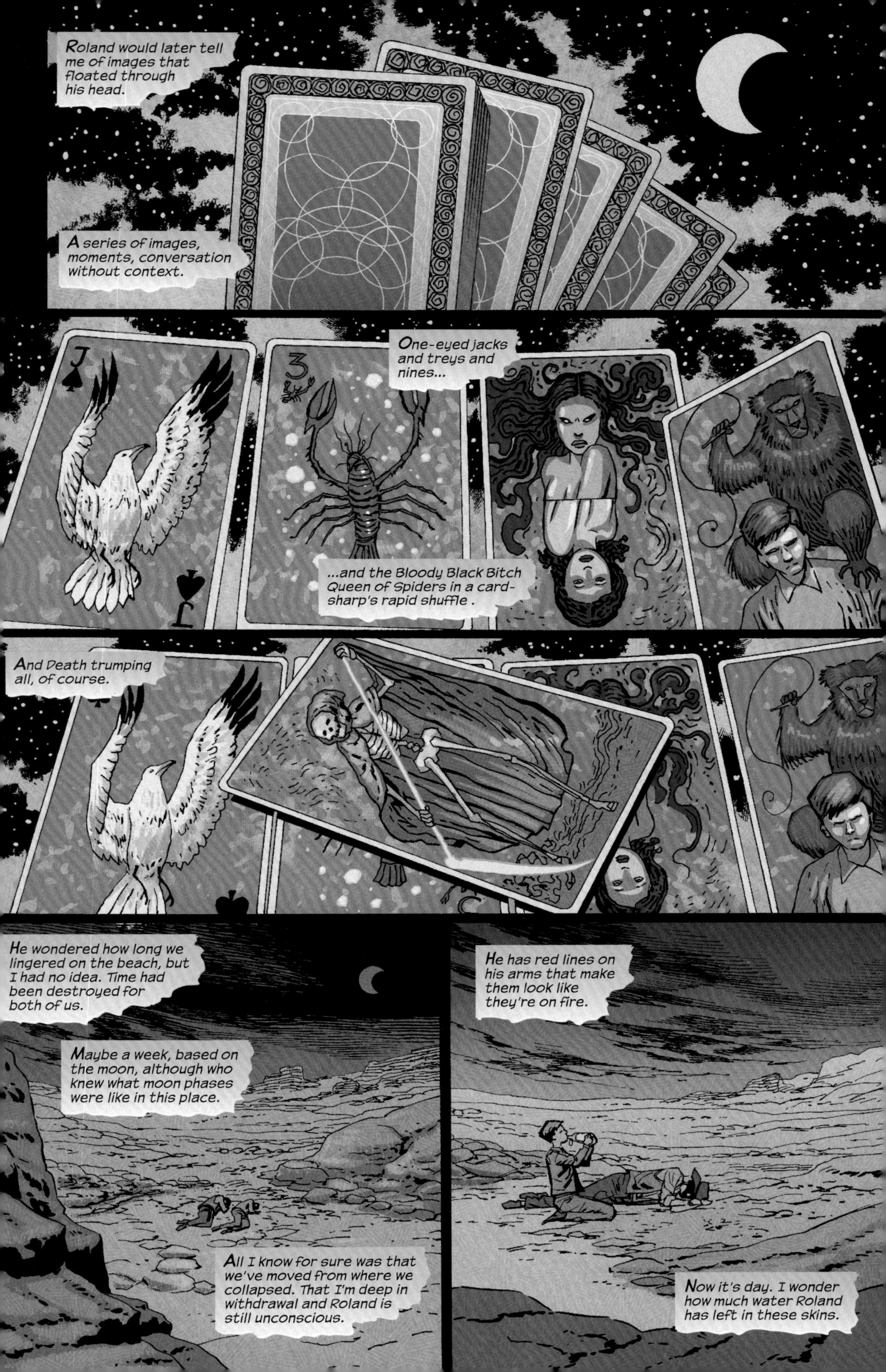
Roland would later tell me of images that floated through his head.
A series of images, moments, conversation without context.
One-eyed jacks and treys and nines...
...and the Bloody Black Bitch Queen of Spiders in a card-sharp's rapid shuffle .
And Death trumping all, of course.
He wondered how long we lingered on the beach, but I had no idea. Time had been destroyed for both of us.
Maybe a week, based on the moon, although who knew what moon phases were like in this place.
All I know for sure was that we've moved from where we collapsed. That I'm deep in withdrawal and Roland is still unconscious.
He has red lines on his arms that make them look like they're on fire.
Now it's day. I wonder how much water Roland has left in these skins.

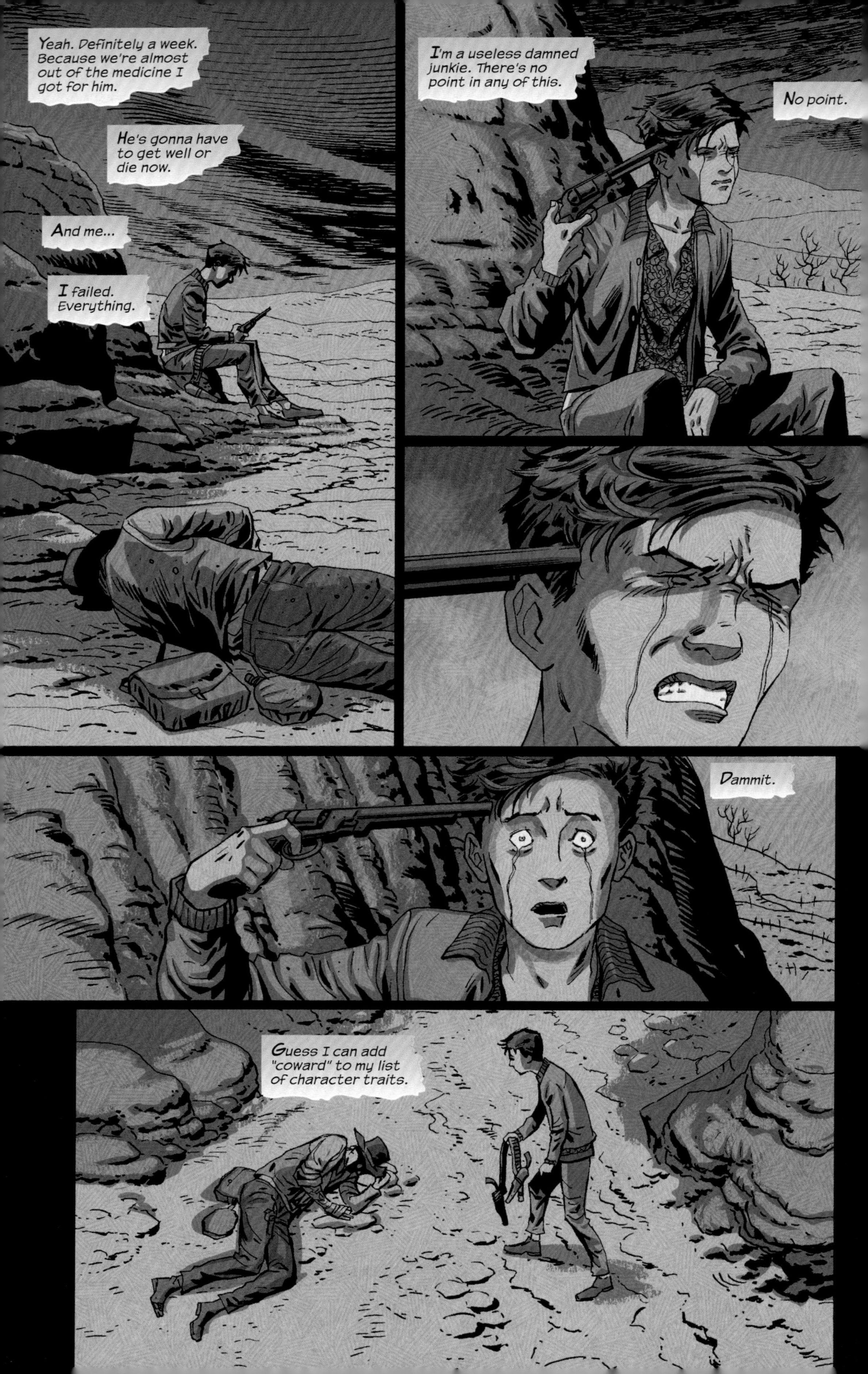

Yeah. Definitely a week. Because we're almost out of the medicine I got for him.
He's gonna have to get well or die now.
And me...
I failed. Everything.
I'm a useless damned junkie. There's no point in any of this.
No point.
Dammit.
Guess I can add "coward" to my list of character traits.

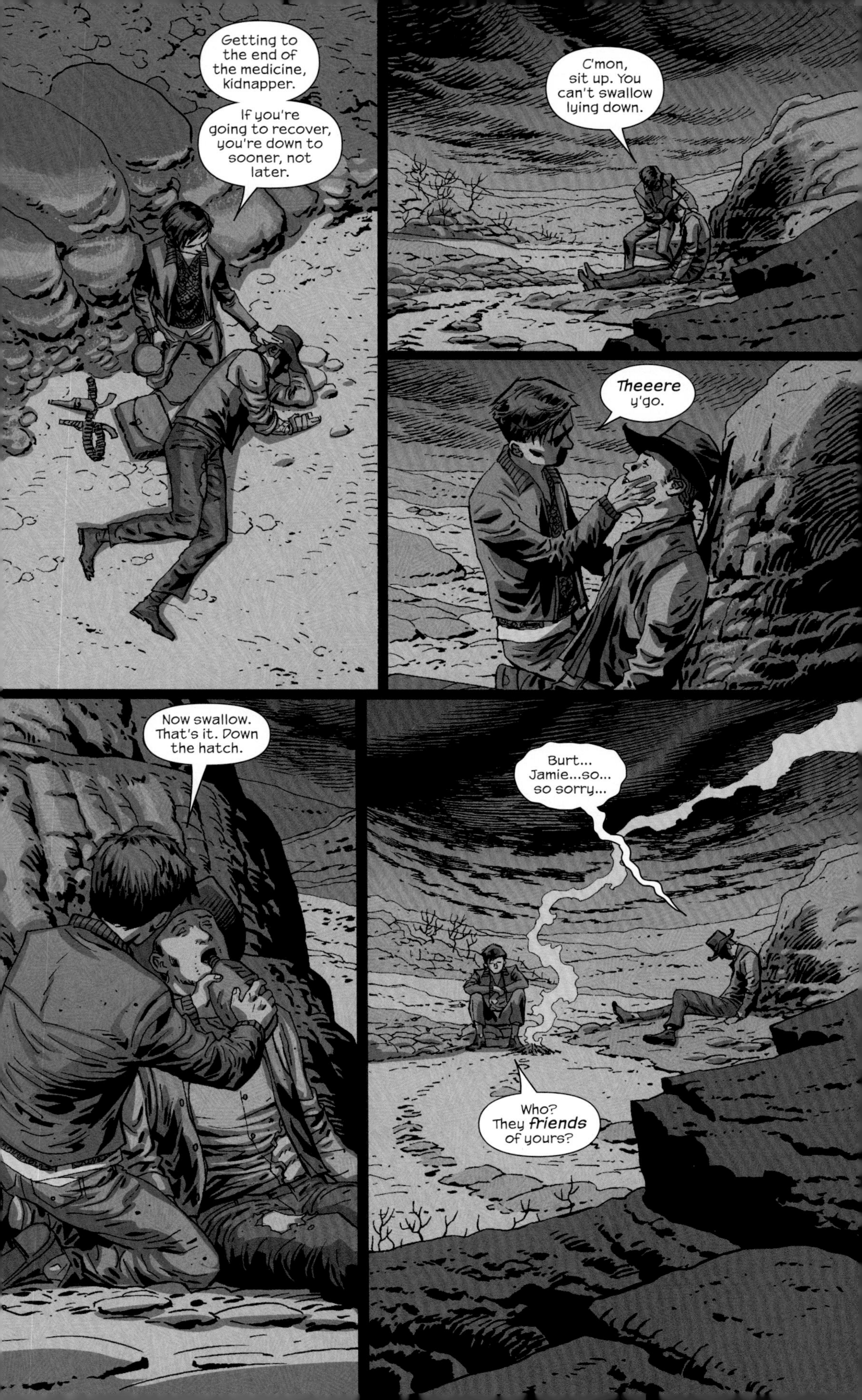
Getting to the end of the medicine, kidnapper.
If you're going to recover, you're down to sooner, not later.
C'mon, sit up. You can't swallow lying down.
Theeere y'go.
Now swallow. That's it. Down the hatch.
Burt... Jamie...so... so sorry...
Who? They friends of yours?

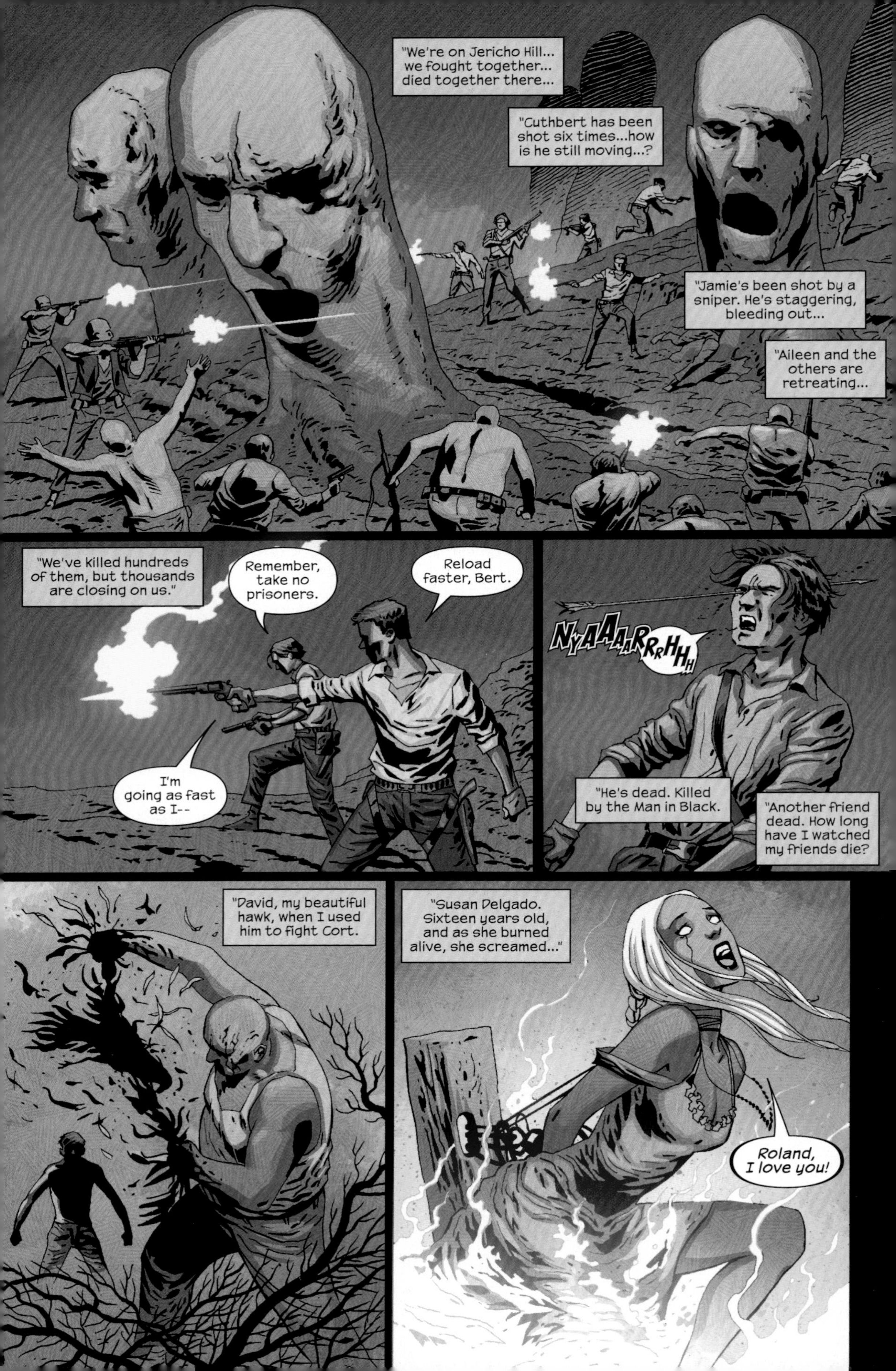
"We're on Jericho Hill... we fought together... died together there...
"Cuthbert has been shot six times...how is he still moving...?
"Jamie's been shot by a sniper. He's staggering, bleeding out...
"Aileen and the others are retreating...
"We've killed hundreds of them, but thousands are closing on us."
Remember, take no prisoners.
Reload faster, Bert.
I'm going as fast as I--
NYAAAARRRHHH
"He's dead. Killed by the Man in Black.
"Another friend dead. How long have I watched my friends die?
"David, my beautiful hawk, when I used him to fight Cort.
"Susan Delgado. Sixteen years old, and as she burned alive, she screamed..."
Roland, I love you!

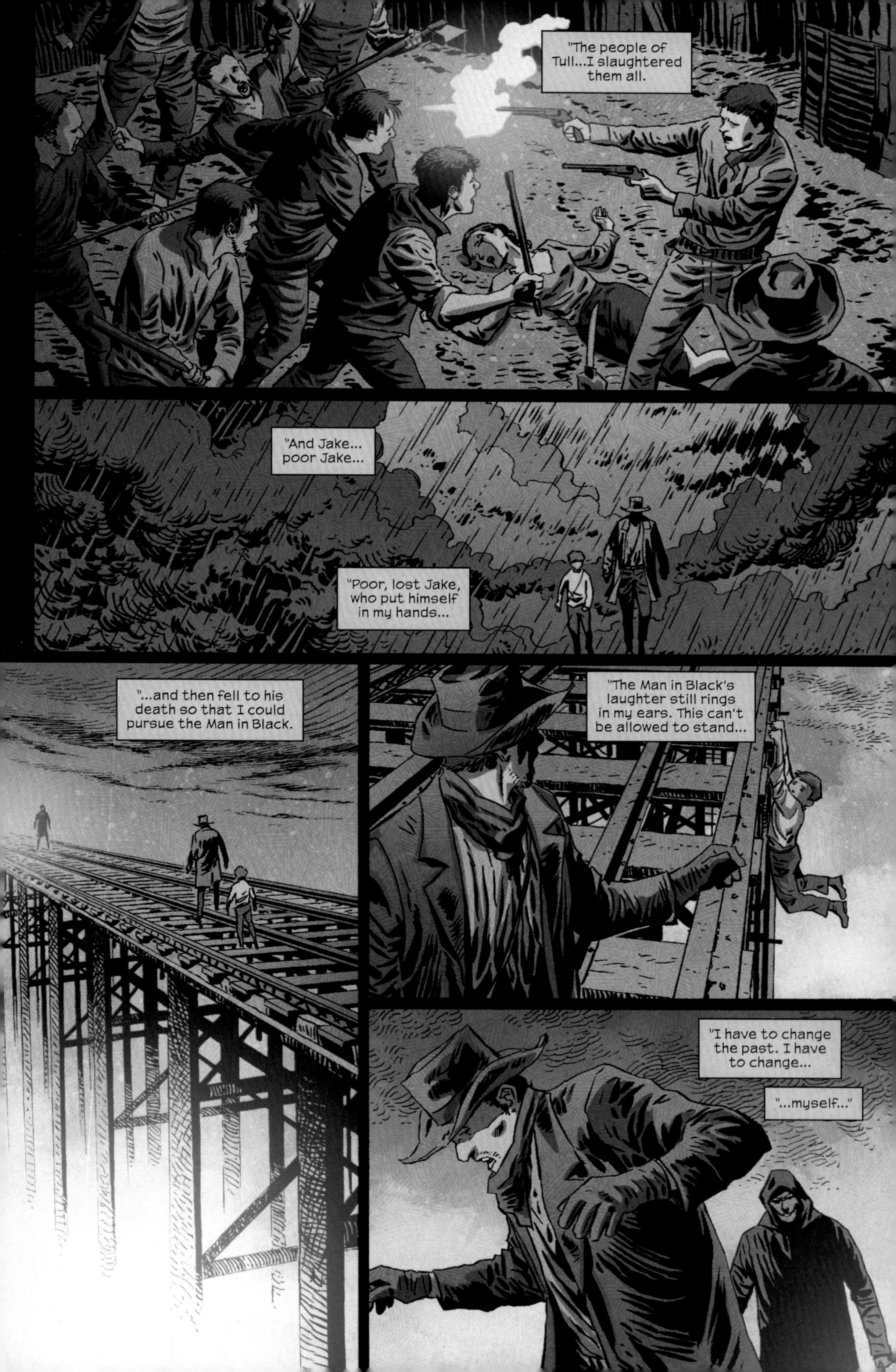
"The people of Tull...I slaughtered them all.
"And Jake... poor Jake...
"Poor, lost Jake, who put himself in my hands...
"...and then fell to his death so that I could pursue the Man in Black.
"The Man in Black's laughter still rings in my ears. This can't be allowed to stand...
"I have to change the past. I have to change...
"...myself..."

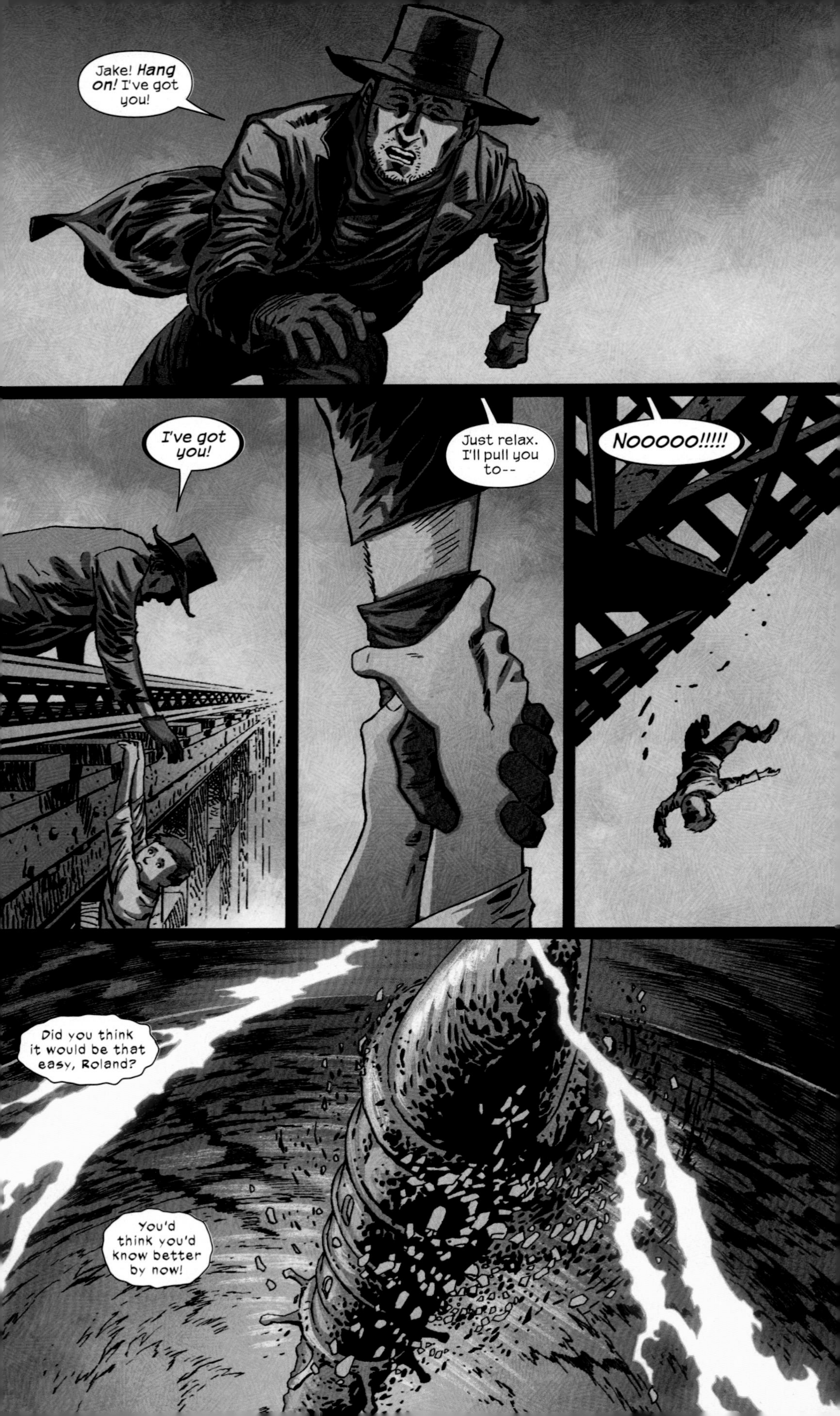
Jake! Hang on! I've got you!
I've got you!
Just relax. I'll pull you to--
Nooooo!!!!!
Did you think it would be that easy, Roland?
You'd think you'd know better by now!

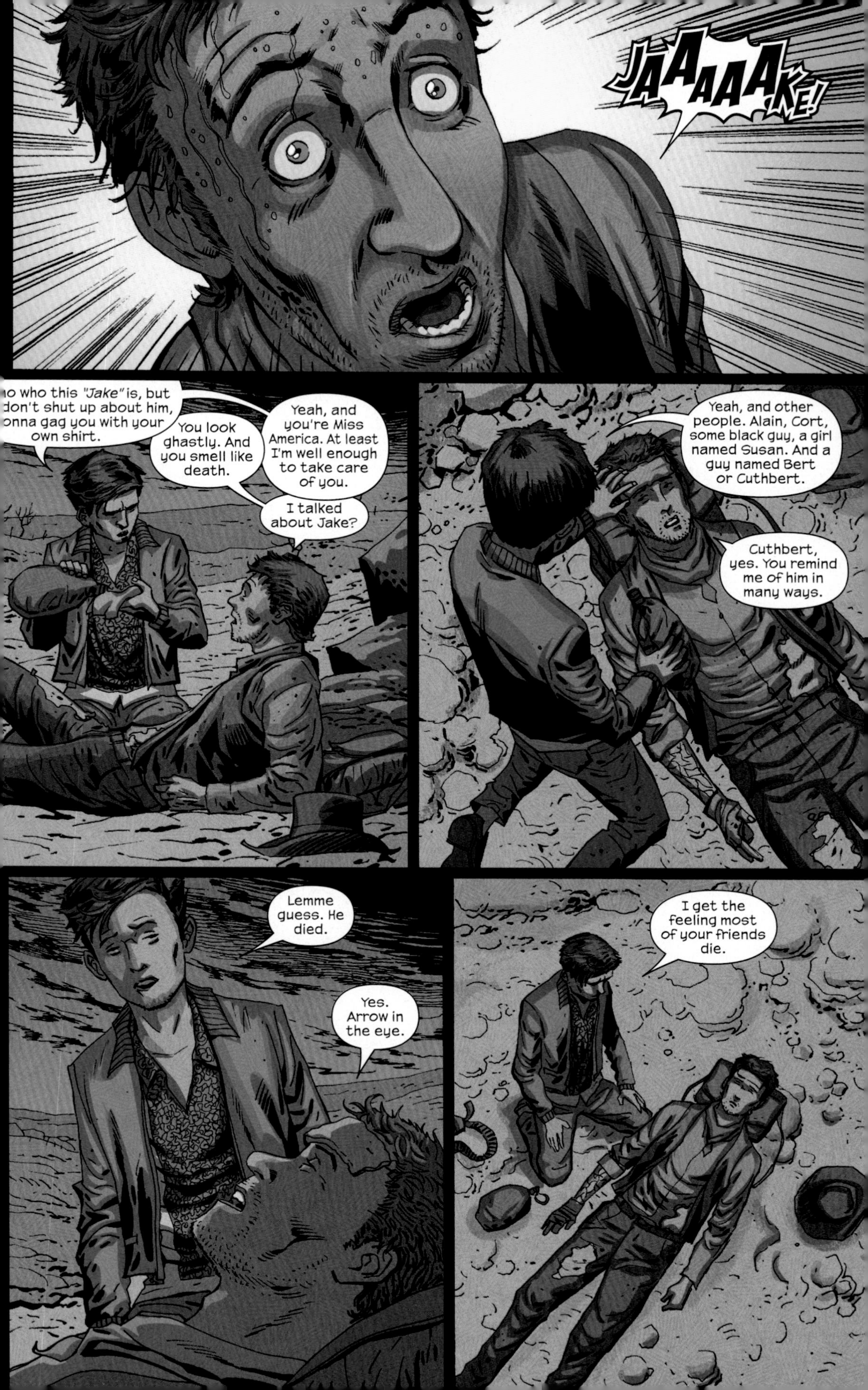
JAAAAAKE!
o who this "Jake" is, but don't shut up about him, onna gag you with your own shirt.
You look ghastly. And you smell like death.
Yeah, and you're Miss America. At least I'm well enough to take care of you.
I talked about Jake?
Yeah, and other people. Alain, Cort, some black guy, a girl named Susan. And a guy named Bert or Cuthbert.
Cuthbert, yes. You remind me of him in many ways.
Lemme guess. He died.
Yes. Arrow in the eye.
I get the feeling most of your friends die.

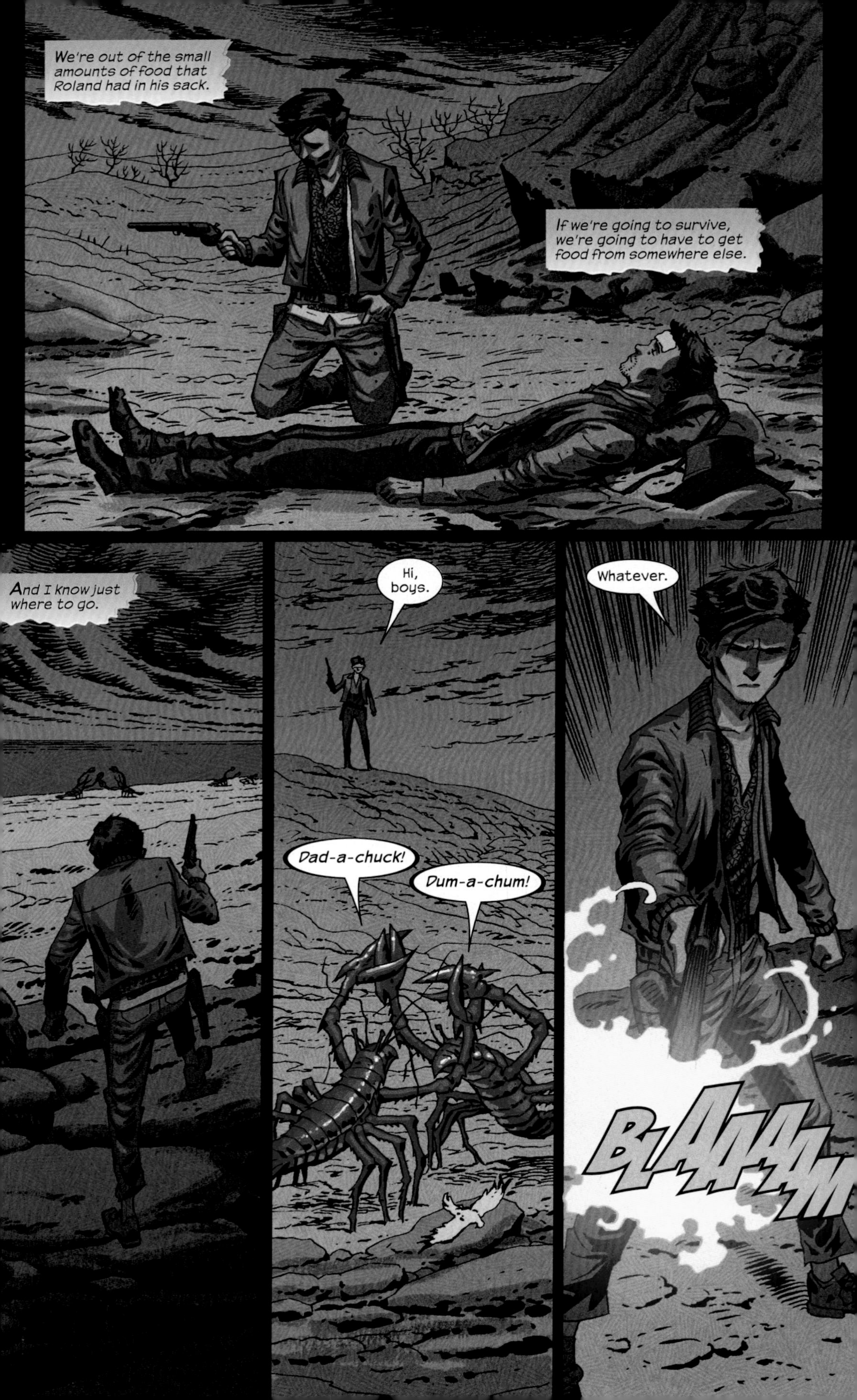

We're out of the small amounts of food that Roland had in his sack.
If we're going to survive, we're going to have to get food from somewhere else.
And I know just where to go.
Hi, boys.
Dad-a-chuck!
Dum-a-chum!
Whatever.
BLAAAAM

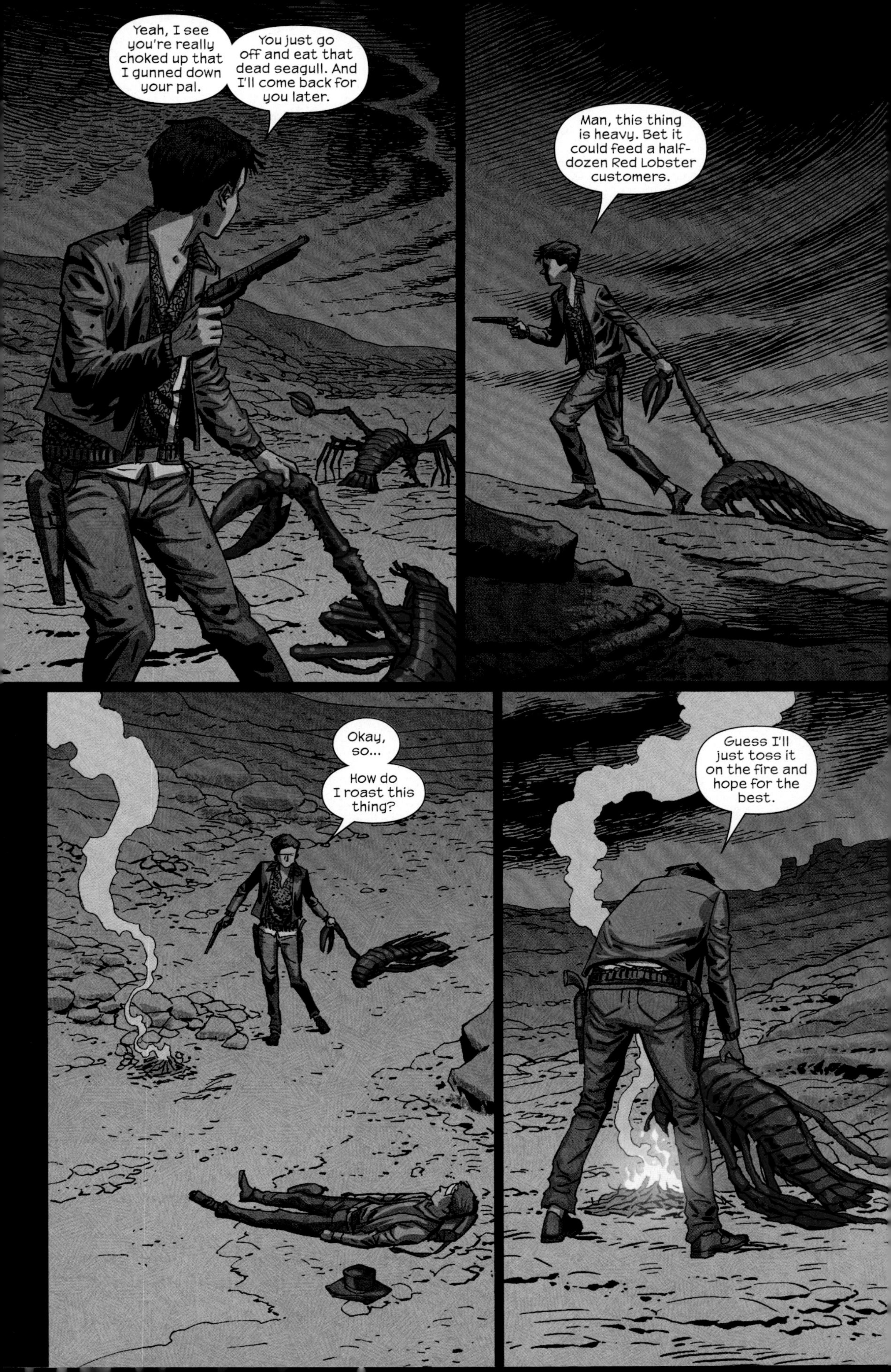
Yeah, I see you're really choked up that I gunned down your pal.
You just go off and eat that dead seagull. And I'll come back for you later.
Man, this thing is heavy. Bet it could feed a half-dozen Red Lobster customers.
Okay, so...
How do I roast this thing?
Guess I'll just toss it on the fire and hope for the best.

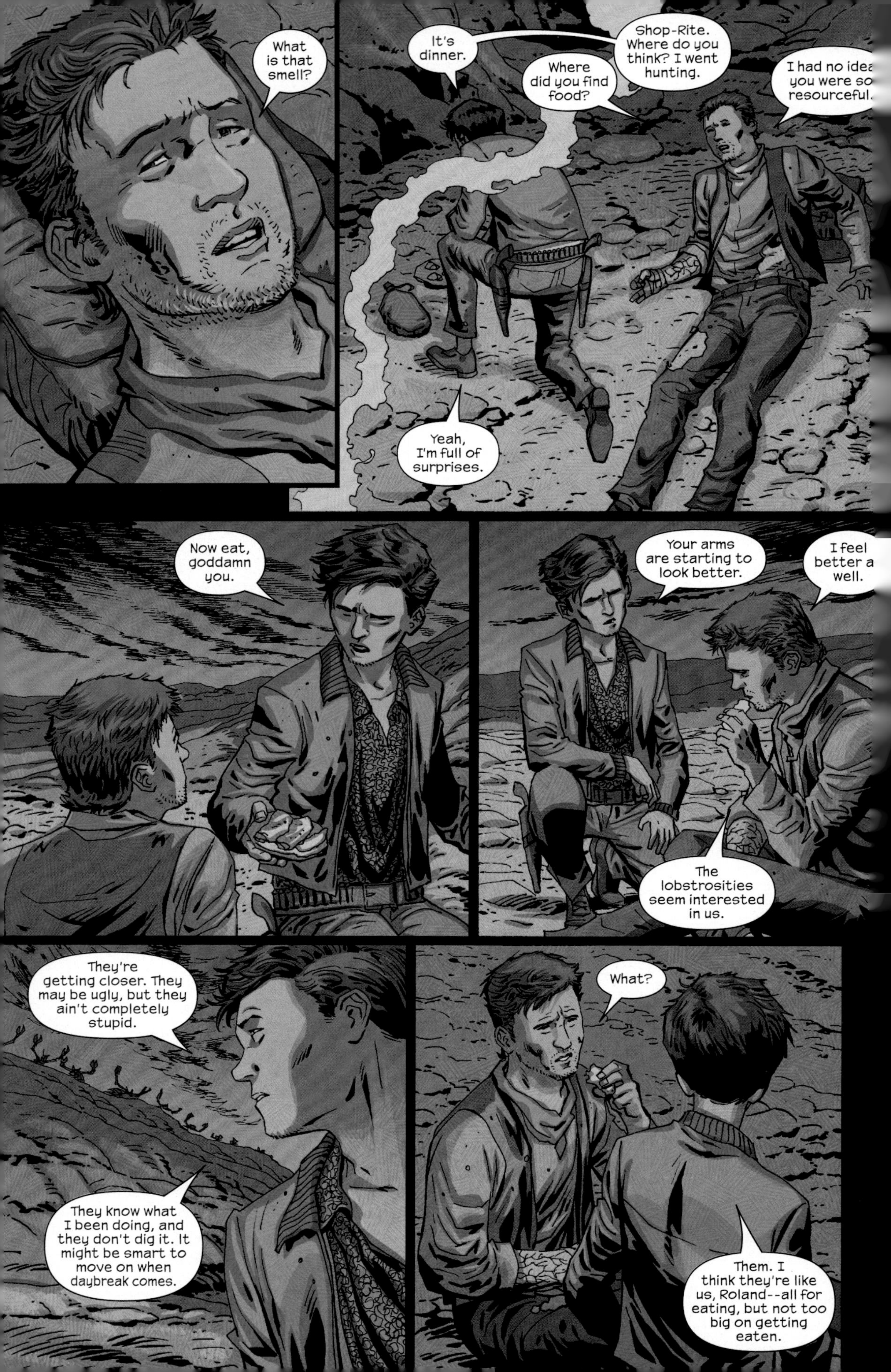
What is that smell?
It's dinner.
Where did you find food?
Shop-Rite. Where do you think? I went hunting.
I had no idea you were so resourceful.
Yeah, I'm full of surprises.
Now eat, goddamn you.
Your arms are starting to look better.
I feel better as well.
The lobstrosities seem interested in us.
They're getting closer. They may be ugly, but they ain't completely stupid.
They know what I been doing, and they don't dig it. It might be smart to move on when daybreak comes.
What?
Them. I think they're like us, Roland--all for eating, but not too big on getting eaten.

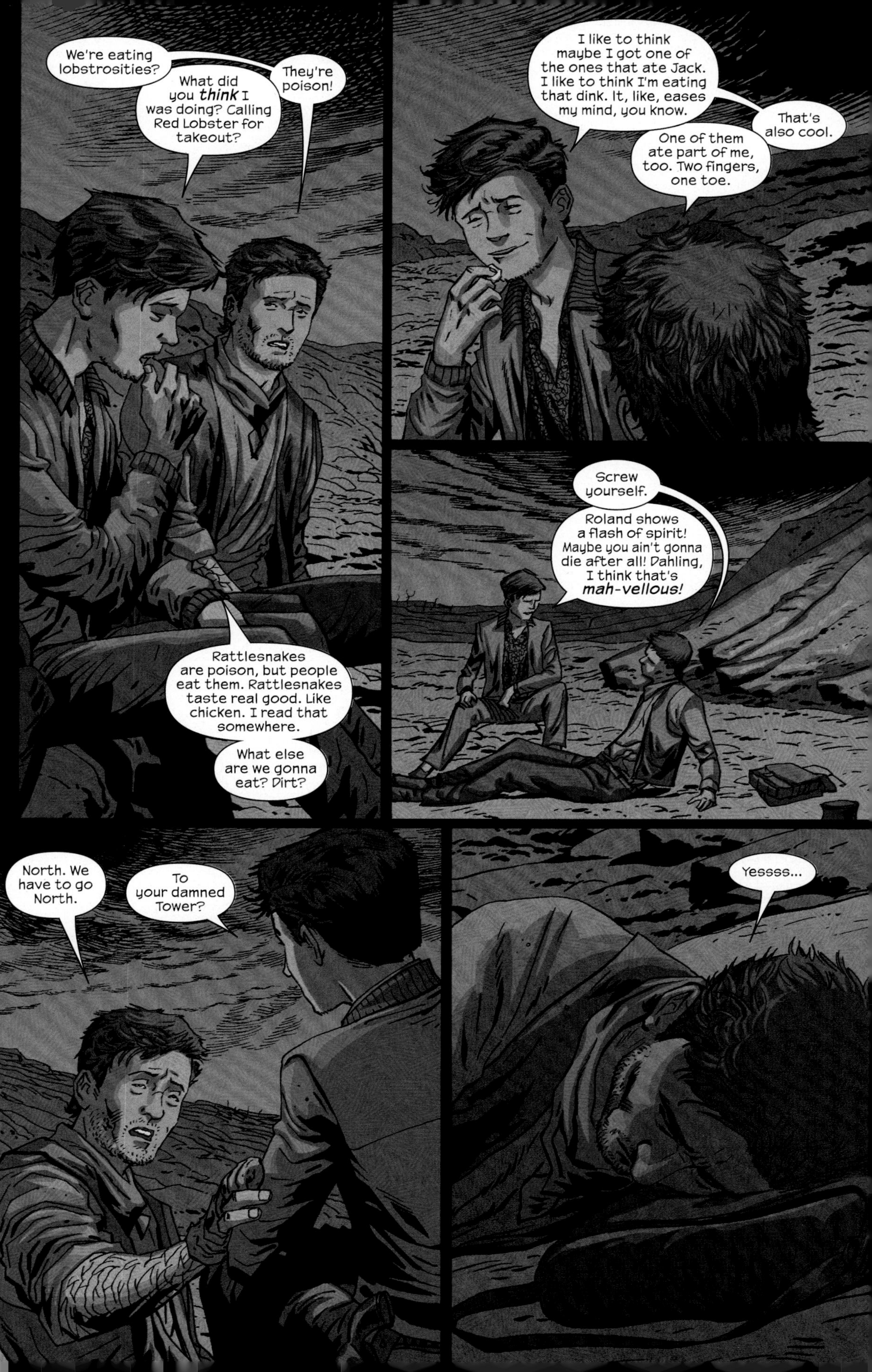
We're eating lobstrosities?
They're poison!
What did you *think* I was doing? Calling Red Lobster for takeout?
Rattlesnakes are poison, but people eat them. Rattlesnakes taste real good. Like chicken. I read that somewhere.
What else are we gonna eat? Dirt?
I like to think maybe I got one of the ones that ate Jack. I like to think I'm eating that dink. It, like, eases my mind, you know.
That's also cool.
One of them ate part of me, too. Two fingers, one toe.
Screw yourself.
Roland shows a flash of spirit! Maybe you ain't gonna die after all! Dahling, I think that's *mah-vellous!*
North. We have to go North.
To your damned Tower?
Yessss...

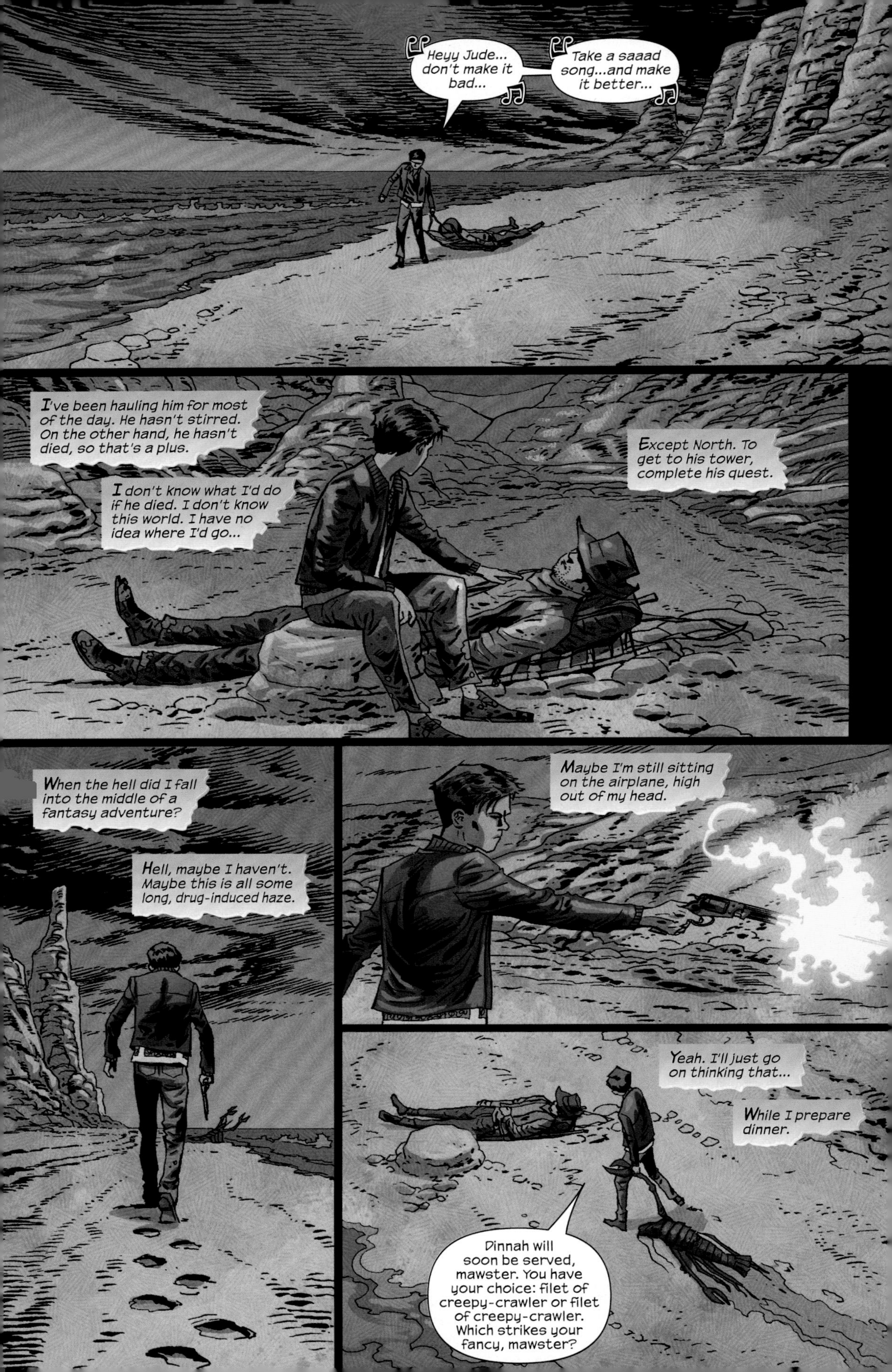
Heyy Jude... don't make it bad...
Take a saaad song...and make it better...
I've been hauling him for most of the day. He hasn't stirred. On the other hand, he hasn't died, so that's a plus.
I don't know what I'd do if he died. I don't know this world. I have no idea where I'd go...
Except North. To get to his tower, complete his quest.
When the hell did I fall into the middle of a fantasy adventure?
Hell, maybe I haven't. Maybe this is all some long, drug-induced haze.
Maybe I'm still sitting on the airplane, high out of my head.
Yeah. I'll just go on thinking that...
While I prepare dinner.
Dinnah will soon be served, mawster. You have your choice: filet of creepy-crawler or filet of creepy-crawler. Which strikes your fancy, mawster?

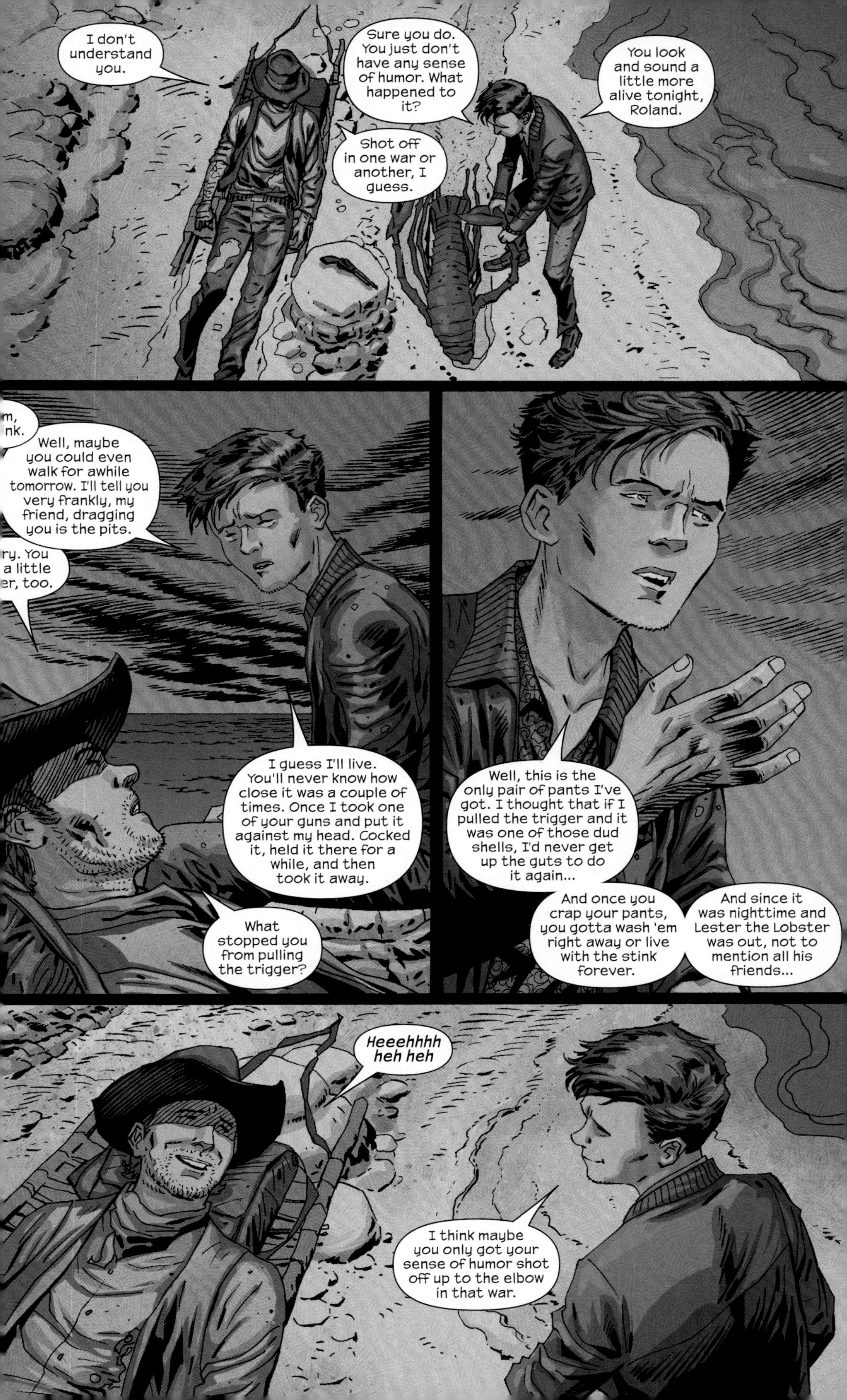
I don't understand you.
Sure you do. You just don't have any sense of humor. What happened to it?
Shot off in one war or another, I guess.
You look and sound a little more alive tonight, Roland.
m, nk.
Well, maybe you could even walk for awhile tomorrow. I'll tell you very frankly, my friend, dragging you is the pits.
ry. You a little er, too.
I guess I'll live. You'll never know how close it was a couple of times. Once I took one of your guns and put it against my head. Cocked it, held it there for a while, and then took it away.
What stopped you from pulling the trigger?
Well, this is the only pair of pants I've got. I thought that if I pulled the trigger and it was one of those dud shells, I'd never get up the guts to do it again...
And once you crap your pants, you gotta wash 'em right away or live with the stink forever.
And since it was nighttime and Lester the Lobster was out, not to mention all his friends...
Heeehhhh heh heh
I think maybe you only got your sense of humor shot off up to the elbow in that war.

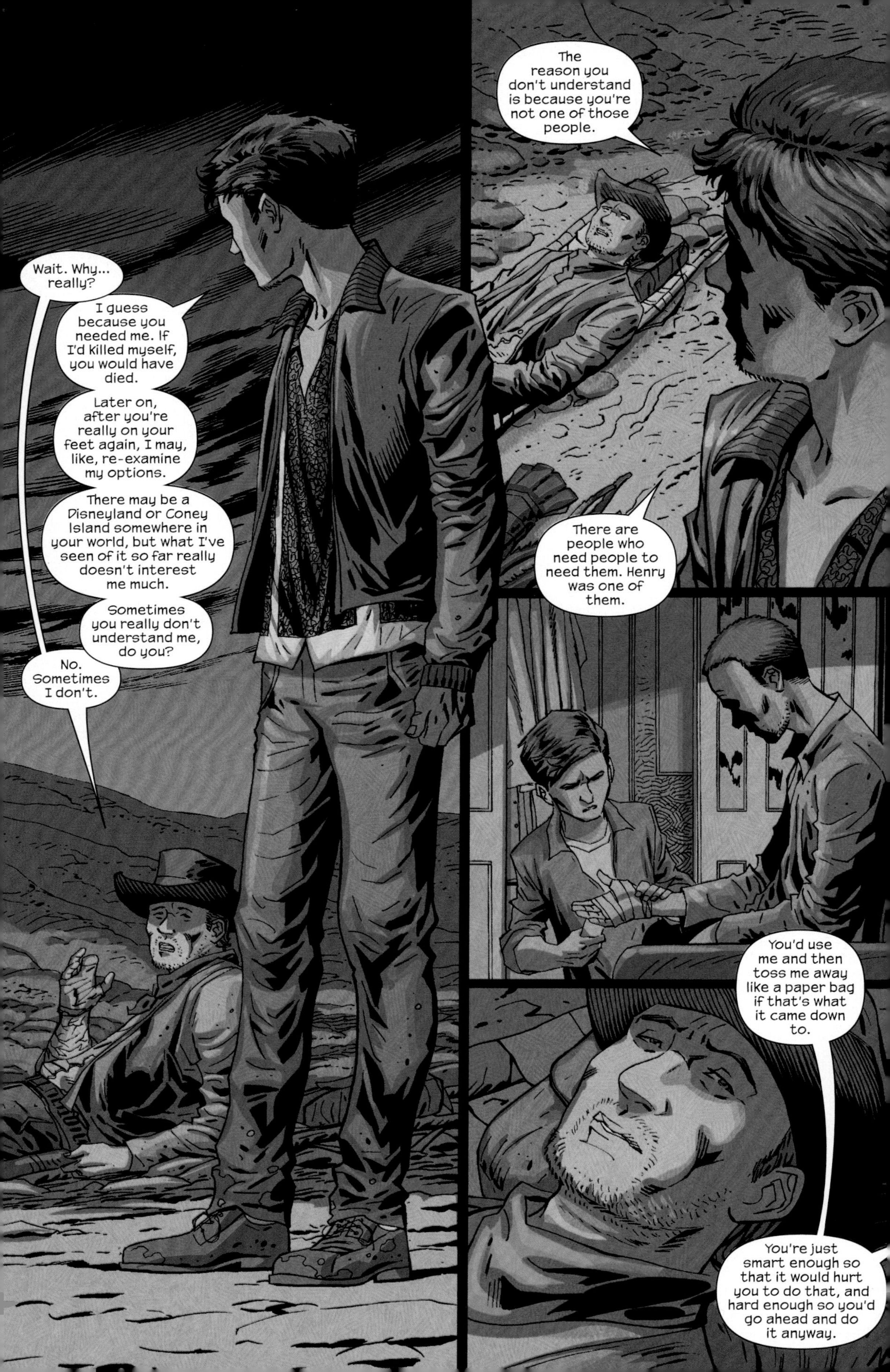
Wait. Why... really?
I guess because you needed me. If I'd killed myself, you would have died.
Later on, after you're really on your feet again, I may, like, re-examine my options.
There may be a Disneyland or Coney Island somewhere in your world, but what I've seen of it so far really doesn't interest me much.
Sometimes you really don't understand me, do you?
No. Sometimes I don't.
The reason you don't understand is because you're not one of those people.
There are people who need people to need them. Henry was one of them.
You'd use me and then toss me away like a paper bag if that's what it came down to.
You're just smart enough so that it would hurt you to do that, and hard enough so you'd go ahead and do it anyway.

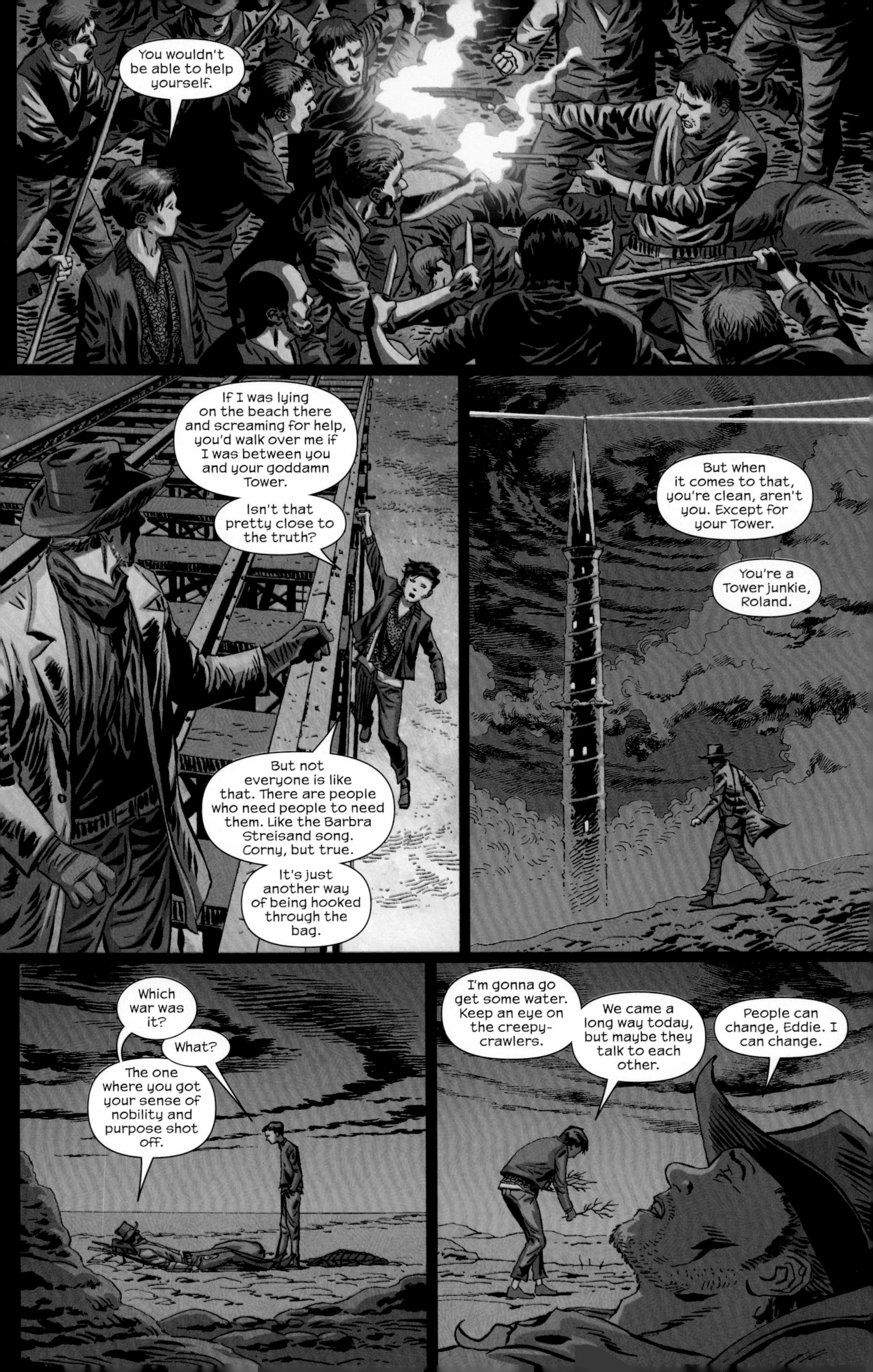
You wouldn't be able to help yourself.
If I was lying on the beach there and screaming for help, you'd walk over me if I was between you and your goddamn Tower.
Isn't that pretty close to the truth?
But not everyone is like that. There are people who need people to need them. Like the Barbra Streisand song. Corny, but true.
It's just another way of being hooked through the bag.
But when it comes to that, you're clean, aren't you. Except for your Tower.
You're a Tower junkie, Roland.
Which war was it?
What?
The one where you got your sense of nobility and purpose shot off.
I'm gonna go get some water. Keep an eye on the creepy-crawlers.
We came a long way today, but maybe they talk to each other.
People can change, Eddie. I can change.

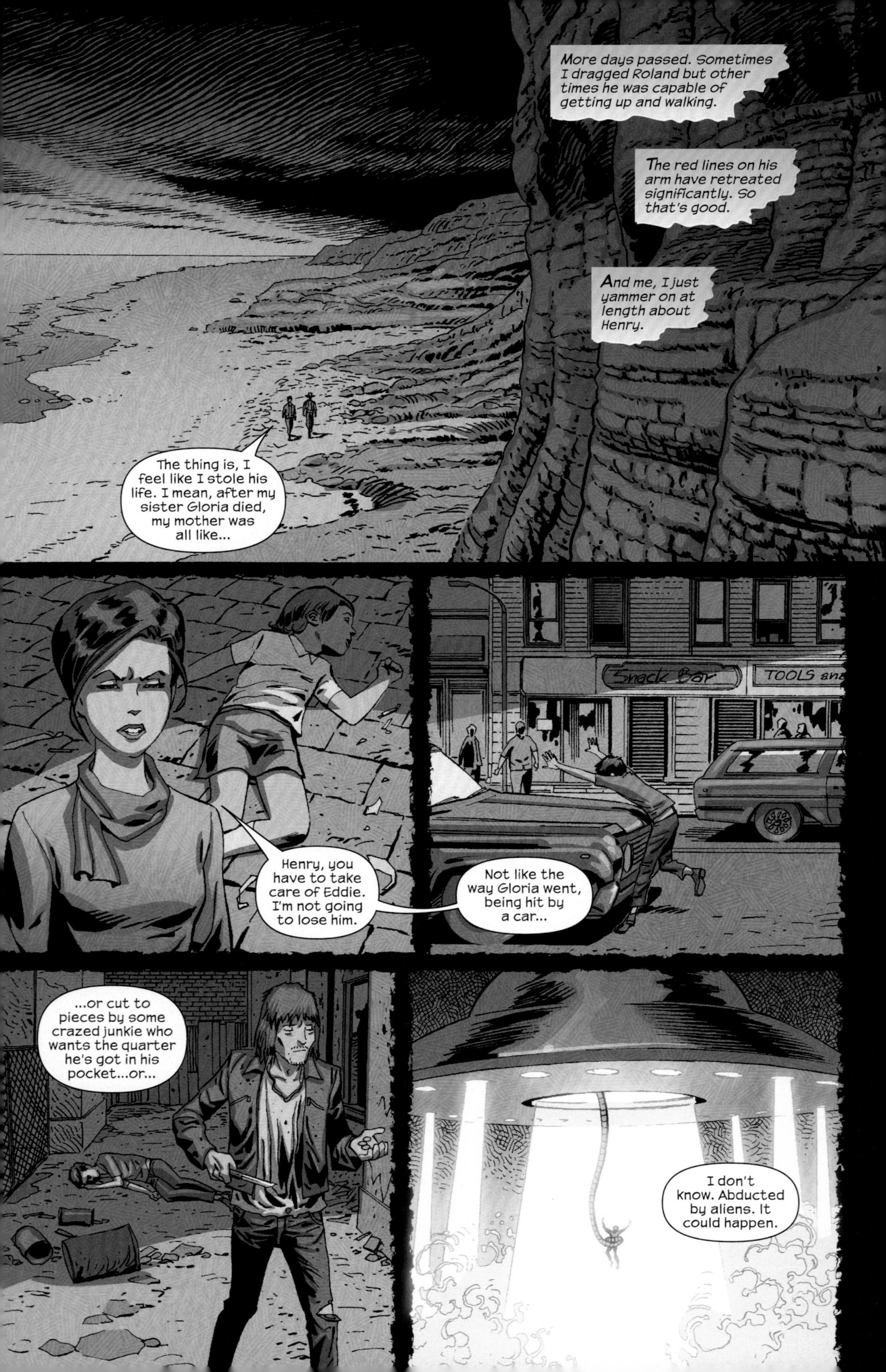
More days passed. Sometimes I dragged Roland but other times he was capable of getting up and walking.
The red lines on his arm have retreated significantly. So that's good.
And me, I just yammer on at length about Henry.
The thing is, I feel like I stole his life. I mean, after my sister Gloria died, my mother was all like...
Henry, you have to take care of Eddie. I'm not going to lose him.
Snack Bar
TOOLS an
Not like the way Gloria went, being hit by a car...
...or cut to pieces by some crazed junkie who wants the quarter he's got in his pocket...or...
I don't know. Abducted by aliens. It could happen.

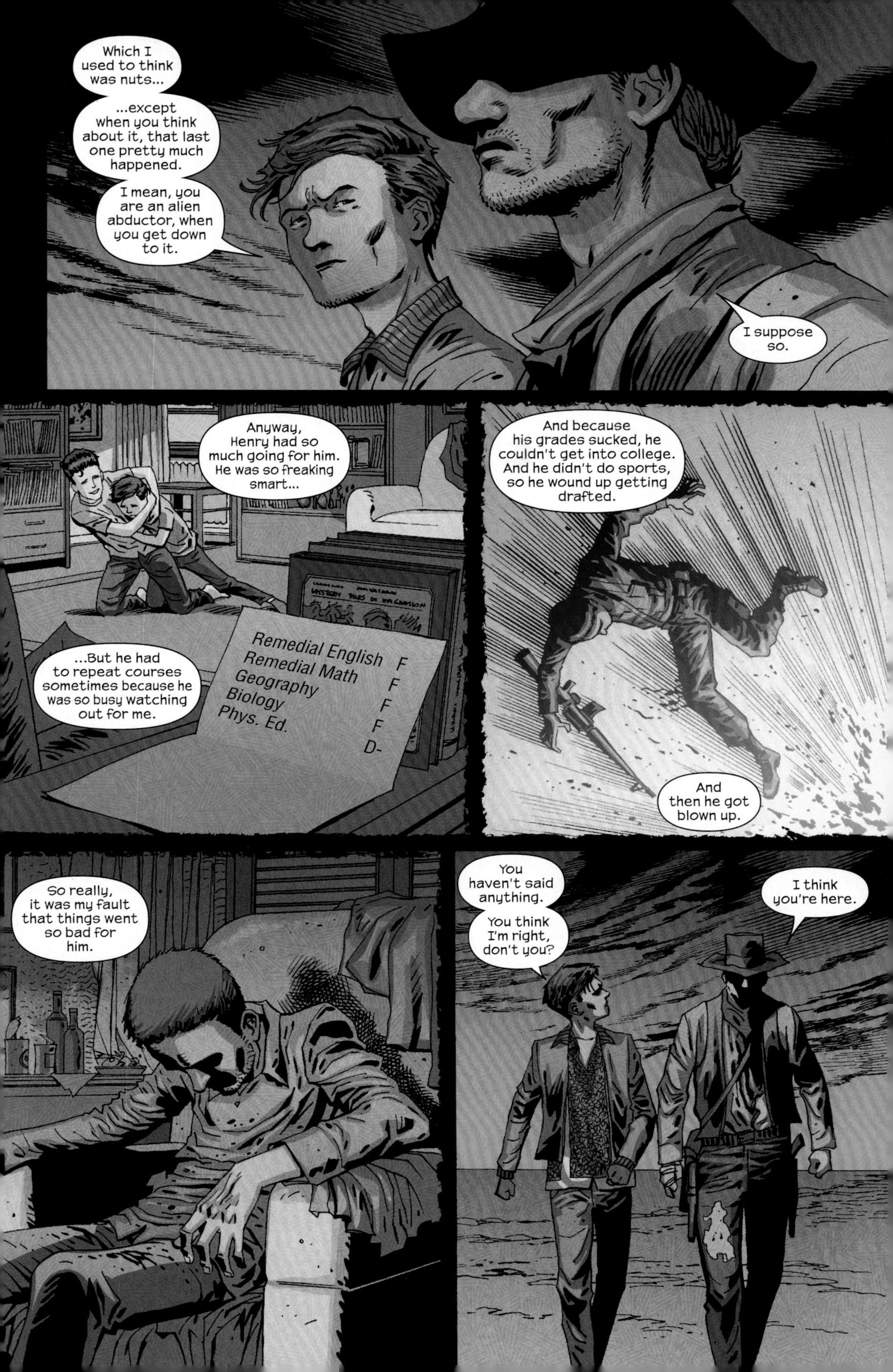
Which I used to think was nuts...
...except when you think about it, that last one pretty much happened.
I mean, you are an alien abductor, when you get down to it.
I suppose so.
Anyway, Henry had so much going for him. He was so freaking smart...
...But he had to repeat courses sometimes because he was so busy watching out for me.
Remedial English F
Remedial Math F
Geography F
Biology F
Phys. Ed. D-
And because his grades sucked, he couldn't get into college. And he didn't do sports, so he wound up getting drafted.
And then he got blown up.
So really, it was my fault that things went so bad for him.
You haven't said anything.
You think I'm right, don't you?
I think you're here.

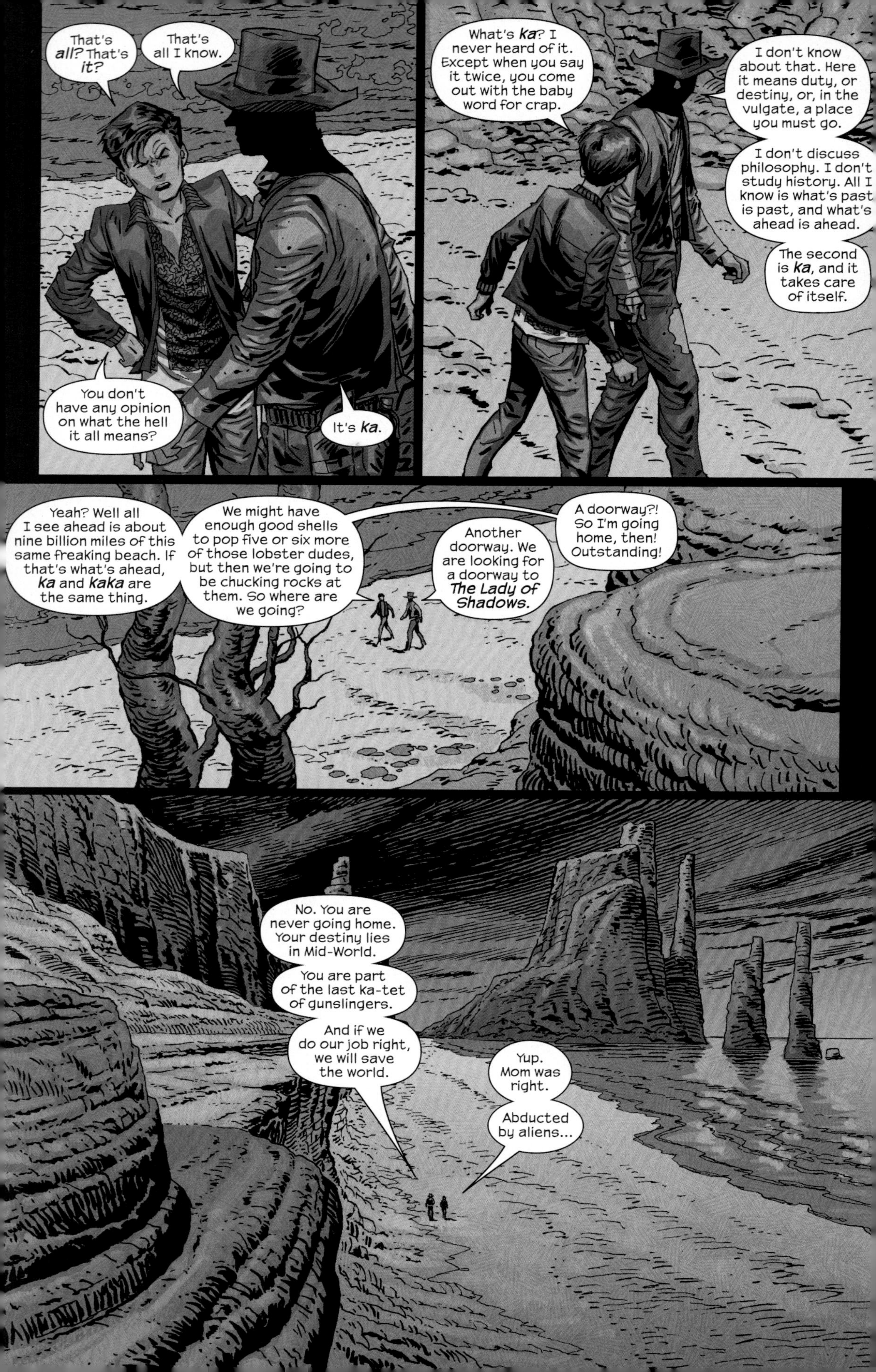
That's all? That's it?
That's all I know.
You don't have any opinion on what the hell it all means?
It's ka.
What's ka? I never heard of it. Except when you say it twice, you come out with the baby word for crap.
I don't know about that. Here it means duty, or destiny, or, in the vulgate, a place you must go.
I don't discuss philosophy. I don't study history. All I know is what's past is past, and what's ahead is ahead.
The second is ka, and it takes care of itself.
Yeah? Well all I see ahead is about nine billion miles of this same freaking beach. If that's what's ahead, ka and kaka are the same thing.
We might have enough good shells to pop five or six more of those lobster dudes, but then we're going to be chucking rocks at them. So where are we going?
Another doorway. We are looking for a doorway to The Lady of Shadows.
A doorway?! So I'm going home, then! Outstanding!
No. You are never going home. Your destiny lies in Mid-World.
You are part of the last ka-tet of gunslingers.
And if we do our job right, we will save the world.
Yup. Mom was right.
Abducted by aliens...

The story continues in *The Dark Tower: The Drawing of the Three — Lady of Shadows*

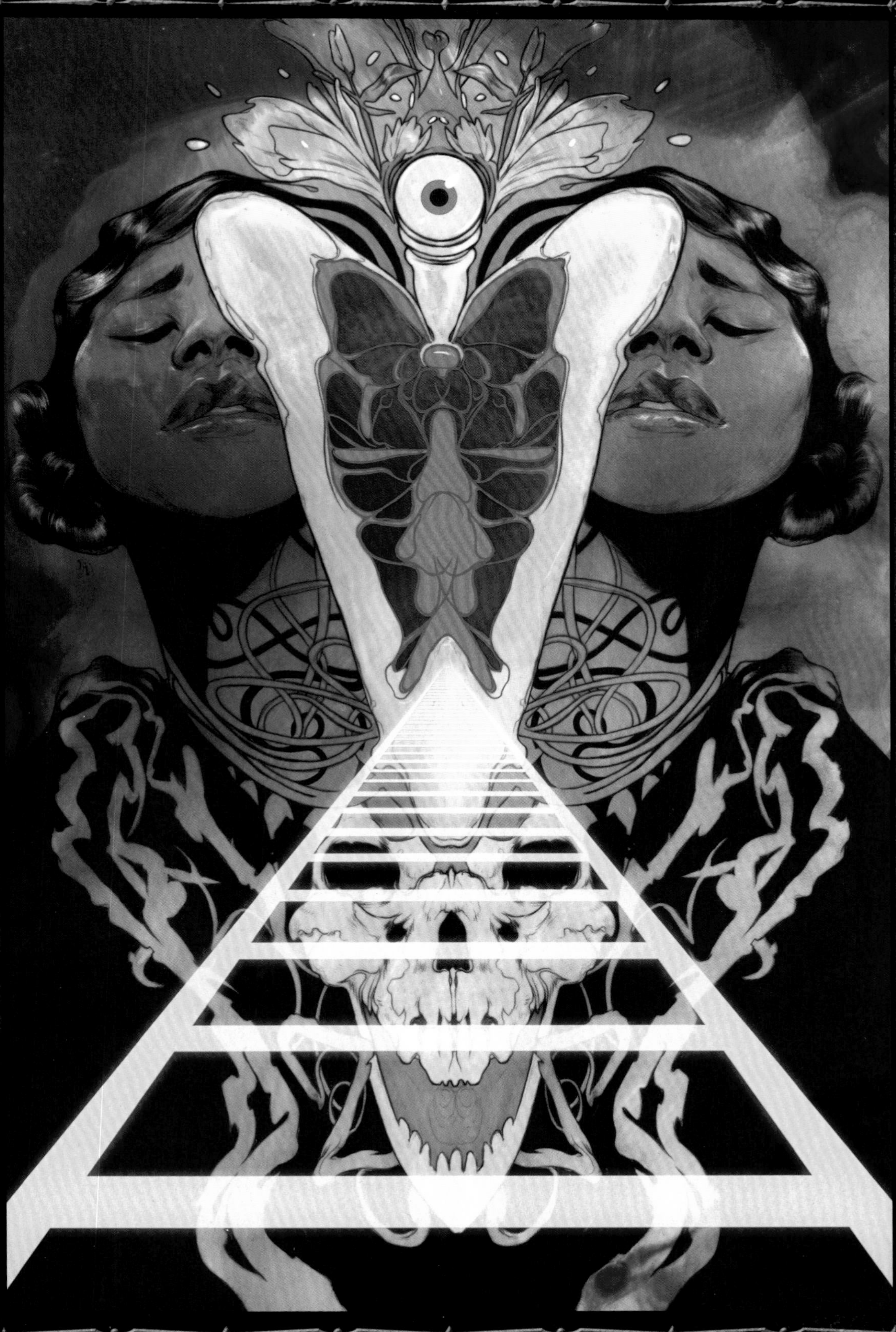

*The Dark Tower: The Drawing of the Three — House of Cards #1* **Cover by Julian Totino Tedesco**

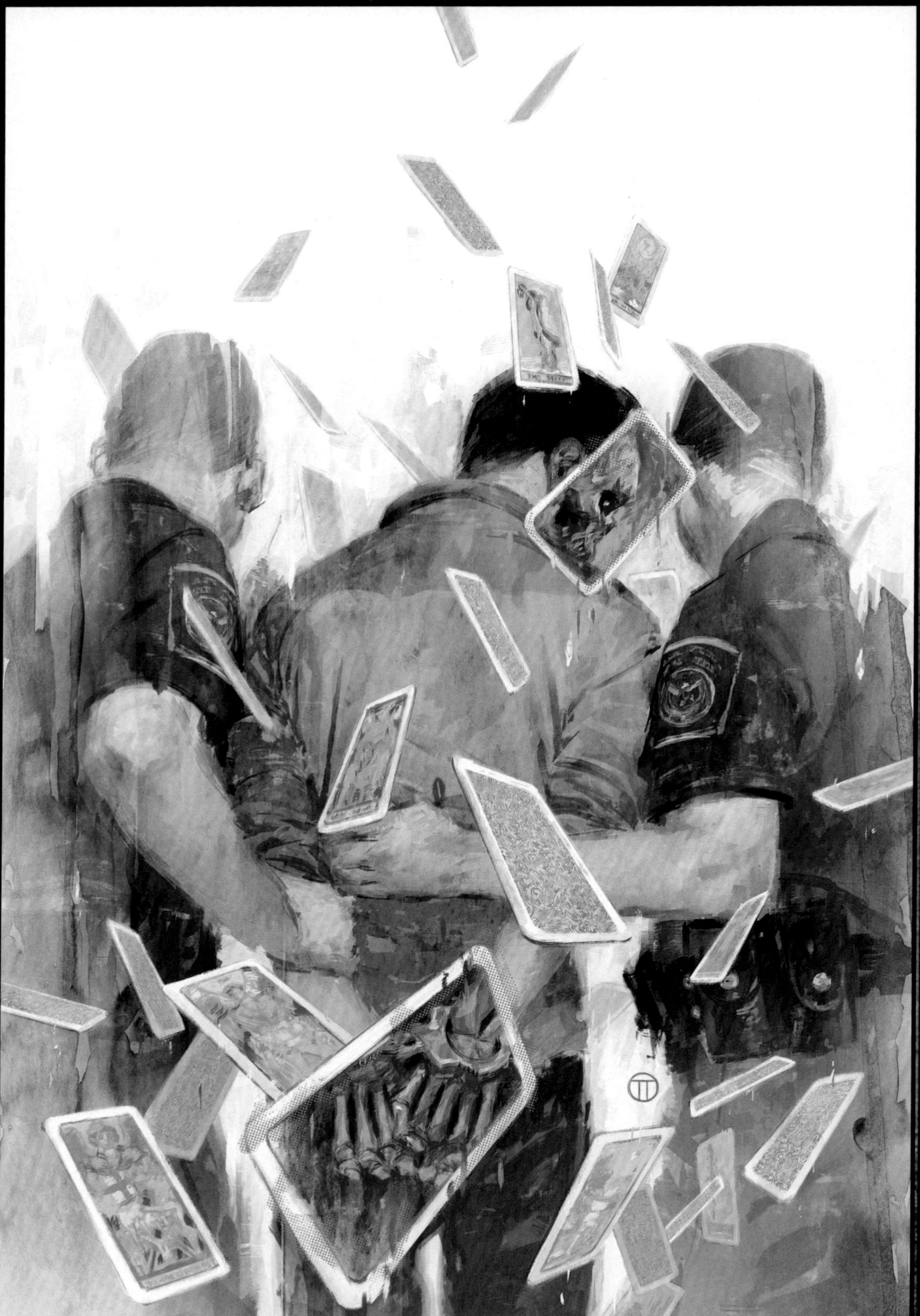

*The Dark Tower: The Drawing of the Three — House of Cards* #1 Variant Cover by Mike McKone & Jordan Boyd

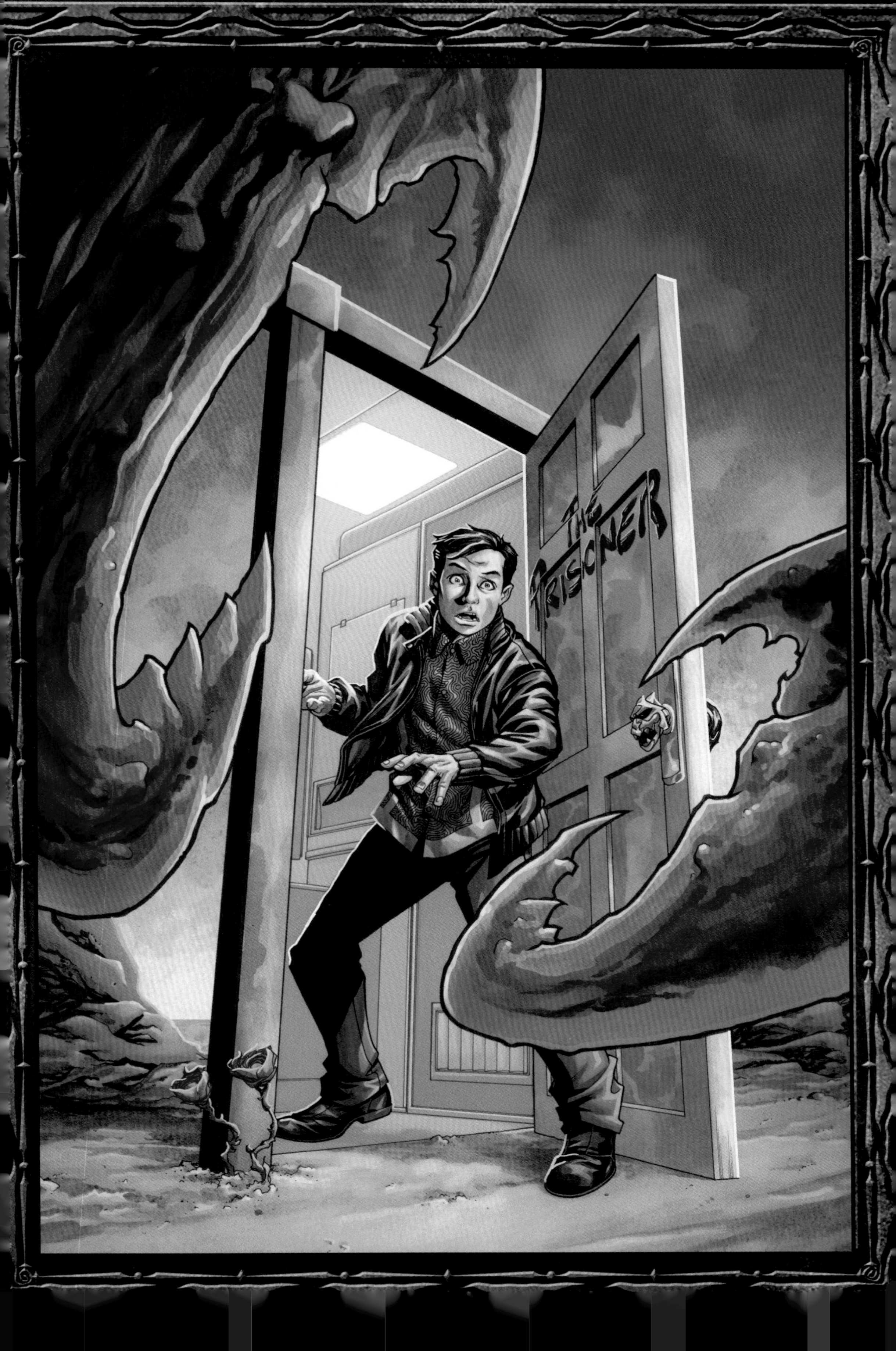
THE PRISONER

*The Dark Tower: The Drawing of the Three — House of Cards* #2 **Cover by Julian Totino Tedesco**

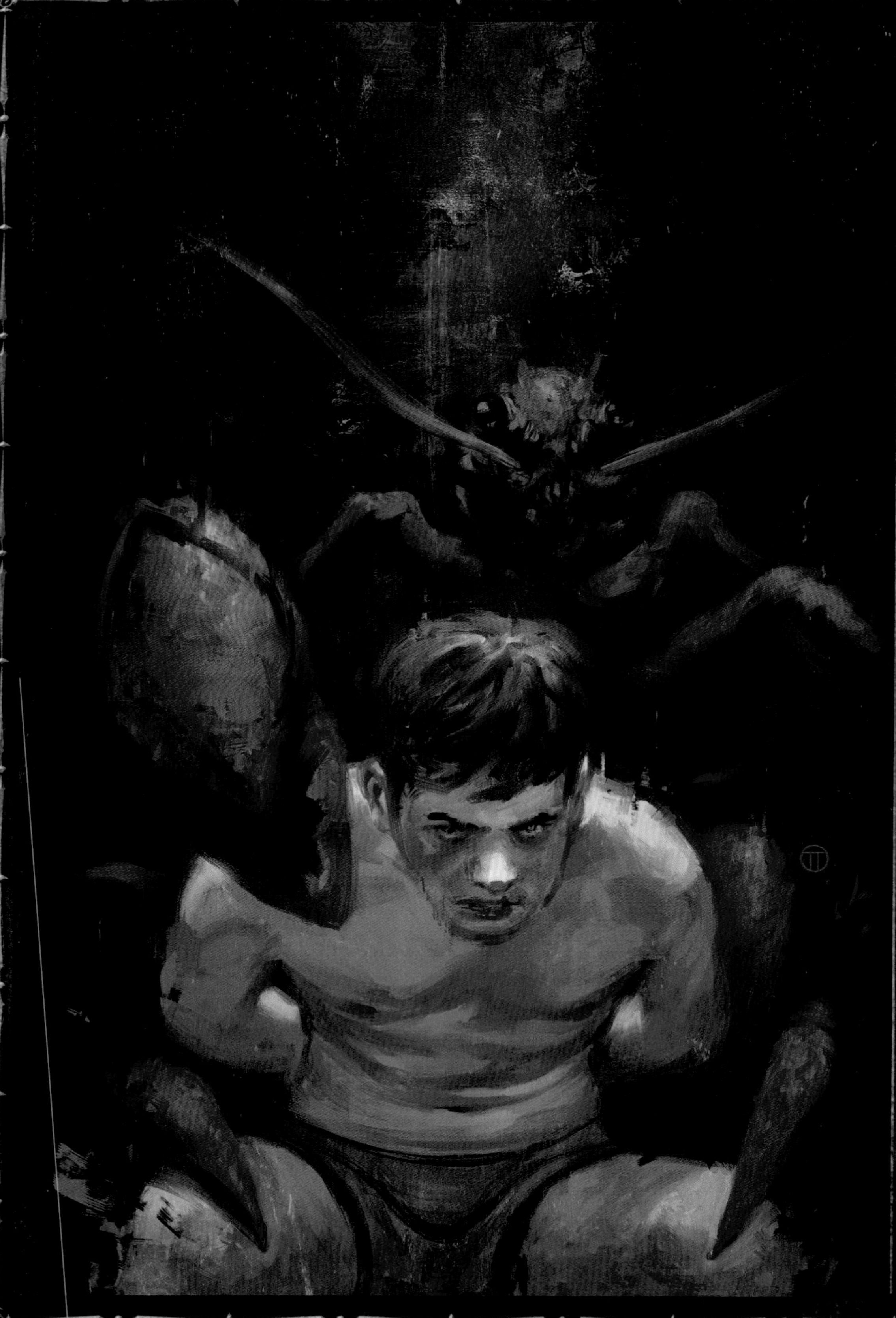

*The Dark Tower: The Drawing of the Three — House of Cards #3* **Cover by Julian Totino Tedesco**

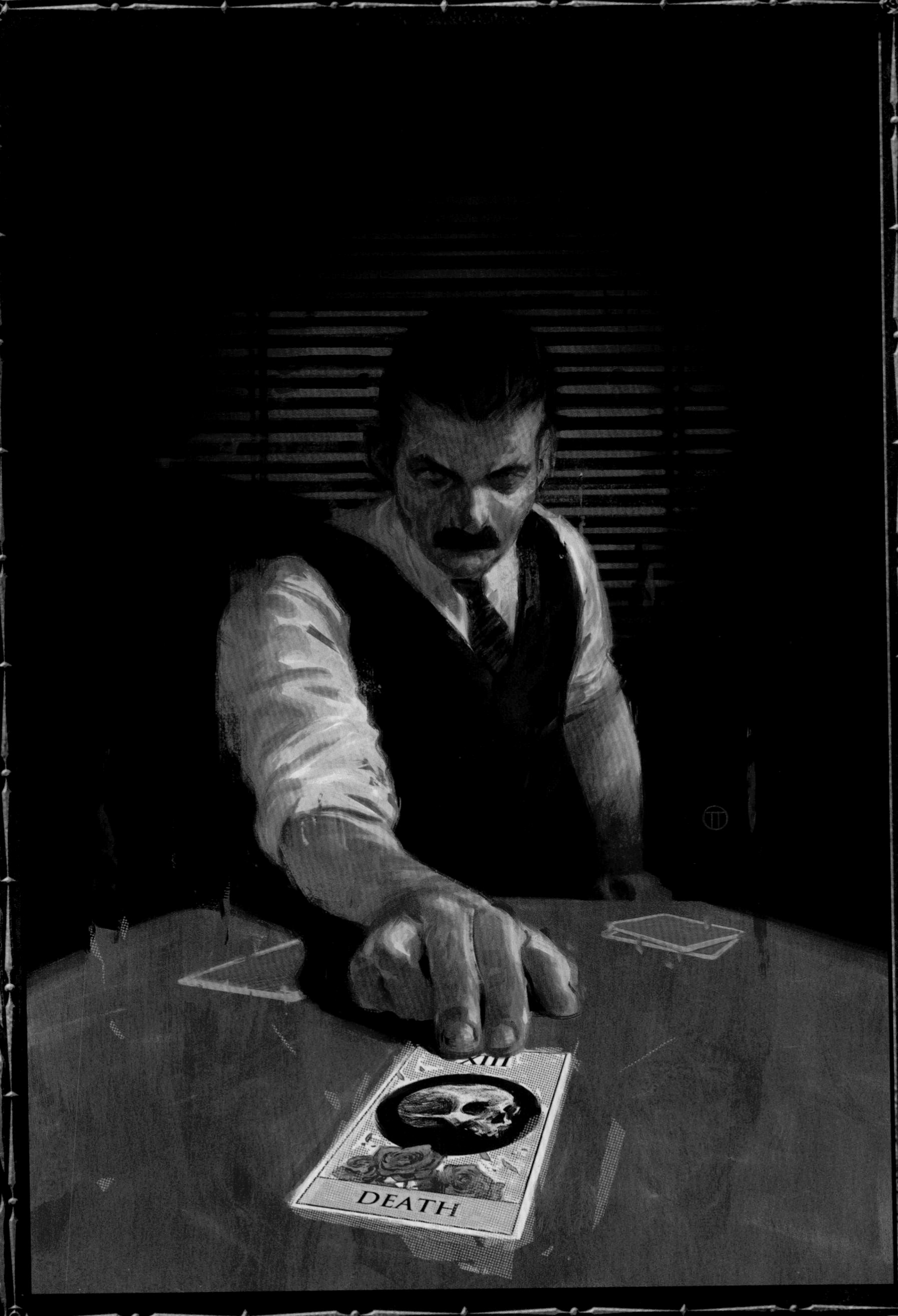

*The Dark Tower: The Drawing of the Three — House of Cards #4* **Cover by Julian Totino Tedesco**

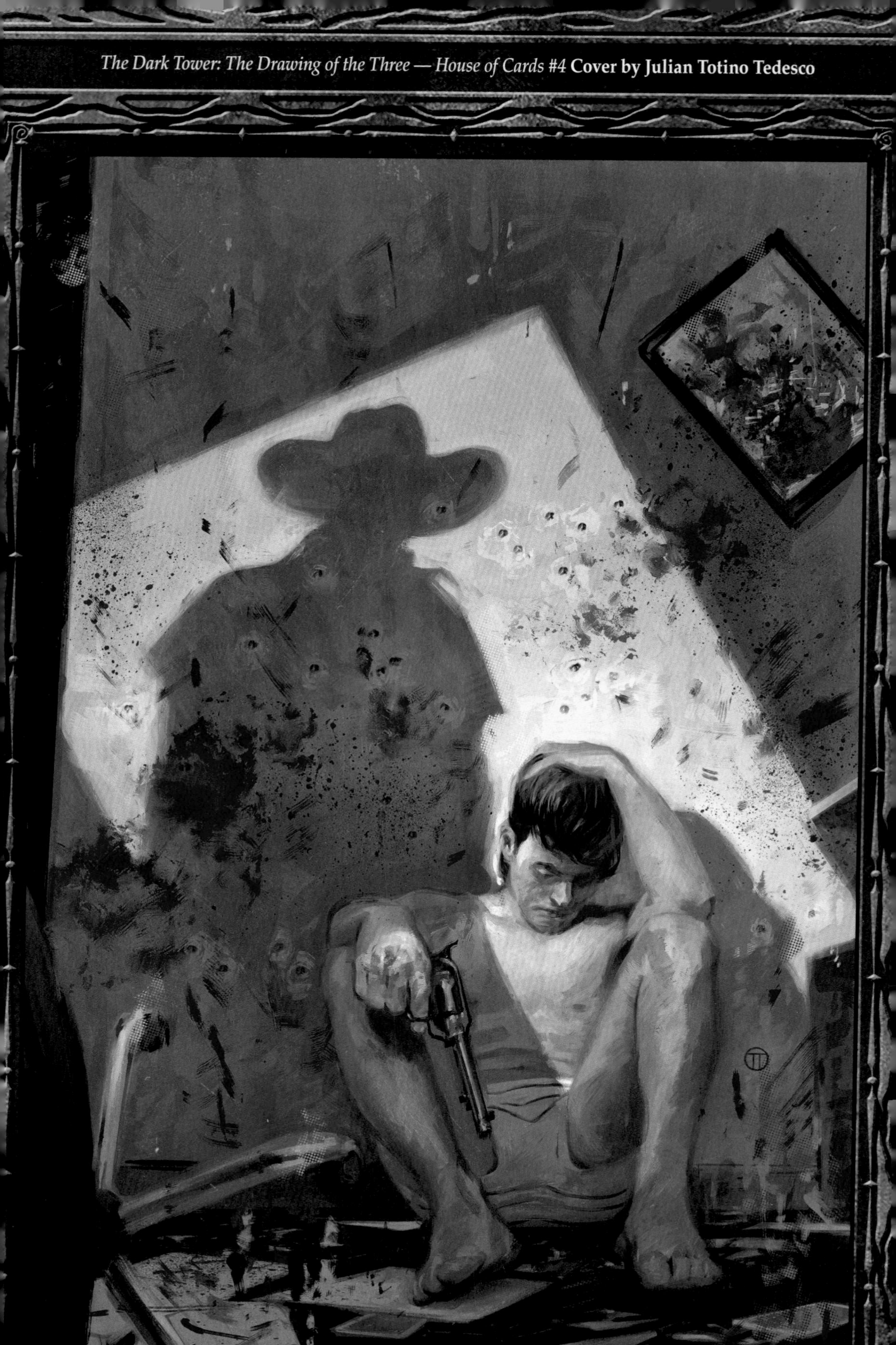

*The Dark Tower: The Drawing of the Three — House of Cards* #5 **Cover by Julian Totino Tedesco**

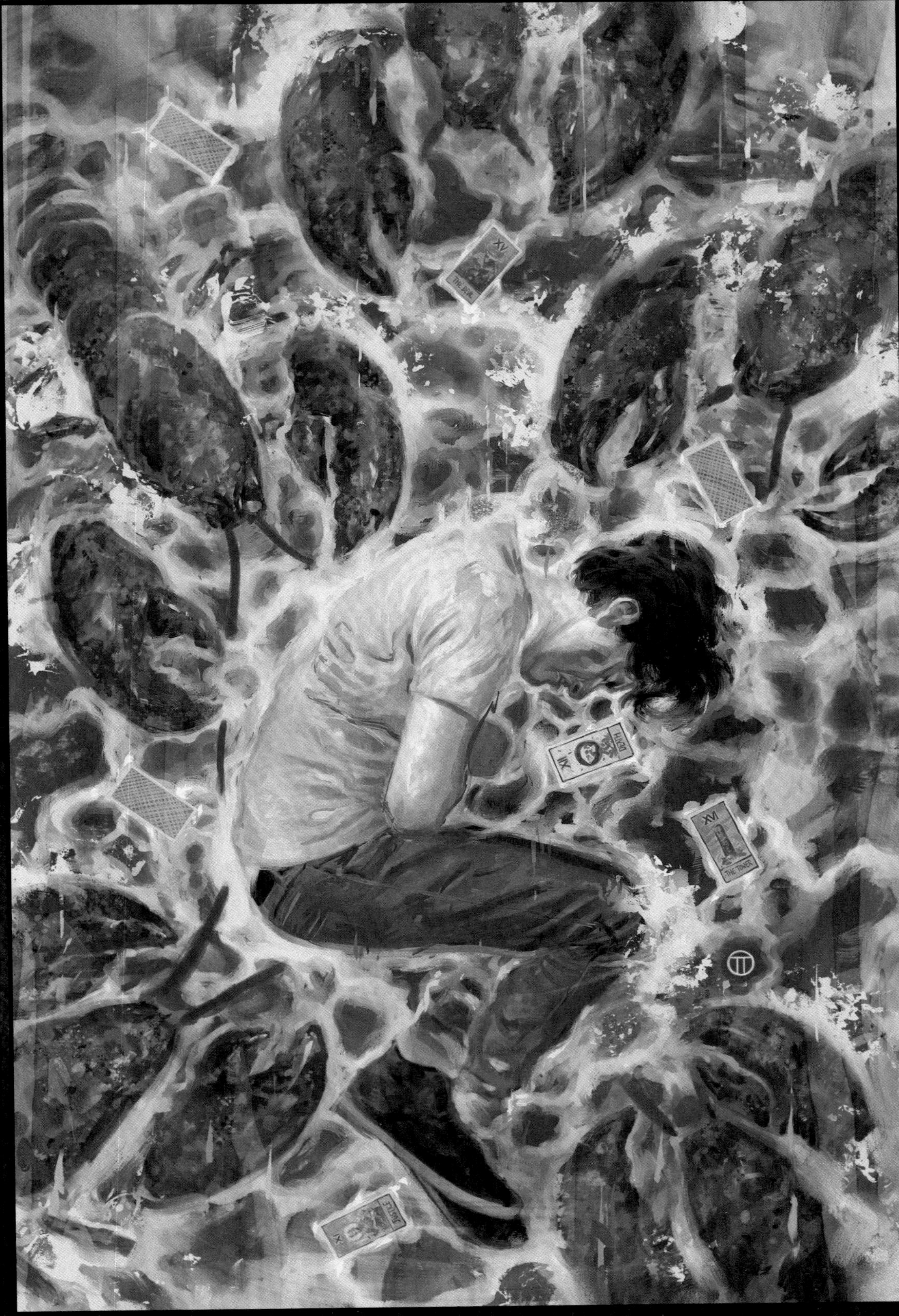

## Page 13

1. Andolini is following Eddie into the bathroom. He is holding the gun in the air because he thinks Eddie is hiding a trick. (NOTE: The medicine cabinet door should be hanging open. This will become important in the next issue.) Eddie tells Andolini to close the door. Andolini says no. Eddie says "shut the door or no dope." From outside the bathroom, Balazar says, "Shut the door, Jack!"

2. As Jack kicks the door shut behind him, Eddie makes a wisecrack.

3. Snarling, Jack raises his gun, butt-forward to pistol-whip Eddie across the mouth.

4. Jack freezes, his gun in the air. His snarl has become a slack-jawed gape. Eddie's eyes have transformed from hazel to ice blue. Jack just has time to say, The kid's gone schizo—when...

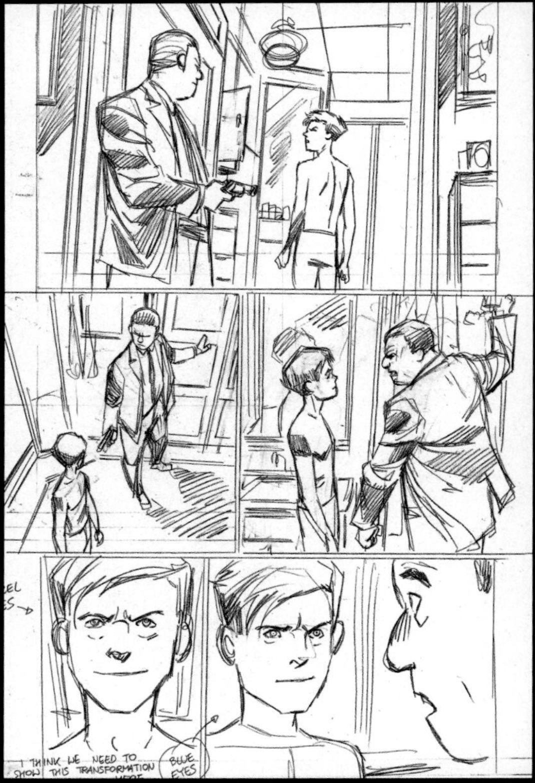
I THINK WE NEED TO SHOW THIS TRANSFORMATION
BLUE EYES

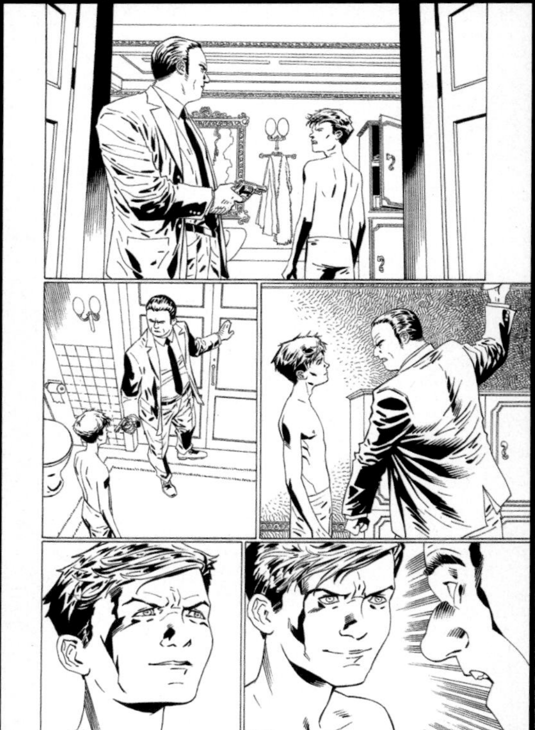

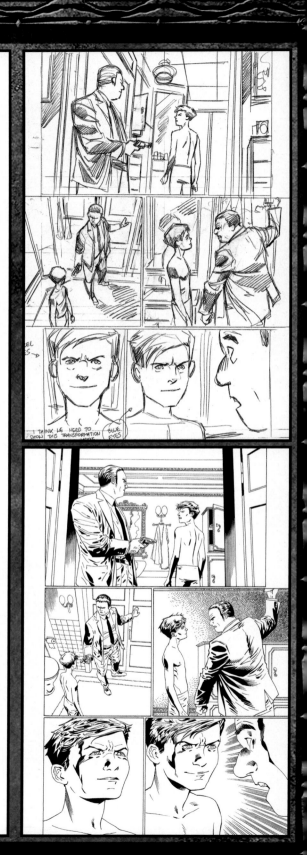

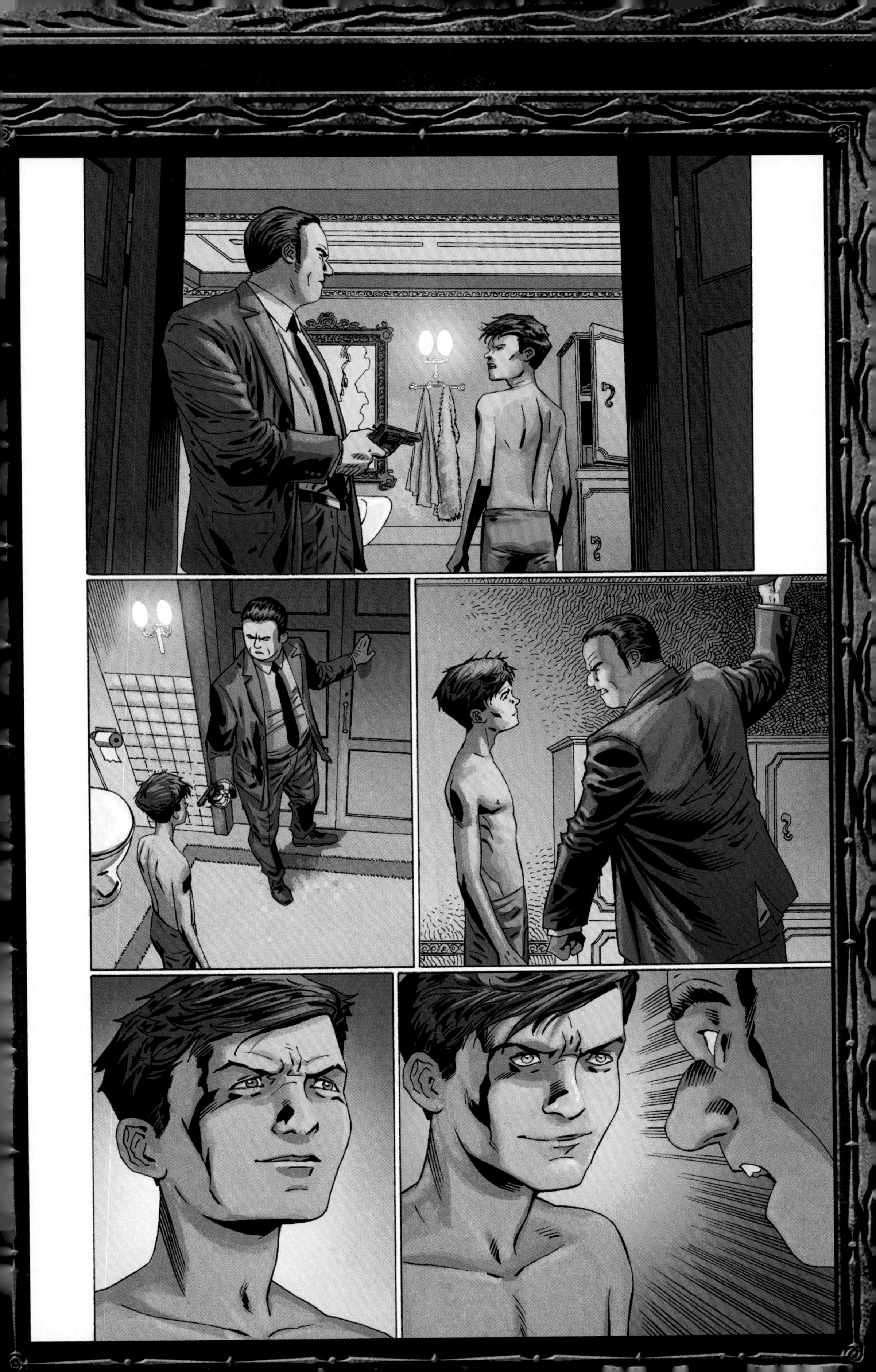

**Page 14**

FULL PAGE. Eddie is grabbing Jack by the shoulders, and so now Jack can see the glowing door behind Eddie. It hangs in space about a foot or so above the floor in front of Balazar's private shower.

Through the door Jack can see a dark beach, which slopes down to crashing waves. The beach is crawling with lobstrosities. Jack is jabbering, Hail Mary fulla grace...

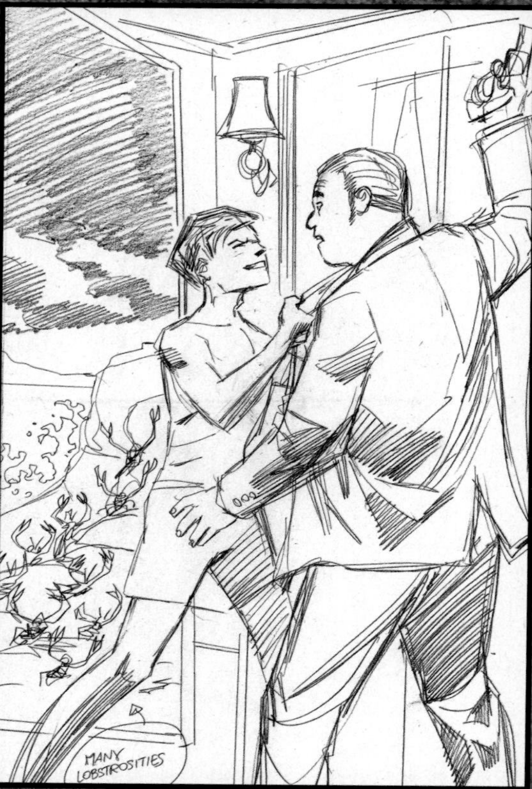
MANY LOBSTROSITIES

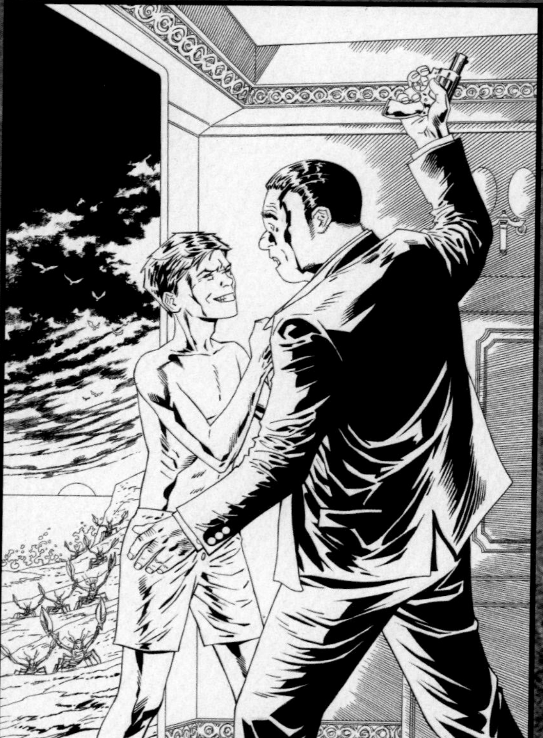

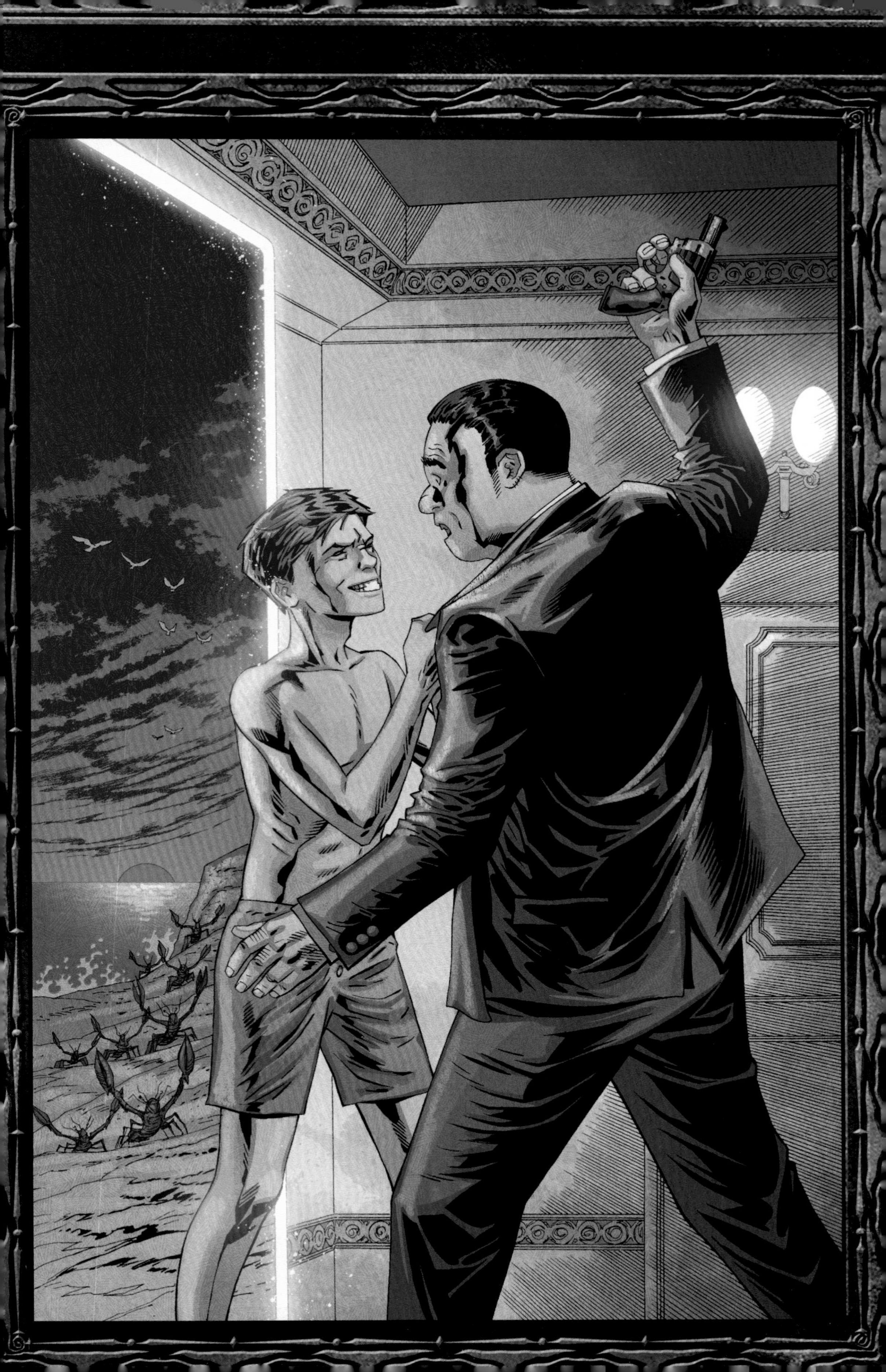

## Page 15

1. Jack is trying to smash his gun butt into Eddie's teeth but the strength has run out of him. Sagging, he just manages to bloody Eddie's lip.

2. Through his bloody mouth, Eddie says, 'I TOLD you I was gonna knock your socks off, Jack."

3.  Eddie is yanking Jack backwards through the doorway. Jack is screaming as he falls through the door.

4. Eddie and Jack are now rolling down the rocky scree that edges the beach. They are fighting over Andolini's gun.

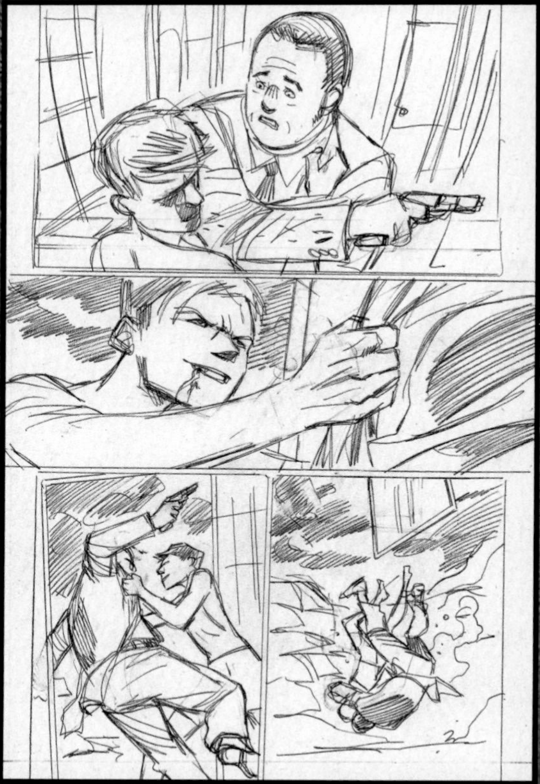

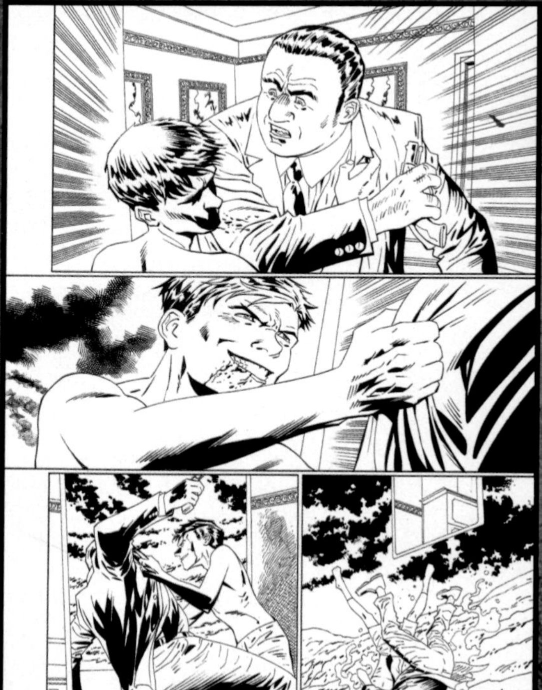

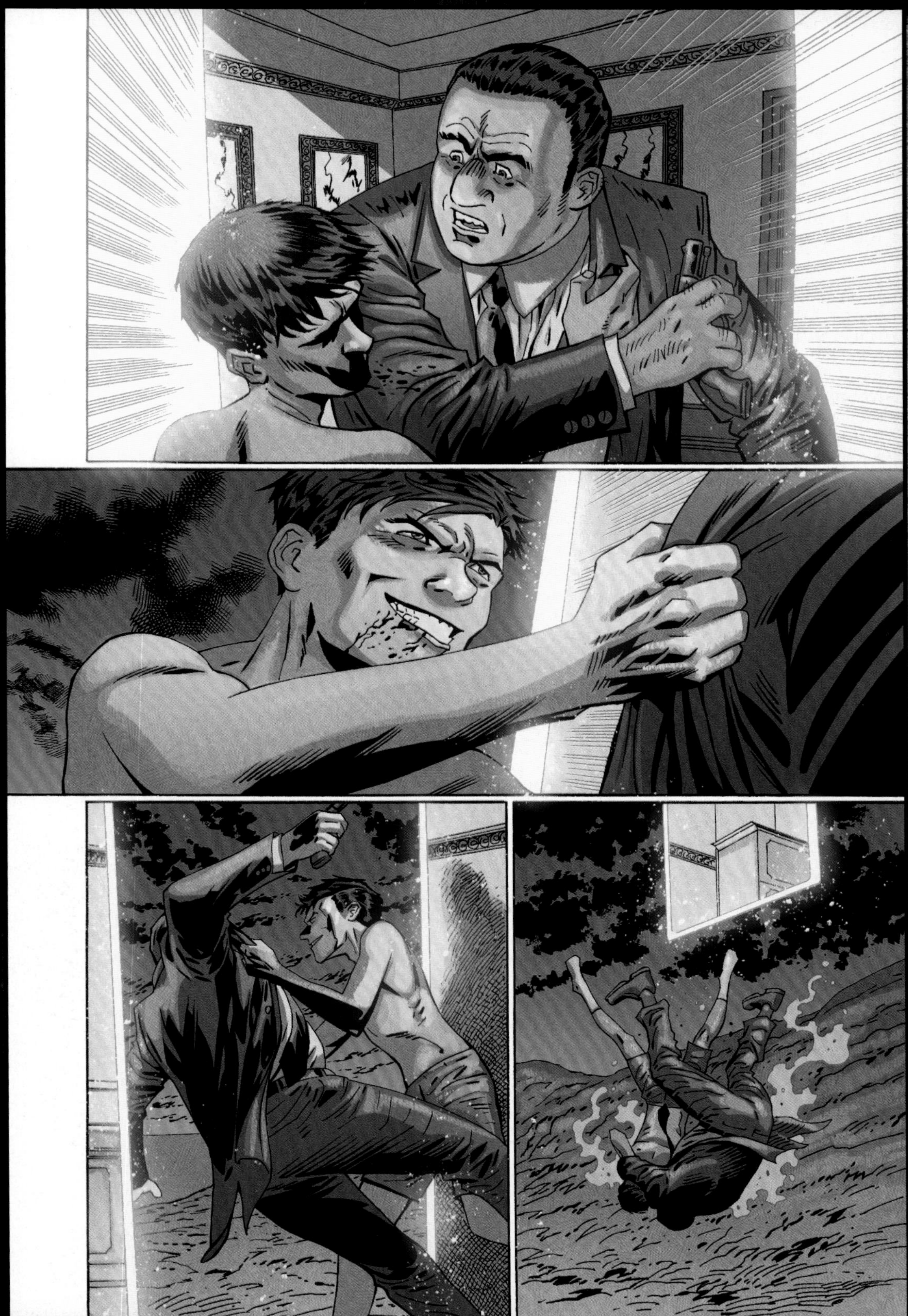

**Page 16**

1. Eddie is grabbing Jack's gun (it's a Colt Cobra).

2. Jack knees Eddie in the big muscle of his right thigh. Eddie screams for Roland's help.

3. Still holding Eddie (but now with his gun in his hand), Jack's head has snapped around. His expression is one of shock.

4. Let's have a shot of Roland, from Jack's perspective. Roland looms over him like a vengeful ghost. His haggard white face is rough with beard-stubble. His shirt is in tatters and shows the starved stack of his ribs. A filthy rag is wrapped around his hand, and on his hips he wears a pair of guns that look like they came out of a Wild West museum. Roland is sick and dying, but he is so hard that he makes Andolini look like a soft-boiled egg. Roland is pointing his gun at Andolini.

5. As Roland shoots with his left hand, Andolini snap-rolls to the right. An edge of rock tears open his five-hundred dollar sport jacket. But Roland's gun is giving a dry snap. The dud bullet has misfired! (Many of Roland's bullets got wet when he was drenched with seawater. Most of his bullets were located in the loops of his gunbelt.)

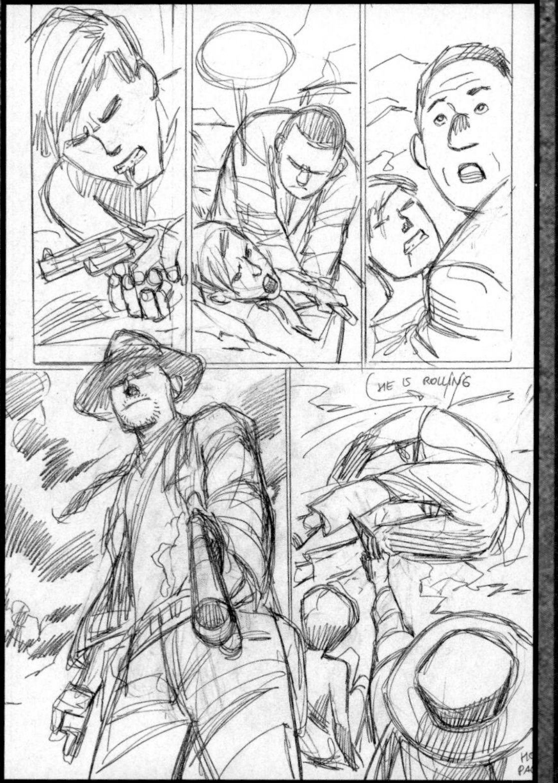
HE IS ROLLING

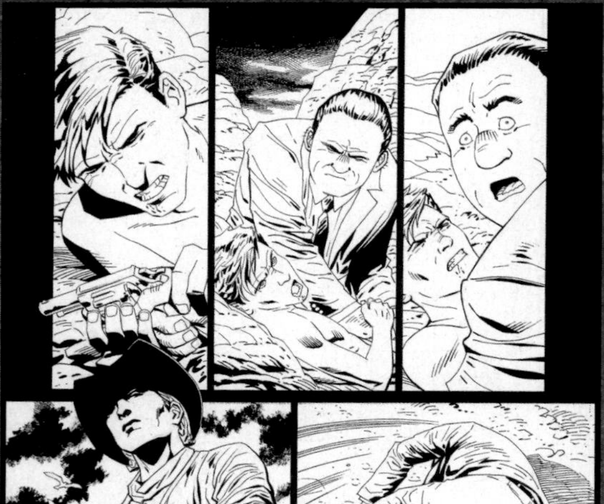

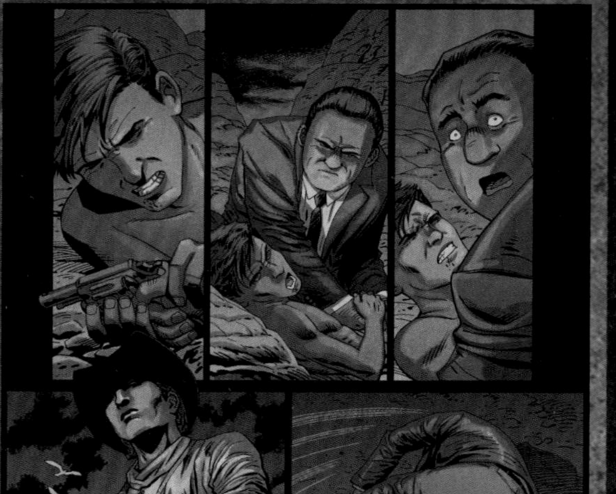

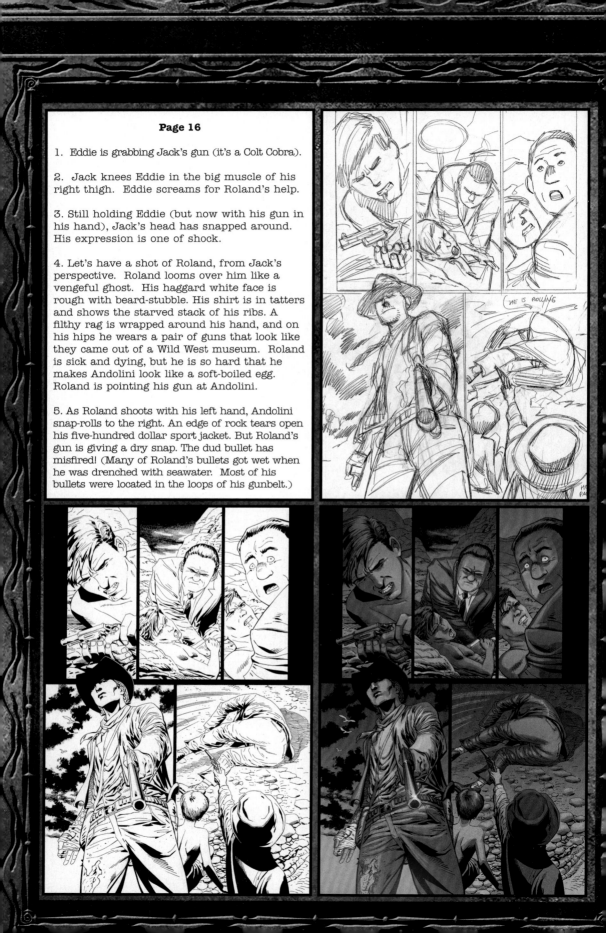